The Cure For Pentecostalism

Other books by Howard W. Boldt:

The Gospel of the Rainbow Sign (2018) ISBN 9781773540665
The Real Biblical Elder (2018) ISBN 9781773540672
Judge For Yourselves (2021) ISBN 9781773543642

The Cure For Pentecostalism

Why Pentecostal and Corinthian believers never spoke unlearned languages or unknown tongues

Howard W. Boldt

ISBN: 978-1-77354-363-5

Published by Howard W. Boldt

Publishing Assistance and digital printing in Canada by

PAGEMASTER
PUBLISHING
PageMaster.ca

DEDICATION

To Marilyn, whose diligent, thoughtful service to family and friends, whose unwavering faith in the Lord and love for His Word only begins to explain why I am so grateful to God that she is my loving wife and best friend!

DEDICATION

[illegible]

Table of Contents

ACKNOWLEDGMENT

My thanks to everyone who took the time to read all or portions of this manuscript, which I had previously entitled *Charismatic Reality Check*. Your suggestions, comments and critique are all very much appreciated.

PREFACE

Some years ago, I watched a debate between two prominent pastors on the subject of cessationism and continuationism. In my opinion, the cessationist could not defeat his opponent's argument. That exchange, along with the Strange Fire conference, has prompted me to personally examine this subject again. I wholeheartedly agree with the stand of the cessationist, but his arguments seemed flawed.

While delving into Paul's letter to the Corinthians, I came upon some studies by Robert Zerhusen on Pentecost in Acts chapter two. After comparing his work with the Scriptures, my views on some of the events of that Pentecost have changed. The supernatural manifestations of that great day were real, but not what I had presumed they were.

Lacking the degreed credentials readers look for, in an author of a book such as this, a dismissive response to a 'new' approach is quite normal and even expected. Indeed, we should be wary of any 'new' teaching. Yet, well-respected, conservative theologians, who know Hebrew and Greek, are not always in agreement on Bible interpretation!

Since church teaching does not always line up with the Bible, it is my hope, that the reader would objectively answer these important questions. Is Pentecostalism 'new' to the Scriptures? Does Pentecostalism impede the salvation of the lost, or the growth of believers?

The first edition, entitled, *Charismatic Reality Check*, was printed in 2016. After more than five years of amendments and refinements since then, it is my hope that *The Cure For Pentecostalism* adequately exposes the heresies of charismatic doctrine.

As a sinner, who has been saved, by grace alone, through faith alone, in Christ alone, as revealed through His written Word alone, my desire is that the words of this book do not contradict the Scriptures and that the reader would be greatly blessed for the glory of God.

Howard W. Boldt

DEFINITIONS

CESSATIONISM

Cessationism is the belief that supernatural gifts ceased with the closing of the canon of Scripture at the end of the apostolic era.

CONTINUATIONISM

Continuationism is the belief that some of the supernatural gifts continue beyond the apostolic era to the present day.

CHARISMATIC

Charismatic is the belief that all supernatural gifts continue to this day.

PENTECOSTALISM

Pentecostalism encompasses the charismatic and continuationist error. Though Pentecostalism is centered in Charismatic churches, this movement is present in all Christian denominations.

SUPERNATURAL

Supernatural means that the laws of nature can be observed to be suspended. When the winds and the waves obeyed Christ's command, a supernatural event occurred.

However, inability to be able to explain an event in natural terms, does not necessarily imply that it was supernatural. While it is certain that God also has His hand in every physical 'healing', recovery from illness is not supernatural.

Man is gifted according to God-given abilities. But, abilities are not supernatural.

ABBREVIATIONS

OT is Old Testament; NT is New Testament. Numbers in brackets are references to Strong's Exhaustive Concordance. YLT is Young's Literal Translation. NKJV is New King James Version. NAS is the New American Standard. ESV is the English Standard Version.

INTRODUCTION

The charismatic movement has destabilized and altered much of the evangelical landscape in just a few decades. Even highly respected reformed theologians today sanction 'speaking in tongues', unlearned language-speaking (gibberish) and a distorted view of 'word of knowledge' by which the needs of others are mystically made known. These and other disturbing distortions of the truth impede a biblical understanding of our relationship with Christ and each other.

The Contagion

Radicals of the charismatic movement within professing Christianity have turned churches of various denominations into feeling-based laboratories, where old self-esteem drugs are repackaged with some Christianized religion, then labeled as the solution to a happy life. With tongues of gibberish they claim to pray and speak 'words' from the Holy Spirit. Incapable of biblical diagnosis, these pseudo-pastor-physicians devise their own prescriptions for health and wealth that only help to mask the symptoms of sin. Their medications wear off, but the toxin has done its damage as expectations of recovery from illness give way to hopeless despair. Their 'healings' multiply sorrows. Professing believers have become so anesthetized with charismatic euphoria they are too numb to understand that the tumor for which they really need healing is not physical at all.

The inability to recognize erroneous unbiblical claims of visions and dreams, has also infected many with gullibility. These spiritual cancers have spread like a virus! Having gone into remission, these spiritual cancers can be dormant for a while. Unsuspecting professing believers are still seduced with happy 'spiritual' prescriptions not found in God's medical manual. While cessationism has helped to quarantine many from the ravages of this malady, still, many have caught the continuationist virus. Only the Bible has the remedy for this Pentecostalism contagion.

Relevance

Some may think this subject is passé, because the charismatic influence seems to have subsided. But has it really? Rather, when these issues are no longer discussed among Christians, it is often a sign that they are accepted as normal and no longer considered worthy of further debate. Many professing believers think that six 24-hour creation days are unscientific.

Likewise, 'new' norms among otherwise conservative evangelicals, now tolerate various charismatic notions of the gifts of the Holy Spirit. Differing on important issues such as these, belies the unity of the faith that Christians claim to have. Rather than contend for the faith, believers 'agree to disagree'. (Eph. 4:13; Jude 3)

Though the cessationist stand against the charismatic is laudable, this argument is flawed. When charismatics and continuationists challenge the cessationist, the matter remains unresolved because the cessationist has also misinterpreted Scripture. Under the banner of 'continuationism', charismatic doctrine and practice is allowed to flourish within otherwise conservative settings.

Purpose

Since the springboard of the Pentecostalism movement is primarily Acts chapter two and Paul's first letter to the Corinthians, this book will revisit these scriptures in considerable detail. The only cure for the doctrinal ailments of the charismatic and continuationist, is the Scriptures. By exposing the fallacies of Pentecostalism, it is my purpose that more people would come to fellowship with one another and Christ.

Another purpose for the exposure of these heresies is to honor the person and work of Christ and the Holy Spirit.

INTERPRETATION PRINCIPLES

I hold that the scriptures are inspired by God and without error as they were written in the original autograph. For this reason, all translations and commentaries, though valuable, must be compared with the original text.

Grammar and Context

I hold that scripture must be interpreted in its grammatical and historical context. Unless the writer indicates allegory, everything must be taken literally. For example, there is no indication that the six creation days are allegorical so they must be taken as six literal 24-hour days. On the other hand, we know that the animal sacrifices were only given as shadows or copies to depict Christ's sacrifice of Himself for sinners.

Ordinary, everyday words may also describe a supernatural event, depending on context. For example, the word 'touch' does not normally imply a supernatural occurrence, but it does when the woman touched the hem of Jesus' garment, because her hemorrhage stopped. The context reveals that this was an extraordinary 'touch' of faith. Many people would have touched Jesus and not been healed. (Lk. 8:46,47) Jesus and Peter did indeed walk on water but 'walking' is not supernatural. Similarly, all the gifts of the Spirit are handled first, from the normal use of the word. ('Heal' is not normally supernatural.) 'Miracle', as translated from the Greek, does not necessarily imply a supernatural occurrence. Only with clear contextual evidence, may a word be assigned a supernatural meaning.

NT Scripture Does Not Replace The OT

The NT writers of scripture must never be presumed to replace OT Scripture. Instructive by example, the Bereans verified what they heard by comparing it with OT Scriptures. NT authors often quoted and repeated truth from the OT and added commentary as the Holy Spirit guided them. But they did not 'correct' or revise the OT.

The best commentaries on any book in the Bible are the other 65! The best commentary on the OT is the NT.

'Natural' Reading Versus 'Actual' Reading

The notion among some that a 'new' biblical interpretation cannot contradict a 'normal' or 'natural' reading of the passage is presumptuous.

A prominent example of how a 'normal' reading of a text that gets the professing believer into serious theological problems is the doctrine of works. Misunderstanding James' teaching of faith and works, theologians continue to default to the 'natural' reading of the text, that one is saved by means of both faith and works. (Jas. 2:14, 24) Upon careful examination, the 'natural' reading of the text is not the actual meaning of the text. James was describing the character of faith. He said that the result of true faith in God is works. Saving faith is always accompanied by works. This accords with Paul, who writes that no man can contribute to his salvation by his own works. (Eph. 2:8,9)

Baptism is another doctrine where professing Christians are distracted with the 'normal' or natural reading of a text. Most of Christianity so-called, believe baptism is necessary for salvation. When Paul preached to the gospel to the Philippian jailor, the normal reading of the passage seems to indicate the necessity of baptism for salvation. (Ac. 16:31) But when compared with other Scripture, it becomes clear that Paul could not have intended baptism as a step to conversion. The thief on the cross went to Paradise without being baptized. It is important to comprehend the 'actual' reading of the text.

Even Christ's disciples had not understood that His kingdom would not obliterate the Roman empire. The disciples needed the 'new' interpretation, which was that Christ came to die for a kingdom that was not of this world. They, like us, read or hear presumptively.

TRANSLATION ISSUES:

Unfortunately, *glossa* in most Bibles is mistranslated to read 'tongue(s)' when it should read 'language.' Other words not in the original will also be addressed to show how the context of the passage has been altered with a distorted dynamic equivalence.

SUMMARY

Credible interpretation is not based on assumptions or bias or a natural reading of a text. Translation, grammar, and context help to determine if one's 'natural' reading of many puzzling scriptural passages, is also the 'actual' reading. The relevance of this discussion will become particularly apparent in the detailed analysis of Pentecost. From a 'natural' reading of Acts 2, the reader infers that the Galileans spoke unlearned languages. But what is the 'actual' reading?

THE CHURCH FATHERS

After the Apostles, Christendom drifted into various doctrinal fallacies. The "theology of the fathers is much less than ideal, since it does not recognize the Pauline writings on par with the Old Testament scriptures, and at times, it seems to have an inadequate emphasis on grace." [1] Admittedly, sound theology not specifically affirmed in the writings of the Church Fathers, does not necessarily indicate that sound theology was denied. Nonetheless, some of their writings directly conflict with sound theology.

DID THE FATHERS RECOGNIZE THE ETERNAL SECURITY?

The doctrine of eternal security, or what might also be called 'the perseverance of the saints', was not carefully delineated by the early church Fathers. In fact, NT references vital to this doctrine were scarce in over 5000 pages of Ante-Nicene writings. (100 AD to Council of Nicaea in 325 AD) For example, John 3:16 is referenced twice; Rom.8:33,34, once; John 6:37,39, four times; Jn.10:28,29, twice; Eph.1:13-14, seven; Phil.1:6, zero;

---

[1] Dr. Peter A. Lillback, *Testamentum Imperium, An International Theological Journal* , p.3 http://www.preciousheart.net/ti/2007/005_07_Lillback_Early_Saints.pdf

1 Pet.1:4,5, zero. Though eternal security is not explicitly denied, it is credibly argued that when all the extracts of pertinent scripture are surveyed, the 'fathers' had no clear understanding of what they were trying to teach, consequently, falling into contradictions.[2]

THE CHURCH FATHERS HELD ERRONEOUS DOCTRINE

Church Fathers held to some very erroneous views.

> "Clement and Tertullian had ascribed eternal virginity to Mary. Augustine believed that the mother of the sinless Christ had never committed actual sin. Monasticism, with its emphasis upon virginity, strengthened the idea of the virginity of Mary."[3]

Clement contributed to the false doctrines of purgatory and mysticism.[4] Tertullian became ensnared in Montanism, which claimed a 'new era of prophecy and continuing revelation.'[5] Irenaeus, Origen, Tertullian and Ambrose taught that baptism is necessary for salvation.[6]

Revered among the 'fathers' is Augustine, who lived three centuries after the apostles. First a cessationist but toward the end of his life changed to a continuationist.

> "But there is still a major problem with Augustine's report of miracles. His description is highly mystical and replete with superstitious elements. In recording these healings, he attributes them to things like prayer to the saints, the power of relics, and the use of religious symbols. Such descriptions are deeply troubling and call into serious question the veracity of his supposed miracles. Added to that, most of what he reports is from second or third-hand sources, which again casts doubt on the factual accuracy of his interpretations."[7]

Augustine's understanding of faith, grace and practice are fundamentally conflicted.

---

[2] ibid. p.14

[3] Earle Cairns, *Christianity Through the Centuries*, 1964 P. 174

[4] Howard F. Vos, *Exploring Church History*, Thomas Nelson Publishers, 1994, p.19

[5] Ibid., P. 18, 32

[6] Christian Apologetics and Research Ministry https://carm.org/church-fathers-quotes-topic

[7] Nathan Busenitz, *Augustine and Miracles in History*, Point #7. The Cripplegate https://thecripplegate.com/augustine-and-miracles-in-history/

Conclusion

The notion that since the church fathers lived closer to the time of the Apostles, doesn't necessarily mean that the Fathers have the best understanding of the Scriptures. Even they were not in agreement with one another. The doctrinal digression of the Church Fathers drifted toward Roman Catholicism. Having failed to heed the apostolic warnings, Christianity today continues to be a laboratory where people continue to get infected with spiritually deadly doctrinal viruses.

Though the Church Fathers may be fundamentally correct on doctrines such as the depravity of man and the substitutionary death of Christ, there are other essential doctrines. Augustine and other church Fathers promoted doctrines that interfere with the salvation of the lost and the growth of believers. Having failed this test of orthodoxy, they must be considered suspect for anything they have written about 'Pentecostalism'.

SCHOLARSHIP

Since the Reformation, sound scholarship flourished, enabling believers to know biblical truth that for centuries remained hidden. Yet, scholars did err.

Scholarship Contends For Truth

Negative commentary expressed in this book on biblical scholarship requires a proviso. While scholars have taught error, they have also been greatly used of God in the defense of the faith of our Lord. In this book, I have referenced degreed individuals who know Hebrew, Greek and are experts in disciplines that I am not. I appreciate them. And I need them to help me understand various portions of scripture, especially in regards to grammar and history.

Scholarship Can Mislead

The intelligence of scholars is not enough. Satan is also very smart. Knowing what God had said to Adam, he was able to twist his words to deceive Eve. Scholars believe in evolution. Some rehash Satan's temptation to Eve that she could become as gods with the 'new' teachings of psychology and self-esteem. Acquainted with Scripture himself, Satan stands ready to deceive believers, therefore it is important to identify the thresholds of error where scholars become false teachers.

THE TEST OF SCHOLARSHIP

I think conservative Christians would mostly agree that there are some incorrect doctrines that do not interfere with the salvation of the lost and the growth of the believer. Whether one's eschatology is ammillennial or dispensational, though important, such differences do not contribute to a false gospel of eternal salvation. However, when reputable reformed theologians who teach salvation by faith alone insist, that praying gibberish for private worship is biblical, a believer's growth is directly affected. It's essential to know from Scripture how this doctrine negatively impacts the Christian's walk with God.

SUMMARY

Notable, reputable, conservative scholars differ on a variety of biblical doctrine. Opposing views testify to the fact that not all scholars have it all right. Therefore, the reader should hold every commentator, including this author, accountable to the Scriptures, not to other commentators.

NOVELTY

There is another hurdle to a better understanding of Scripture. Novelty. After beginning this study, I discovered that a very few students of Scripture essentially held to some of the same views as mine on 1 Corinthians 12 to 14. Another scholar, differed with the common interpretations of Acts 2. Not only are these views different, they are apparently 'new'. After two millennia of church history, should there not be a record somewhere of the views of this book?

Because commentary aligned with the major themes of this book are few, reluctance to accept what appears to be 'new' views regarding the pouring out of the Spirit at Pentecost and the gifts of the Spirit in Corinth, is expected. With the preponderance of false teaching, the discerning believer's natural impulse is to reject teaching he or she has not heard before. However, if we believe that the Bible alone is the word of God, then all commentary, new and old, must be subject to critique. Are all 'new' views false? Are some views 'new' because they are unknown, or because they are contrived?

'OLD' TRUTH MIGHT BE 'NEW'

Very 'old' truth had been known in Israel. But as they drifted from the Lord, His word became unknown. King Josiah was alarmed when he heard the newly discovered Book of the Law read to him. (2 Kg. 22:8-13) To

King Josiah, the scripture was 'new', but it had been given long ago. Though some biblical truth may elude us today, it is not new truth. Some truth may need to be rediscovered.

CAN A 'NEW' TEACHING BE 'OLD' TRUTH?

The Scriptures alone are the source of all divine revelation. In them believers are warned to be wary of false teaching, not 'new' teaching.

After explaining to Nicodemus, a teacher in Israel, that one must be born again to enter the kingdom of God, He asks him, 'Are you a teacher in Israel, yet do not know these things?' Jesus implied that the doctrine of the new birth is taught in the OT. (Psa. 87) This teaching was 'new' to Nicodemus, but not new to Scriptures. It was and is still 'old' truth!

At the Last Supper Jesus gave His disciples a 'new' commandment to follow. (Jn.13:34) They argued with one another who would be the greatest in the kingdom of heaven. Washing one another's feet was the last thing on their mind. (Lk.22:24) But long ago, Moses had commanded the people to love their neighbor as themselves, so it was not new. (Lev. 19:18,34) By their behavior, the disciples demonstrated that this commandment was new to them, not new in existence.

Therefore, to say that a 'new view cannot be true', is false.

A 'NEW VIEW' MIGHT BE FALSE

Peter warned believers that false prophets would arise to introduce heresies about the Lord. (2 Pe. 2:1-2) Paul was amazed at how quickly the Galatian churches had succumbed to a 'different' gospel. (Ga. 1:6,7) Believers were to reject 'new' views that twisted the gospel of the Lord Jesus Christ.

AN 'OLD VIEW' MIGHT BE FALSE

For centuries it was believed that the sun revolved around the earth. In the third century BC, Aristarchus of Samoa proposed that the earth revolved around the sun. Evidently, it was not until the 16th century that Copernicus challenged the geocentric model, proposing that the earth revolved around the sun.[8] Interestingly, when heliocentrism was first made known, it was not well received by the 'Church' because it was 'new'. Yet, what was 'old' and believed to be true, was false.

---

[8] McKay, Hill, Buckler, *A History Of Western Society, Sixth Edition*, Houghton Mifflin Company, P. 96,126

Wrong doctrine began with Satan's temptation of Eve in the Garden of Eden. (Ge. 3:5) The devil's theology that man can be like gods continues to this day in cults like Mormonism. The older a doctrine is, does not make it more likely to be true.

Both Old And New Views Can Be True Or False.

As a Catholic monk and theologian, Luther had gained popularity with the people and notoriety with the Roman church by nailing the 95 theses to the castle door in Wittenberg. Luther's prominence gained him a preferred status among printers because his books were easily sold. From the time of Luther, printing houses search for marketable material.

Contemporary publishers, likewise, look for reputation and potential for sales. Is the 'author' well-known? The 'praise' pages evidence the author's need to gain academic credibility with the endorsement of other well-educated professionals. Publishers favor fame.

But the 'views' of famous theologians can be wrong. Both right and wrong teachings may be 'new' because they have been rediscovered or contrived. Luther published right views against indulgences, penance, etc., considered 'new' by many in his day. His correct published views on the "bondage of the will' were also 'new' at the time. However, Luther's publication of 'new' doctrines on the Lord's Table, known as consubstantiation, are wrong.

To the extent that publishers have ministered the gospel of salvation and sanctification, true believers should be grateful. Yet, every Christian publisher has, in some measure, failed to correctly discern 'old' biblical truth. Then, when generally unknown 'old' biblical truth becomes known, it is thought to be 'new'. Biblical truth is 'new' when 'old' truth is rediscovered. Therefore, every 'teaching' ought to be tested according to the 'old' truth of the Scriptures, not when it was discovered or published.

Summary

Gaging the veracity of apparently 'new' teaching, such as found in this book, based on opinions of what is 'old' or 'new', does not determine truth. If a teaching is deemed to be 'new', it is either because it is contrived or because it is rediscovered. 'Old' doesn't make doctrine right any more than 'new' makes doctrine wrong. A 'new' teaching might be 'new' because 'old' truth had been unknown. All views, both right and wrong, have at one time been 'new'. Whether 'old' or 'new', **therefore, it is vital to know whether the teaching is 'new' to the Scriptures**.

Therefore, adages such as 'what's new is probably not true' or 'what's older is probably true', in the quest for the truth of the Scriptures are of absolutely no value. These are not biblical principles.

CONCLUSION

The teaching of this book may be new to Christians, but is it new to Scripture? If the teachings of this book do not contradict the Scriptures, it is absolutely certain that this author has not been the first to teach it. Believers, acquainted with the Bible through the centuries, would have known and expressed exactly what Paul had been teaching on the gifts of the Holy Spirit. Obscured by faulty translations, presumptive interpretation, and Church Fathers, some correct views remained unpublished and thus became isolated and generally unknown. A view not found in centuries of published Christian literature does not, in and of itself, make it wrong.

It is therefore important to highlight the fact that sound biblical scholarship is not dependent on published opinions. It is dependent on the illumination of the Holy Spirit, who is not restricted to Bible colleges and Seminaries. Ultimately, the Bible is the only published 'view' that matters, because it's God's revealed truth.

A Basis For Critical Analysis

A credible critique of this book is not based on what centuries of ecclesial authorities have taught. However, the basis of a biblical critical analysis of this or any other book about the Bible must pertain to its two central themes – the salvation of the lost and the sanctification of the believer.

Does Pentecostalism cause people to believe they are converted, when they are not? Or, does a wrong view of the gifts of the Spirit impede the growth of the believer? Only the Bible has the final answer.

CATEGORIES OF GIFTS

Students of Scripture agree that Paul was not intending to provide a complete list of gifts. However, the classification of gifts differs among writers. They are variously categorized as 'edifying', 'sign gifts', 'service gifts' or alternatively, 'for believer's needs', 'for revelation' and 'for witnessing'.[9] The categorizations of the gifts in these two systems bear little resemblance to each other, yet both are claimed to be biblical. 'Signs and wonders' are confused with 'gifts', when neither definitions nor context allow it.

But Paul does make us aware of three ultra-distinct categories of giftedness. Gifts are defined by abilities. Gifts are defined as persons: apostle, prophet and teacher. And, gifts are defined by character.

RECOMMENDED SOURCES

Robert Zerhusen provided some insights why the Galileans spoke learned languages at Pentecost. After revisiting Acts 2, I have also come to the same conclusion that unlearned languages is an incorrect inference. The following references show that others have had similar views.

Daniel M. Brown, *A More Covenantal Approach to Pentecost*,
http://www.federationorc.org/Pentecost_2.pdf

Robert Zerhusen, *The Problem of Tongues in 1 Corinthians 14*,
http://www.alliancenet.org/a-new-look-at-tongues
http://www.alliancenet.org/the-problem-of-tongues-in-i-corinthians-14

Clyde McCone, *The Phenomena of Pentecost*,
http://www.asa3.org/ASA/PSCF/1971/JASA9-71McCone.html

Renton MacLachlan, *Tongues Revisited, a Third Way*

[9] Larry D. Pettegrew, The New Covenant Ministry of the Holy Spirit, , Kress Biblical Resources c. 2001, pg.160-161

1. 'GREATER WORKS'?

Charismatics and continuationists assert that all believers have the potential to do supernatural works based on Christ's words at the Last Supper. The following Scripture is used to support this supposition:

> "Believe Me that I am in the Father and the Father in Me, or believe Me for the sake of the works themselves. Most assuredly, I say to you, he who believes in Me, the works that I do He will do also; and greater *works* than [of] these he will do, because I go to My Father." (Jn. 14:11,12, NKJV, brkts. added)

Pentecostalism holds that believers may still perform miracles.[10] They think that the miracles of Jesus provide the context for 'greater works'. Unfortunately, the Cessationist's answer to this error supposes that this text applies only to the Apostles, assuming that 'greater works' is the power He would grant His disciples to perform miracles after His ascension to authenticate their apostleship. (Jn. 14:25,26; 16:13) This view infers that 'greater works' must be supernatural.

Others believe that 'greater works' pertains to the sudden increase in the number of souls saved after Pentecost. Are the works of prophets like Jeremiah then to be considered not so great because of a lack of conversions? Even unbelievers have preached and brought some to Christ. Have they then also participated in His 'greater works'?

Though the Cessationist is correct in his stand against the Continuationist, his argument also assumes these greater works to be supernatural. Were they, really? Or, might Jesus have prophesied to these disciples that the works they would do, were not supernatural at all? If so, what were they?

THE GRAMMAR

There are two main features of the grammar that help us to identify the works that Christ had in mind. What was the work Jesus was speaking about when He said, "the works that I do he will do also." And, could

---

[10] Matt Waymeyer, Michael Brown, *Authentic Fire & John 14:12*, http://thecripplegate.com/michael-brown-authentic-fire-john-1412/

any of these works be deemed to be "greater"? (Jn. 14:12) Though His visible supernatural work had almost come to an end, His works had not. When Christ said these words, He was still doing 'works.'

Present Tense

Commentaries teach that this is a reference to Christ's supernatural miracles, but this interpretation ignores the tense and mood, which is present indicative active. If Jesus had meant to refer to all His miracles, then certainly we would expect Him to have stated instead, 'the works I have done, he will do also.' Therefore, Jesus must have been doing some very important works, not normally considered to be supernatural.

Possessive and Comparative

Translations render part of John 14:12 as 'greater works than these shall he do; because I go to the Father.'[11] This is a distortion of the text.

An Interlinear parses 'these' as genitive and therefore should be translated **'greater of these shall he do'**, not "than these". In other words, no believer will do greater works than Christ was doing or would be doing, but **of** the greater works He is doing, the believer will do some. (Jn. 14:12)

Summary

It is not stated that the disciples would do all the 'greater' works of Jesus. However, since Jesus was speaking about what was happening presently, a review of the works of Jesus at this Passover is essential to evaluate what work the disciples would be doing.

WORKS IDENTIFY WHO JESUS IS

Moses, the most revered Jewish Prophet, did miracles that Israel believed were real. But, as much as the Jews professed admiration of Moses, they showed by the things they said and did, that they really didn't believe him. If they had, they would have believed Christ because he wrote of Him. (Jn. 5:45-47; De.18:15, 18) God had given His people the OT prophecies by which they would know who Jesus is. Like Moses, this Prophet would perform miracles to verify His claims about who He was and what he came to do. He came to fulfill the Law that Moses taught.

---

[11] Jesus also used the comparative/possessive in His defense against the accusation for working on the Sabbath. (Jn. 5:20) Literally, it says, 'For the Son is being fond of the Son and all is showing to Him, which He is doing and greater of these He shall be showing to Him works that you may be marveling.' Please refer to *Scripture4all.*

This much awaited Prophet had almost finished His earthly ministry and was about to leave His disciples. However, despite His three and a half years of ministry, they still had major theological challenges regarding the identity of Christ and His ministry. Thomas had not understood that the only way to the Father was through Christ. Despite Jesus' advice on how to come to the Father, Philip requested to see the Father. Jesus replied, "Have I been with you so long, and yet have not known me, Philip?" Jesus explained that the words that He speaks and the works that He does, are from the Father, and for that reason you can believe that the Father is in the Son and the Son is in the Father. (Jn.14:6-11)

What works did Christ have in mind?

CHRIST'S REFERENCE TO HIS 'WORKS'

All the disciples were acquainted with His works. They had seen Him leave the scribes and Pharisees as He answered their trick questions. Jesus rebuked the Pharisees who were intent on stoning the woman caught in adultery, 'Let him who is without sin cast the first stone'. And, they had seen Jesus preach to the spiritually impoverished woman at the well in Sychar. (Jn. 4:31-33) They saw 5000 hungry people fed with one lad's lunch, the blind see, and demons cast out. Philip would have heard about the time Jesus said to the paralytic, 'Your sins are forgiven', and then healed him to show that He had the power to forgive sins. (Matt. 9:1-8)

When John the Baptist had heard of the 'works of Christ' while in prison, he sent two of his disciples to ask Jesus if He was the last Prophet. Jesus told John's disciples that the blind see, the lame walk, lepers are cleansed, the deaf hear and the dead are raised, and the poor have the gospel preached to them. (Matt. 11:1-5) After His temptation in the wilderness, Jesus went back to His hometown of Nazareth. In the synagogue on the Sabbath, Jesus stood up to read from the scroll of Isaiah where it is stated, "The Spirit of the Lord is upon me, because He has anointed me to preach the gospel to the poor." (Lk. 4:18)

SUMMARY

Even the Pharisees themselves believed that Jesus healed the lame, but they criticized Him for healing on the Sabbath and rejected His claims about who He said He was. Jesus exhorted Philip to believe Him on account of His works. By Jesus' own definition, works includes both miracles and preaching. He taught as one having authority. (Mk.1:22)

THE WORKS OF THE DISCIPLES

Jesus said, 'He that believes on me, the works that I am doing, he shall do also.' After years of sitting under His teaching, Jesus implies that they were not yet doing His works. (14:12) In fact, they were not even supportive of Jesus' own ministry.

THEY SCHEMED

Two disciples, vied for control when they, together with their mother, asked to sit on the right and left hand of Jesus in the kingdom. Jesus rebuked them for it. (Matt. 20:21,26; Lk. 22:25-27)

THEY DISPUTED

They disputed among themselves who would be the greatest in the kingdom of heaven. (Mk. 9:34) They also argued at the Lord's Table.

THEY COMPLAINED

The disciples wondered why Jesus would even talk with a Samaritan woman. On another occasion they complained when Jesus blessed the children.

THEY DID NOT SERVE OTHERS

They did not wash one another's feet as the custom was. Humble service was not part of the disciples' work resume.

THEY DID MIRACLES

During their time with Christ, the disciples had participated in public ministry to the Jews. The 12 disciples themselves had already personally worked miracles under the authority of Christ. And, they had also preached that the kingdom was at hand. (Matt. 10:1-8; Lk. 9:1-6)

SUMMARY

When Christ said, 'the works that I do he will do also', He implied that they were not doing the works He was presently doing and the works they would be doing was something other than miracles. Later that evening Peter nearly killed Malchus.

CHRIST'S WORKS AT THE PASSOVER

A review of His works at this Passover helps us to discern the works that were missing from the lives of the disciples, and to understand how the works that Jesus was doing presently, were 'greater' than miracles.

The Work of Passover Preparation

Jesus organized and presided over the Passover meal. (Lk.22: 7-22)

Jesus was motivated to eat this Passover because it would be His last on earth. He desired to eat it with them before He suffered. In the future the disciples would repeat this ordinance in remembrance of Him. However, since the disciples followed Christ's instructions to secure the Upper Room, and prepare the meal, this could not have been one of the 'greater' works, because this 'work' was yet future. (Lk. 22:8-18)

The Works of Teaching

Notably, He was teaching His disciples at the time He spoke these words. (Jn.14:1-7) This was obviously a work that Jesus was doing that the disciples might recognize as a future occupation. Later, Jesus explained to His disciples that the Holy Spirit would help them to remember what He had taught them. (Jn. 14:26) In the absence of Jesus, the Holy Spirit would do the revelatory teaching through His chosen Apostles. (Jn. 16:12,13)

Despite a lack of understanding that Christ's kingdom was not of this world, they would eventually do the same work of teaching others as Christ did. They would do this work of teaching with authority and accuracy, without differences of opinion.

After His resurrection, Jesus met with the disciples a third time. Three times Jesus asked Peter if he loved Him, to which he answered that indeed he had a 'brotherly' affection for Jesus. Each time He said, "Feed My sheep." (Jn. 21:12-17) Feeding His sheep was what Jesus was doing at the Passover, obviously, one of the 'greater' works His disciples would do when He would go to the Father.

The Works of Humble Service

Jesus was doing the humbling work of washing feet. (Jn. 13:6) He exhorted them to follow His example,

> "So when He had washed their feet, taken His garments, and sat down again, He said to them, "Do you know what I have done to you? You call Me Teacher and Lord, and you say well, for so I am. If I then, your Lord and Teacher, have washed your feet, you also ought to wash one another's feet. For I have given you an example, that you should do as I have done to you. Most assuredly, I say to you, a servant is not greater than his master; nor is he who is sent greater than he who sent him. (Jn. 13:12-16; NKJV)

How could this not be another one of the 'greater' works of Christ? Here is the King of kings, the Lord of lords, the Creator of the Universe, the righteous Son of God, stooping to wash the feet of His sinful disciples!

Jesus said to them,

> "A new commandment I give unto you, that you love one another; as I have loved you, that you also love one another." (Jn. 13:34; NKJV)

The Greek word for 'new' means 'fresh', not 'new in existence'. This was truly a sharp rebuke to the disciples. The commandment to love one another was not new in existence, but for the disciples it was new in practice. (Lev. 19:18) If Jesus, the holy One, deigned to wash sinful disciples, then certainly they had no right to claim superiority, making excuses not to serve one another.

This ministry the disciples had not yet done. (Lk. 22:24, 27)

The Work of Exposing Sin

Aware that one of the twelve would betray Him, Jesus also publicly name the traitor among them. (Jn. 13:18-28)

Jesus did not hesitate to expose the deceiver among them. Any work that opposes sin and exposes deception would be one of the 'greater' works His chosen disciples and believers would do. Peter had exposed the lies of Ananias and Sapphira, Stephen exposed the hypocrisy of the Pharisees and died for it, and later Paul censured the man living with his father's wife. Censuring deceivers is also a 'greater' work.

John wrote to the elect lady, instructing her that she had a right to censure deceivers. (2 Jn. 7-10)

The Works Of The Priesthood

At this Passover Jesus did the work of praying for His people. (Jn. 17) He prays that those who the Father gave Him may behold His glory, which the Father had given Him. (Jn.17:24) These were the friends He loved. (Jn. 15:12-17) He was doing the 'greater' and greatest work of the priesthood. Trapped in his own sin, man could not be forgiven without the sovereign work of God and the offering of our High Priest in his behalf. As our High Priest, Jesus interceded for the salvation of His people. (Jn. 17:9-18) Man cannot forgive his own sins.

However, having been forgiven their own sins by Him fulfilling the Covenant of Grace, His chosen people can do the 'greater' work of forgiving one another. (Matt. 6:12)

SUMMARY

The disciples were exclusively endowed with the ministry of teaching what Christ had taught them, as the Holy Spirit helped them remember. Giftedness notwithstanding, every believer has the right to dispense what the OT Prophets and NT Apostles wrote and approved: censure deceivers, forgive and humbly serve one another.

Since Christ was not performing supernatural miracles at this particular time, 'greater' must refer in some way to the 'unspectacular' works that He was doing at that time. This rules out any suppositions that this verse teaches that believers were to be endowed with miracle powers.

EVERY BELIEVER HAS 'GREATER' WORKS

The 'greater' works of teaching, censure, forgiveness and service did not begin at the Passover. Jesus only qualified His promise with the words, 'He who is believing...'. These 'greater' works were already evident in true men and women of faith before and during the time of Christ.

'GREATER' WORKS DID NOT BEGIN AT PASSOVER

The woman who anointed Jesus' feet with perfume did the 'greater' works despite the ridicule she faced, even from the disciples, for 'wasting' it. John the Baptist also did these 'greater' works of admonishing Herod for his adultery and lost his life for it. The woman at the well shared the word of Christ with others. Elijah, the Prophet, challenged the Baal worshippers and had them 'censured'. Nathan exposed David's sin. Joseph showed kindness instead of vengeance to his brothers. Believers before Christ did 'greater' works. The man or woman with 'greater' works is 'one who is believing', whether it was Noah, Rahab, Abraham or Stephen, Peter, Aquila and Priscilla.

'GREATER' TEACHING WORKS ARE FOR NT BELIEVERS

The 'greater' works of teaching others did not cease. Believers are still to teach the revealed word of God, warn the belligerent and serve others. Beginning at Pentecost, believers taught that Jesus was the prophesied Messiah. The Apostles, inspired by the Holy Spirit, provided commentary to the OT and revealed truth not known before. Stephen, Philip, the Evangelist, Apollos, Aquila and Priscilla are just a few examples of believers who taught the word as revealed to them by the Prophets and Apostles. These 'greater' teaching works that Jesus was doing have also not come to an end.

HOW BELIEVERS DO THESE WORKS?

The believer has the privilege to do these works by asking for them. A paraphrased rendition from an interlinear Greek translation is as follows:

> 'And which ever any you should be requesting in My Name, I shall be doing, that the Father should be glorified in the Son'.'[12] (Jn. 14:13)

Taken in its immediate context, this is an instruction to pray that we might do the 'greater' works Jesus was demonstrating at this Passover. This is not a blank cheque for health, wealth and prosperity. When we ask Him for understanding to teach, humility to serve and wisdom to censure deceivers, and the love to forgive others, we can be assured, based on His Word that He will answer and provide.

SUMMARY

Any claim that Christ grants Christians license to do supernatural works is patently false. Indeed, signs and wonders were a sign of true apostleship. (Ac. 2:43; 2 Cor.12:12) Since Christ was not performing signs and wonders at this Passover, miraculous works are precluded.

We can never do greater works than Christ. And, of course, believers cannot in anyway contribute to the greatest work our Lord did when He, as our High Priest, placed Himself on the altar for our redemption.

But every believer does some **of** the 'greater works' that Christ was doing – lovingly serving and teaching others.

---

[12] Interlinear Translation, *scripture4all*
https://www.scripture4all.org/OnlineInterlinear/NTpdf/joh14.pdf

2. THE HOLY SPIRIT'S MINISTRY

The ministry of the Holy Spirit before and after Christ has remained the same. Yet, scholars think that Pentecost was a special introduction of the Spirit into NT believers, whereby the 'church' was instituted. If there had been a change in relationship and ministry of the Holy Spirit to believers before and after Christ, we would expect NT writers to point that out from the Law and the Prophets. Scripture, including the OT must be the basis of ecclesiology.

THE HOLY SPIRIT'S OT MINISTRY

Perhaps, not so well known is the fact that the Holy Spirit was at work in OT saints. Was His relationship to people after Pentecost any different?

THE SPIRIT AMONG THEM.

Despite Israel's sin of unbelief, the Spirit was in their midst in the wilderness and stayed among them. (Isa. 63:11,14; Hag. 2:5; Heb. 3,4) He was always present on earth. (Psa. 139:7-13)

THE HOLY SPIRIT WAS GRIEVED.

The Holy Spirit was grieved as He lived among the rebellious people of Israel. (Isa. 63:10,11) The Holy Spirit was resisted before Christ, as he is after. (Ac. 7:51)

THE HOLY SPIRIT MADE THE TRUTH KNOWN

The Holy Spirit was involved in the communication of truth before Christ. This member of the trinity warned Israel concerning the hardness of their hearts. (Psa. 95; Heb. 3:7-9) The Spirit instructed Israel in the wilderness. (Neh. 9:20) Since no prophecy ever came by human will, these communications came from the Holy Spirit, before as well as after Christ. (Ac. 1:16; 28:25; 2 Pe.1:21)

David Prophesied Truth:

The Spirit of the Lord gave God's word to David by which he prophesied truth. (2 Sa.23:2) Luke writes that the Holy Spirit spoke through David. (Acts. 1:16)

Micah had Courage To Preach:

Micah testified that he is filled with power. The Spirit of the Lord had given him courage to make known to Israel their sin and rebellion. (Mic.3:8,9; Ac. 4:13; 13:46)

Jahaziel Encouraged the People:

The Spirit of the Lord came upon Jahaziel to encourage the people. (2 Chr. 20:14,15)

SINNERS WERE BORN AGAIN BY THE SPIRIT BEFORE CHRIST

Jesus asked Nicodemus, 'Are you a teacher in Israel and do not understand these things?' The Holy Spirit's ministry in salvation was the same before Christ as it is after, that even Rahab, a Gentile harlot could be born into this spiritual Zion. (Psa. 87:4-6; Jn. 3:5,6; Heb. 12:22,23)

THE HOLY SPIRIT IS ALSO THE PLEDGE OF OT SAINTS

The scope of the Holy Spirit's ministry was expanded to Gentiles. (Acts1:8; 11:16,17) Writing to believers in Corinth, Paul states that He 'also has given us the Spirit as a guarantee.' (2 Cor.5:5) Gentiles, as well as Jews, are benefactors of the pledge of the Spirit, just like Abraham was. (Gal. 3:14) He was Abraham's guarantee by faith, as He is ours. As Abraham did not receive the Spirit by the works of the law, neither do we! (Ga. 3:2-6)

THE HOLY SPIRIT DWELT WITHIN OT SAINTS

The apostle Peter indicates that the Holy Spirit indwelt the prophets. Thus, the Holy Spirit admonished Israel through the prophets. (Neh. 9:30) The Holy Spirit granted discernment to prophesy the salvation that would come through Christ. (1 Pet. 1:10,11, NKJV)

John the Baptist:

He was filled with the Holy Spirit while yet in the womb. (Lk1:15) He fearlessly exposed Herod's sin and pointed to the Lamb of God.

Mary:

The Holy Spirit came upon Mary. (Lk. 1:30, 35) She gave evidence of the filling of the Spirit by her heartfelt proclamation of the gospel.

Job:

Even in the midst of calamity, Job testified that as he has breath, so also he has the Spirit of God. For this reason, he was able to refrain from wickedness. (Job 27:3,4)

Joshua:

The Lord instructed Moses to commission Joshua, a man in whom is the Spirit. (Num. 27: 18,19) Joshua had the character gifts of faith, hope and love, which we will study later. (Josh.1:9)

Ezekiel:

The Spirit entered this prophet to speak to him. (Ez. 2:2; 3:24)

THE HOLY SPIRIT GIFTED BOTH UNBELIEVERS AND BELIEVERS ALIKE.

Paul affirms that the Trinity is involved in the administration of gifts. (1 Cor. 12:4-6) When the OT specifies God as the giver of the ability, the Holy Spirit is included. The work of the Holy Spirit is not exclusive. Following are some examples of how the Holy Spirit benefited both unbelievers and unbelievers in the OT,

Wilderness Israel:

Artisans who were filled with the spirit of wisdom made Aaron's garments. (Ex. 28:3) God 'gifted' artisans for the articles of the tabernacle. (Ex. 35:10, 35) God specifically called Bezalel and filled him with the Spirit of God in wisdom and understanding for the design and work of the artisans. Moses explains that artisanship was a God-given gift. (Ex. 36:1,2; 1Cor.12:6) God gifted them with the ability to teach others. (Ex. 31:3; 35:30-34) This may be compared to the ability 'gifts' of administrations and helps. It cannot be presumed that the Spirit gave these abilities only to people of faith, since most of this generation died representing a people who rebelled and believed not.

Wilderness Jews were not to forget God who gave them the power to get wealth. (De. 8:18) Without gifts of various natural abilities, Israel would not have been able to get wealthy.

Moses and Jethro:

Though reluctant to assume a leadership role, Moses proved his abilities as a leader. His father-in-law Jethro, also gifted, advised him to share his judicial responsibilities with other capable men. (Ex. 18:13-27) As Jethro exercised his gift of a 'word of wisdom', he showed Moses how others could contribute with their gifts. If Jethro's and Moses' abilities were not Spirit-given, from where did they come?

Joseph:

Pharaoh called for a man in whom was a divine Spirit of wisdom. (Gen. 41:38) Pharaoh rightly saw that the Spirit of Joseph was not of himself.

King Saul:

God chose Saul to be the king of Israel (1 Sa. 10:1, 24) When the Spirit of the Lord came upon Saul, he prophesied together with the prophets. (1 Sa. 10:10-13) The Spirit of the Lord came upon Saul when he expressed anger concerning the aggression of the Ammonites. (1 Sa. 11:6) The Spirit of the Lord departed from Saul and an evil spirit was permitted to torment him. (1 Sa. 16:14) His penitence was based on fear of the people, rather love for God. Samuel perceived his hypocrisy and personally warned him that he had rejected the word of the Lord. (1 Sa. 15:24-26) Saul's sorrow for sin only produced death. (2 Cor. 7:10) Despite the Holy Spirit's work through Saul, he remained faithless.

Daniel:

God gave Daniel and his three friends skill in literature and wisdom. They already had abilities but God augmented their giftedness with skill. (Dan. 1:4,16)

Balaam:

The Lord talked with Balaam. (Num. 22:12,20) The Lord put a word in Balaam's mouth. (Num. 23:5) He was given the ability to communicate God's knowledge and wisdom to Barak. (Num. 22:18,38) Balaam prophesied what God told him. (Num. 23:7,18) He prophesied by the Spirit of the Lord. (Num. 24:2,3) He heard the words of God. (Num. 24:16)

God gave Balaam the ability to understand God's will and to speak it; he did not acquire this on his own. (2 Pe. 2:1) However, Balaam's God-given abilities gained him nothing because he loved wrongly. (2 Pe. 2:15; 1 Cor.13:13) He tried to use his gift of prophecy to comfort and edify Barak rather than the people of God. He failed to exhort Israel about their harlotries. (Num.25:1) Despite the abilities of this prophet, he was a false prophet condemned to the abyss. (2 Pe. 2)

Eldad and Medad:

These two men had remained in the camp when the others had gone with Moses and Aaron. The Spirit of the Lord came upon them also and they prophesied. (Num. 25:26)

The Seventy Elders:

The Spirit of the Lord came upon the seventy elders. (older men) Consequently, they prophesied. (Nu. 11:25)

Azariah:

The Spirit of the Lord came upon Azariah to boldly proclaim the truth of impending judgment if King Asa did not tear down the idols. (2 Chr. 15:1-8)

Zechariah:

The Spirit of the Lord came upon Zechariah to prophesy. (2 Chr. 24:20) The Spirit admonished the people through the prophets. (Neh. 9:30) Many other examples in the OT assert that the Holy Spirit communicated to His people.

SUMMARY

It cannot be denied that OT believers and unbelievers had abilities given to them by the Holy Spirit. Even Balaam prophesied. The Cessationist argument is also compromised here, with its view that the Holy Spirit can gift only believers. Therefore, the believer's special relation to the Holy Spirit, before and after Pentecost, must be based on something more than giftedness.

THE SPIRIT'S APOSTOLIC MINISTRY

The Holy Spirit had always been instrumental in the communication of truth. The same would be true after Christ died and rose from the dead. However, because of Christ's finished work, the Holy Spirit would now pour out of Himself prophesied truth about Jesus' great salvation.

THE SENDING OF THE SPIRIT

When Christ said that the Holy Spirit would not come until He departed, it is incorrectly inferred that the relationship of the Holy Spirit to OT believers was not the same as to NT believers. Consequently, His ministry has been wrongly relegated almost exclusively to NT times.

What did Jesus mean when He said 'I will send Him'? (Jn. 16:7) Most have deduced from the words "send" and "come" an image of Christ returning to heaven to give instructions to the Holy Spirit for Him to go to earth to be a comfort to His chosen people. "Send" as used in John means to 'dispatch'. However, Jesus, <u>not the Spirit</u>, must 'depart' meaning to 'go away.' (Jn. 16:7)

The Spirit Comes To One Already Indwelt

It is impossible to be born again without the Spirit. (Jn. 3) The Spirit has already come to anyone who has life. (Jn. 6:63) One commentary states, "The Holy Spirit was, of course, already at work in the hearts of men, but not in the sense of witnessing as *Paraclete*, which could only take place after Jesus had gone back to the Father."[13] The Spirit 'comes' "to you" for a specific purpose to specific persons: His disciples. (Jn. 14:26)

The Sending Of The Spirit Was Not At Pentecost

Jesus had promised that the Holy Spirit would assist them when He departed, which was before Pentecost, not at Pentecost. (Jn. 16:7, 10) This was spoken to the 11, not the 120 Galileans.

The Spirit Was Dispatched As The Advocate To Aid Their Memory

John's use of the word '*parakletos*' [14], translated as 'Comforter', is a reference to aid given in court by an advocate. An advocate is a lawyer who defends and prosecutes with words. (Jn. 14:16, 26; 15:26; 16:7)

Jesus promised that this Advocate would be dispatched to aid His chosen disciples to remember and teach what Christ told them. So, Christ comforted His disciples with the promise that the Spirit of truth would be "in them" for that purpose. They would not be left as orphans to fend for truth Christ had taught them, but would be aided by the Holy Spirit to accurately remember what He had taught them and reveal truth He had not discussed. The Spirit was 'dispatched' for this specific purpose. (Jn.14:16,17,26;15:26;16:7-14; Ac.1:4; 2:33,39) Understanding this, John wrote authoritatively that those who do not hear the apostolic message are not of God. (1 Jn. 4:6)

The Spirit Was Dispatched To Prosecute The World

But, this Advocate would now also prosecute the world with words spoken through the Apostles because it did not believe on Christ. (Jn. 16:7-9) God, who had graciously written Law in stone to show man's guilt and his inability to justify himself, now reveals the one 'witnessed by the Law and the Prophets' who could. (Rom. 3:19-23) The object of the faith of all true believers from the beginning of time is now clearly revealed in the God-Man, Jesus Christ, who fulfilled the Law. To truly believe in the Law and the Prophets, is to believe in Christ.

When the Spirit comes, He will convict the world of sin no longer by depicting the truths with the Levitical ceremonies. The Spirit would be dispatched to convict men for failing to believe the Person these ceremonies were all about. No longer would the repercussions of their sin

---

[13] A. T. Robertson, *Robertson's Word Pictures in the New Testament*, John 16:7

[14] *Vine's Expository Dictionary of New Testament Words*, Oliphant's, 1940

be depicted with the shedding of animal blood. The Spirit would now convict the world by the Person of Christ. (Jn. 16:7-11) Up to Christ, mankind was judged according to the Law. After Christ, mankind is judged according the Lawgiver, the only One who could fulfill the Law.

Though the Jews held the Law in high esteem, they were incapable of the righteousness of it. The Holy Spirit convicted the wilderness Jews for their unbelief and lawlessness; consequently, they would not enter into His rest. (Heb. 3:7-11) The law convicted them, as transgressors. (Jas. 2:9) Unbelief prevailed among Jews throughout their history and would continue in the world, despite personally beholding the Lamb of God. The Spirit had up to then convicted the world of sin, unrighteousness and judgment based on the Law. God had graciously shown the Jews their sins with the Law but would now show them and the world their sins by the righteousness of Christ. Whether based on the righteousness of God-given Law or the righteousness of Christ, the outcome was the same. In addition to the Law, the Spirit now also prosecutes the world based on the Judge who fulfilled the righteousness of the Law.

The Spirit Indwelt The Apostles Like The Prophets

Peter understood that OT prophets indwelt by the Holy Spirit prophesied of the grace of Christ's suffering. The same Spirit who had also indwelt the OT Prophets, revealing to them beforehand the sufferings of Christ, would assist the disciples also from within. (1 Pe. 1:11,12; Jn. 14:17,26) Informed by the OT, Peter made no distinction between the Holy Spirit <u>in</u> the OT Prophets and <u>in</u> NT Apostles.

But Didn't Christ Say That The Spirit Was Not Yet 'Given'?

Speaking of a future day when the Spirit would be *given*, Christ promised believers that 'out of his inmost being shall flow rivers of living water.' There are several factors vital for understanding this in context. (Jn. 7:37-39)

- On each of seven days the priest would bring a vessel from the pool of Siloam and lead in a joyful procession, then pour the water out at the altar. (Neh. 8:18; Num. 29:12-38) But on the eighth the pouring out of ceremonial water did not take place.[15] On this last day of the feast of tabernacles Jesus prophesied a yet future event, when from believers would flow living water. With

[15] See Henry Alford's commentary on John 7:37-39.

the water ceremony of the past seven days still fresh in their minds, Jesus unabashedly announces that only from those who 'are believing' in Him will flow these rivers of living water. This water has a primary source, a reservoir. Through many believer-vessels would flow 'living water' of words provided by the Holy Spirit upon an unbelieving people.

- Jesus' prophecy pertains to those 'believing in Him'. Having the same source, these believers would all agree on the Person and work of Jesus. All the rivers flow from one water, one source. Every believer represents one river as the woman at the well represented one fountain or well. (Jn. 4:14)
- Peter had explained that what happened at Pentecost was the outpouring of the Spirit from whom gushed out in no small trickle, the words of life of Christ through 120 Galilean believers. The ministry of the Spirit was always evident in various ways throughout Scripture, but never with such an overwhelming display of courage and joy and united perception of who Jesus really was and is and what He did.
- There are three words parsed in the genitive in verse 39: 'the', 'Spirit' and 'whom'. If it were intended in this instance that the Spirit Himself would be 'received', Jesus would have stated that 'He spoke of the Spirit, those who believed in Him were to receive'. But He didn't. It should be translated, 'this moreover He said regarding the Spirit, **of whom** those believing were about to receive, for the Spirit was not yet because Jesus was not yet glorified'. The believers were about to receive <u>of</u> the Holy Spirit truth in His possession. This accords with Peter's understanding of Joel's prophecy when he preached that 'I will pour forth <u>of</u> my Spirit.' (Ac.2:17)
- The word 'given' is supplied. But the Spirit wasn't given in the sense that He wasn't present. Since Christ had not yet been glorified, the Spirit was not yet, meaning he was not yet made apparent by the sudden outburst of many rivers of truth.

This prophesied ministry of the Holy Spirit began with the communication of truth centered on Christ as the only remedy to expiate man's sin. As will be shown in the next chapter, the evidence of the 'given' Holy Spirit was <u>not</u> speaking in unlearned languages.

DIDN'T CHRIST SAY THAT HE 'WILL BE IN YOU?'

It is argued that when Christ would leave, the Holy Spirit would come to indwell believers. (Jn. 14:17) Speaking to the eleven, Jesus said, 'you know Him, for He dwells with you and will be in you.' What is meant with Jesus' words, 'will be in you?' How was this yet future?

In what sense was the Holy Spirit not in them? Jesus explains to them that after He ascended, his disciples would need an advocate, One who would know and rightly understand what they had been taught. They would need the additional internal ministry of the Holy Spirit to teach them and help them remember what Jesus had taught them. (John 14:26; 15:26; 16:13) He had always indwelt believers. But here the Lord affirms the authority of the Apostles with the promise that the Holy Spirit would bring to mind what Jesus had taught them.

Peter States That OT Prophets Were Indwelt

Given the evidence already presented regarding the reality of the work of the Spirit in His people before Christ, it is not feasible that Christ's departure initiated a new internal presence of the Holy Spirit. What is meant by Jesus' words 'in you' is best understood with the words of one of the Apostles, who was present at the Last Supper when these words were spoken. (Jn. 14:17) Peter specifically stated that the Spirit of Christ was '<u>in them</u>', that is, in the Prophets, so that they would prophesy the suffering of Christ. (1 Pe.1:10-12)

'OUTPOURING' IS NOT SYNONYMOUS WITH 'INDWELLING'

The term 'indwelt' represents the biblical teaching that the Holy Spirit abides within true believers. However, limiting the Spirit's inward presence to NT believers, is not logical. If we are to restrict the indwelling of the Holy Spirit to believers after Christ, then we must also limit the scope of His purchase. Were OT saints also not their own and were they not also bought with a price? (1Cor. 6:19,20) If the OT believer did not have the Spirit, how could he belong to Christ? (Rom. 8:9) If the Spirit did not indwell the OT believer, how could he be spiritual? How could he then be raised from the dead? (Rom. 8:11) Did the Holy Spirit not bear fruit in OT believers? (Ga. 5:22,23)

At Pentecost Peter specifically preached that this was a pouring out <u>of</u> the Spirit, which caused believers to prophesy, however, the indwelling presence of the Spirit was already a reality. The fruit of the Spirit had already been a reality in the lives of all believers.

The Spirit Poured Out Of Himself

God poured forth of the Spirit upon 120 believers indwelt by the Spirit. He did not pour out the Spirit. Specifically, the Holy Spirit poured forth that which they saw and heard. The crowd saw the courage and the joy as they proclaimed Christ. (Ac. 2:32-34) In this outpouring of the Spirit, the crowd heard the Galileans witness that Christ was a fulfillment of Scripture. (Joel 2:28; Jn. 7:38,39; Ac.1:8; 2:17,18,33,36) The promise of the Spirit is Christ Himself and the gospel He provided. (Ga.3:14)

Previously committed primarily to Israel, the gospel would be expanded to target the Gentiles, who were "afar off", to also receive the promise of the Spirit by faith, as Abraham did. (Ac. 2:39)

Christ Did Not Imply The NT Church Morally Superior

Some have suggested that the Holy Spirit's ministry is greater after Christ, than before. Before Christ, Daniel and his friends shunned power and money even if it should cost them their lives. Instead of cursing God, Job honored Him, despite losing his family, his wealth and his health. Or, how were NT Ananias and Sapphira 'better' than OT Achan?

OT saints, like David, are believed to be morally inferior to NT saints. Why then did Paul need to admonish the church for tolerating a professing believer who was practicing immorality the Gentiles didn't? (1 Cor. 5) The OT saint Joseph fled from the temptation to commit adultery. And, OT men like Noah and his three sons lived according to God's will in marriage. Yet, today's 'evangelicals' differ little from the world. Even 'pastors' have confessed to pornography.

Before Christ there were false prophets and teachers, like Balaam, but today we have upstaged them with the Charismatics, 'spiritual formation' gurus and the religious idolatry of Catholicism.

No difference is evident in the sinful highs and lows of the believer's life before and after Pentecost.

Summary

The Holy Spirit inspired men to preach and write truth before Christ, as He did after. It was necessary to be 'born again' by the Spirit before Christ, as it was after. The Holy Spirit was/is the same Agent of conversion and sanctification of all believers before and after Christ. Before or after, anytime there is less sin in the believer's life it is because of the presence and work of the Spirit. Believers have always needed to be illumined by the Holy Spirit to understand the truth and live it.

The Holy Spirit was dispatched to be in His Apostles to accurately speak and write about the gospel of Jesus Christ. This was not a location change. Therefore, Pentecost is not the beginning of the Spirit's ministry in believers. It was, however, a predicted manifestation of the Holy Spirit in which He would shower power upon timid believers to boldly witness that Christ was indeed who the Prophets wrote about.

DID THE SPIRIT START THE 'CHURCH'?

Further discussion is needed, regarding the institution of the 'church'. Did the Lord start a new society of believers with the pouring out of the Spirit at Pentecost?

Christ Prophesied That He Would Build The Church

Partly based on Christ's prophecy, "...and upon this rock 'I will build My church", it is alleged the church began at Pentecost, when the Holy Spirit 'came'. (Matt. 16:18) It is important to note that Jesus uses metaphors to describe non-physical reality. 'Build' is a verb used to describe the construction of a house. The foundation for this 'house' is the Rock. The components of the house on the Rock are people who have been called out to be separated from the world.

The Prophet Zechariah employed a similar metaphor. While the physical temple was nearing completion under Zerubbabel, he prophesied that a future Temple of the Lord would be built by the "Branch". (Zech. 3:8; 6:12,13) Since "Branch" is a metaphor referring to Christ, the "temple of the Lord", in this context, is not a physical structure.[16]

Paul explains that believers of all ages are 'fitly framed together' as part of one holy temple in the Lord. (Eph. 2:18-22) Peter states that this temple is built with lively stones into a spiritual house. 'Called out of darkness into His marvelous light', His peculiar people are chosen to be part of His spiritual house, His church. (1 Pe. 2:5, 9,10)

The Meaning Of 'Church'

'Church' means 'called out ones'. Individuals are 'called out' from one's physical locale to one specific location for the purpose of assembly. When Paul addresses the 'church', he includes every individual assembled, saved or unsaved. (Rom. 16:1,5; 2 Cor. 1:1) The context determines whether a monogamous group of 'believers only' is intended. (Acts.2:47)

---

[16] The Branch and the Temple of the Lord are exposited as metaphors of Christ and a non-physical temple. (Zech. 6:12) (Barnes' Notes, Keil & Delitzsch and Gill's Bible Exposition)

DO BELIEVERS BELONG TO ONE 'CHURCH'?

Paul taught that even Gentiles, who are 'far off', are citizens with the saints and members of the household of God. (Eph. 2:17-20) There is one body consisting of Jews and Gentiles, as there is one Spirit. (Eph. 3:5,6; 4:3,4) All believers are one with the heavenly Jerusalem, the church of the first born, Zion and with just men made perfect. (Heb. 12:22,23) All believers, before and after Christ, are members of this one assembly.

WHERE WAS THE CHURCH TO BE BUILT?

When Jesus said, "Upon this rock, I will build My church", He was referring to a project that had not yet happened when He spoke these words. Dispensationalists teach that Jesus began to build His church on earth at Pentecost. This is problematic because predeceased believers are excluded from the 'church', making two bodies of believers necessary. One 'body' must include all believers, before and after Christ.

With a quote from Isaiah, 'in Zion is being laid a stone, a chief cornerstone', Peter implies that this has been fulfilled. God would take this very precious Stone that the builders rejected for a construction project in the heavenly Zion. (Isa.28:16; 1 Pe. 2:6-8) With the death and resurrection of Christ, the foundation of His church, the Rock of our salvation, was located in Zion.

If Christ is the Rock, the Foundation and located in Zion, then this must also be the destination of all believers before and after Pentecost. Zion is the ultimate location of the "church". Though this Cornerstone was set in place after Christ's resurrection, He was and is the object of faith for all saints before and after Christ.

WHAT IS THE CHURCH?

Paul reminds believers that they are the 'holy temple of God' in which the Spirit dwells. (1 Cor. 3:16,17) Still under construction, this spiritual structure is maturing 'into a holy temple unto the Lord'. The church is a temple of people, 'built together into a dwelling place for God by the Spirit.' The Cornerstone is Jesus the Rock upon which an assembly, consisting of all saints before and after Christ, would be built. (Eph. 2:19-22; Heb. 12:22,23)

Christ's church consists of all who have been born again. Jesus counseled Nicodemus to be born again, something this rabbi should have known from Scripture. (Jn. 3:3,10) The status of citizenship in our heavenly Zion is acquired by birth. (Psa. 87:4-6; Heb. 12:22,23)

Nicodemus had already been born into an earthly Zion, but he needed to gain his citizenship in the heavenly Zion.

The church is an assembly of the redeemed. Christ gave Himself for the "church". (Eph.5:25,27; Titus 2:14) The church is a redeemed people. (Lk. 1:68) David declares that he has been redeemed. (Psa. 31:5; 71:23) The Psalmist declares that the congregation of Mt. Zion has been purchased and redeemed. This is the church of God both in the Old and New Testaments.[17] (Psa. 74:2) There is only one church of the redeemed.

WHAT IS THE EVIDENCE OF CHRIST'S CHURCH?

First and foremost, the evidence of the redeemed is faith. (Heb. 11:1) Saints before and after Christ trust Him to give them the righteousness they need, for acceptable works. (Isa. 64:6) Evidence of membership is incomplete without the fruit of the Spirit. God-honoring works is the result of true faith before and after Christ. (Heb. 11:1-40)

SUMMARY

As the context allows, 'congregation' in the OT is representative of the NT 'church'. Cleansed from sin, the saints before and after Pentecost belong to Christ. OT saints are no less 'called-out' ones than NT saints.

Paul asked Corinthian believers, "Do you not know that you are the temple of God and that the Spirit of God dwells in you?" (1 Cor. 3:16, NKJV) The Apostle knew that the Branch would build the temple of the Lord. (Zech. 6:12-13) This is one spiritual structure, which Paul also calls the household and building of God. (Eph.2:20) This is the temple to which Old and New Testament saints belong. This is the same spiritual assembly which Christ stated He would build with Himself as the Rock. (Matt. 16:18) All the saints before and after Christ are part of the same household, the same building and the same temple to the Lord. (Eph. 2:17:22) His building is still in progress.

Prior to Christ, saved sinners believed that God would fulfill His Covenant; after Christ, saved sinners believe that God had fulfilled His Covenant of Grace. (Heb. 6:17,18)

THE SPIRIT'S MINISTRY OF THE WORD

Did the ministry of the Holy Spirit change at Pentecost? Have believers made unbiblical assumptions about the ministry of the Spirit?

---

[17] John Gill, *John Gill's Exposition of The Whole Bible*, (Psa. 74:2)

BEFORE PENTECOST

John the Baptist was filled or **influenced by the Holy Spirit** before he was born. As the last Prophet, he incapsulated the message of the Prophets, "Behold the Lamb of God who takes away the sins of the world." The OT message was that sin needed a remedy and John prophesied Jesus to be that remedy. The terms of this remedy, first given in the Garden of Eden, then repeated in more defined terms throughout the OT, is known as the New Covenant. (Gen. 3:15; Isa. 53)

DURING PENTECOST

Just before the launch of the NT apostolic ministry, there was an important prophesied interlude. The Galileans, including the disciples, waited in Jerusalem until they would be clothed with power. At Pentecost, the Holy Spirit confirmed to these believers that Jesus was indeed the fulfillment of OT prophecy, that He was the long-awaited Messiah. Consequently, they began to boldly and joyously broadcast this phenomenal news. (Ac. 2:17, 32) These believers prophesied, as Joel had predicted! Puzzled and disturbed, the crowd was at first antagonistic to what they thought were the shenanigans of people who had too much wine. The apostolic era would now begin.

Peter, the one who cut off Malchus' ear, who denied the Lord just 50 days ago, now got up to speak to the entire crowd! He showed them from Scripture that this event had been prophesied by Joel and that this Jesus whom they crucified, was their Savior. Three thousand souls were saved and were taught the 'apostles' doctrine'. All the Apostles had now become involved. (Ac. 2:41-43)

According to Joel, the Holy Spirit would be poured out upon all mankind. This was essentially fulfilled at Pentecost, when the Holy Spirit enabled believing 'sons and daughters' to prophesy the fulfillment of the New Covenant in Christ to Jews and Gentiles in their own languages. (Joel 2:28, 29; Ac. 2:17,18)

AFTER PENTECOST

However, as emissaries of Christ, these selected Jewish believers were also enabled by the Holy Spirit to communicate the Gospel in subsequent 'outpourings'. The Father directed the promise of the Spirit to be heard and seen first in Jerusalem, then in Judea, Samaria and in the Gentile world. (Ac. 1:7,8) This ministry of the word by the Spirit continued upon "all flesh", those who were 'afar off'. (Ac.2:17, 39)

SUMMARY

The Holy Spirit revealed truth to the OT Prophets. After the resurrection, the Holy Spirit would help His chosen Apostles remember what Christ had taught them. As always, the Holy Spirit reveals truth.

Fifty days before Pentecost, the promise of the New Covenant was fulfilled. God confirmed this Covenant with the outpouring of the Holy Spirit, as Joel prophesied. The ministry of the Spirit changed only in regards to perspective. Before Pentecost, He confirmed the promise of the New Covenant; after Pentecost, He confirmed its fulfillment.

KEY OBSERVATIONS OF THE HOLY SPIRIT'S WORK

Following are a few basic statements that summarize the ministry of the Holy Spirit before, during and after Pentecost.

1. The Holy Spirit was never absent from the earth, neither did He leave earth when Christ came and then return to earth when Christ left. The Holy Spirit was present when Jesus talked to Nicodemus. (Jn. 3:5,8)
2. But He would be dispatched to communicate and confirm Christ's work of salvation prophesied in the OT, as Joel predicted.
3. The Holy Spirit would be sent as the Advocate to the disciples, who would bring the truth to their mind to preach and record.
4. He would now be commissioned to convict the entire world, not just Israel, of sin, righteousness and judgment because they would <u>not believe on Christ</u>. (Jn. 16:8,9; Ac.2:37)
5. The Holy Spirit fulfilled the promise to clothe these timid disciples with power from on high. (Lk.24:49; Ac.1:8) OT Prophets, including John the Baptist, displayed this same extraordinary courage, indicating that the Holy Spirit had also caused them to be bold.
6. The 'pouring out of the Spirit' was a prophesied event.
7. The outpouring of the Holy Spirit did not initiate the indwelling of the believer, neither was it the beginning of the 'church'.
8. The pouring out of the Holy Spirit was **not** an endowment of ability gifts.
9. The 'pouring out of the Holy Spirit' was initiated and expedited through the direct intervention of God alone.
10. Strictly speaking, the <u>only</u> 'outpouring of the Spirit' occurred at Pentecost. Without the intermediary of a teacher, the Spirit directly and simultaneously poured knowledge of Christ upon each of the Galilean believers. (Lk. 24:49)

11. The ‘pouring out of the Spirit’ disclosed the person and work of Christ as per OT prophesy.

12. The Holy Spirit caused believers to prophesy in learned languages.

13. The outpouring of the Spirit was evident by what was seen and heard. People saw the believers’ joy and courage. People heard the truth about Jesus, as taught in the OT.

14. The evidence of the indwelling Holy Spirit begins with faith in Jesus Christ. (Ac. 15: 7,8)

15. The baptism of the Holy Spirit may also occur when ministers ‘pour’ the gospel upon those who hear.

16. At Pentecost, the Holy Spirit showed His ‘power’ by causing many to come to the same understanding of Christ at the same time.

17. Christ bore witness of Himself; the Father bore witness of Christ. The Holy Spirit bore witness of Christ through believers. (Jn.8:18; Ac. 1:8)

A Guiding Perspective

The Holy Spirit’s ministry throughout Scripture must serve as our guiding perspective in the review and analysis of The Outpouring of Pentecost that follows in the next chapter.

3. THE OUTPOURING OF PENTECOST

At the outset of this project, I had intended to focus on Paul's teaching on gifts in his letter to the Corinthians. But during this study, one author's perspective of Pentecost caused me to reexamine mine.[18]

Most of Christianity has deemed Corinthian 'giftedness' to be an extension of the manifestation of the Spirit at Pentecost. 'Speaking in tongues' is held by Cessationists to have been a supernatural gift. However, since many views of supernatural giftedness in the church flow from our understanding of Pentecost, we must be certain that we have the facts right.

A Preview Of The Events

Approximately 120 believers were assembled together on the day of Pentecost when the sound of a might rushing wind from heaven interrupted their prayers. Tongues "as of fire" sat upon each one. Filled with the Holy Spirit, they began to speak "other" languages as the Holy Spirit gave them "utterance". Rushing to the source of the sound, the multitude discovered Galileans speaking to one another the mighty works of God in 'other' languages. But others accused them of having too much wine. Peter answers them from Scripture based on a prophecy of Joel. (Ac. 2:1-15) This was all according to God's plan for a very special Pentecost.

HISTORICAL BACKGROUND

Jesus had instructed His disciples to wait in Jerusalem where they would be clothed with power, not languages. (Lk.24:49) Knowing this special unction would not occur at just any location, they were continually in the temple praising God. (Lk. 24:53) Luke records that when they returned to Jerusalem they were devoting themselves to prayer. (Ac.1:14) Approximately 120 believers were already gathering regularly together before the Day of Pentecost, continuing to meet day by day in the temple and breaking bread from house to house. (Ac. 2:46) Meeting for prayer and fellowship had already become routine.

---

[18] Robert Zerhusen, *A New Look at Tongues*. Other supporting authors have quoted him. Though my thoughts may vary slightly, I take his position that languages in Acts were not miraculous.

THE PLACE OF GATHERING

There were about 120 believers present when they selected Mathias to replace Judas. (Ac. 1:13,15; 2:1) A private house large enough to accommodate this size of a gathering was extremely unlikely. Crammed among other residences, say, a block or two away, how would this multitude swarm this indoor meeting, and make the observations it did?

Since the Galileans 'continued daily in the temple', they would have been in the Temple on the day of Pentecost. Going to the temple to pray was a habit of the believers in Jerusalem. (Ac. 3:1) The time of the 'filling' of the Spirit on the Day of Pentecost was the third hour, one of those times of prayer in the Jewish day. (Ac. 2:15)

Luke writes that "they were all together" when Pentecost had fully come. (Ac. 2:1,2) The text does not tell us where this 'place' or 'house' was. Some believe it might be the 'upper room', where the disciples lodged. The text says that they were in a "house". "House" is also used in reference to the 'house of God'. (Matt. 12:4, Mk. 2:26) God's house was to be a house of prayer, not a house of merchandise. (Lk. 19:46; Jn. 2:16) Luke uses the same Greek word to refer to the 'house' Solomon built for Him. (Ac. 7:47,49)

There are two things specific to their location: they were in one place and they were sitting in the house. Since the temple area was large, 120 people could be in a lot of places, yet not be together. The 'house' must have been large enough for them to be in one 'place'. Halls and porches around the Court of the Gentiles were convenient places for meetings.[19]

THE GALILEAN

Following is a brief assessment of the Galilean's status, reputation, education and linguistic abilities. (Ac. 2:7)

Status:

Jesus and His disciples were Galileans. Some thought that Jesus might be the Prophet, but the Pharisees insisted that Christ's hometown of Nazareth was not prophetically important. (Jn. 7:41,52) Nathanael also wondered if anything good could come out of Nazareth. (Jn. 1:46) The religious establishment in Jerusalem disparaged the Galileans.

---

[19] *Bible History Edersheim – Within The Holy Place*, The Temple Porches https://www.bible-history.com/jewishtemple/jewish_templeedersheim__within_the_holy_place.htm

Reputation:

The Galileans had a dubious reputation. Judas (not Iscariot), a Galilean, had tried to lead a rebellion. (Ac. 5:37) Aware that some had reported seeing Jesus alive after being in the tomb for three days, the multitude might have wondered if these Galileans were attempting a coup in His name. Was this another band of zealots? Now proclaiming Jesus as the Messiah, who everyone would know, why were they disturbing the worshippers?

Education:

The Galileans were 'unschooled' according to the standards of the Pharisees, though many of their claims to know the Law and the Prophets were exposed by Jesus as ignorance. (Matt. 12:1,2; 15:8,9) Their perception of Peter and John as 'untrained' was based on the gospel they preached.[20] No Pharisee was trained in the way Jesus taught the disciples. (Ac. 4:8-13)

So, who really were the 'uneducated and untrained'? Peter explained that these Galileans were speaking as a fulfillment of prophecy. (Ac. 2:16,17) These believers had the boldness to educate the rulers, elders and all the "devout" gathered, that the Person they crucified, who arose from the dead, was the Christ prophesied by David! (Ac. 2:29-35) Only through Christ could they be saved! (Ac. 2:21; 4:8-13)

The only language, which might determine education status in the eyes of the Pharisees, would be Hebrew. Otherwise, education had little to do with how many Gentile languages one knew.

Language:

Galileans were recognized by their accent. The servant girl knew Peter's origin by his accent. (Matt. 26:73) After they heard them speaking, not before, they wondered, "Behold, are not all these which speak Galileans?" (2:7) Their accent gave away their identity.

The Galileans were able to speak the same languages as their listeners. Clyde McCone cites R.H. Gundry who states that "proof exists that Hebrew, Aramaic and Greek were commonly used by Jews in first century Palestine."[21] Latin was also spoken. Three major highways intersected Galilee from Syria, Egypt and Arabia. Because of Galilee's proximity to

---

[20] Two schools of religious thought prevailed under the conservative Shammai and the liberal Hillel.

[21] Clyde McCone, *The Phenomena of Pentecost*, http://www.asa3.org/ASA/PSCF/1971/JASA9-71McCone.html

trade routes and commerce of the Gentiles, it is likely they knew more languages than Jews in Jerusalem. It is believed that they were proficient in at least four languages and also had some limited skill in minority dialects as well. McCone states that "in a multilingual world, Galileans were the most multilingual of all."[22]

Summary

The Galilean status and reputation was part of the reason for the crowd's bewilderment. The view that the Galileans were simple and uneducated because they were monolingual, clashes not only with the text but with history.[23] Actually, Galileans were derided for lack of education, not language proficiency. Given the strategic location of Galilee and exposure to languages, no other province could match the linguistic abilities of the Galileans.

THE MULTITUDE

The identity of the multitude helps us not to read into the text. What can we know about the multitude?

Identity

Dwelling in Jerusalem were devout Jews and proselytes from every nation under heaven. (Ac. 2:5,10) The places of their origin are specifically listed. (2:8-11) As 'devout' devout Jews, they likely understood Hebrew, the language of the scriptures. Jerusalem remained the center of Judaism for all Jews, including the Dispersions, both East and West, and so devout Jews and proselytes travelled a great distance for these feasts.

Languages

The view that the number of provinces listed represent a total of more than 15 languages is an erroneous presumption.[24] He does not say what the languages were. However, by identifying these provinces, both the shared and the different languages would be known. For example, if we would say that devout Jews and proselytes assembling at Jerusalem came from Canada, Britain, Australia, U.S, Ireland, Jamaica, New Zealand, Philippines, France and Mexico, we would know that they likely knew

---

[22] ibd.

[23] *John Gill's Exposition*, on Acts 2:7 'never learned any language except their 'mother -tongue.' *Albert Barnes Notes on the Whole Bible* on Ac 2:7, also derides the Galileans for their accent. These comments cannot be supported with the history or the text.

[24] Robert Zerhusen, *A New Look At Tongues*, page 1. Horton and Henry assume more than 15 languages. http://www.onthewing.org/user/Tongues%20-%20Zerhusen.pdf

English, French and Spanish. The devout Jews, who came from the areas listed, were hearing the Galileans speak 'English, French and Spanish', by way of illustration.

Apollos, a Jew from Egypt, preached in Ephesus and later in Achaia and Corinth. Visitors from these countries would know and understand the same language Apollos spoke – Greek. Men from Cyrene, Alexandria, Cilicia and Egypt disputed with Stephen. (Ac. 6:9,10) Jews and proselytes from these different countries understood common languages.

Not every province of the Roman Empire was represented. The provinces of Macedonia, Moesia, Thrace, Epirus, Bithynia among others existent in his day are excluded.[25] Had there been visitors from these areas, the language repertoire of the Galileans may have been insufficient.

Prophetic Purpose of Luke's List

This list serves as a record of regions represented at this Pentecost that would have been impacted with the Gospel. (Ac. 2:17) Prior to this, God had 'poured' His truth out in Hebrew to Israel through the Prophets. Now, God would spread the gospel in Gentile languages the people already knew. These listed nations serve as documented evidence of the fulfillment of Joel's prophecy of the Spirit's outpouring of His word upon all flesh, not just "Judea". Jews and proselytes saved on the day of Pentecost would return home to share the gospel with Gentiles as well.

SUMMARY

This background of the habits of believers before Pentecost, where they gathered, who the Galileans and the multitude were, are elements essential to gaining a biblical perspective of this event. The notion that ignorance was based on the lack of knowledge of languages is untenable. Without this context we become vulnerable to charismatic legends.

THE HOLY SPIRIT'S MINISTRY TO GALILEANS

Luke writes about how the Holy Spirit affected the Galileans,

> 'And they were all filled of the Holy Spirit and began to speak in other languages as the Spirit gave them utterance'. (Ac. 2:4)

Spirit is in the genitive, meaning that the Galileans were filled with something in the Holy Spirit's possession.

---

[25] *Holman Bible Atlas*, B&H Publishing Group, c1998, map 116, page 241

LANGUAGES

Glossa used in 2:4,11 and *dialektos* in 2:6,8 both mean 'language'. Our English word 'dialect' originates from *dialektos*. These are synonyms because they both require linguistic familiarity to speak them. Indeed, the Galileans elicited a surprised response from the crowd, when they spoke 'other' languages. (2:6) But, why?

THE SPIRIT GAVE 'UTTERANCE'.

It is inferred that 'utterance' is synonymous with 'language'. (2:4) But, it does not say that the Holy Spirit gave them 'languages'. It says He gave them 'utterance'. 'Utterance' means, "to utter or declare oneself, give one's opinion." (Thayer's Lexicon) 'Utterance' and 'language' have entirely different meanings.

A 'Miracle' Of Comprehension

As Paul was not given a new language when he 'utters' to Festus and King Agrippa, so also, were Peter and the Galileans not given unlearned languages when they spoke in other languages. Language was the vehicle by which the 'utterance', or the opinion was conveyed. In all three instances, it means to "declare" something. In this context, they understood and declared the mighty works of God. (Ac. 2:4, 11, 14; 26:25)

A 'Miracle' Of Boldness

But there is another aspect to 'utterance', which explains some added jeopardy their conduct exposed them to. These believers were emboldened to authoritatively declare His wonderful works, not in the Hebrew language, appropriate for the day of Pentecost, but in their own languages. The pouring out of His Spirit illumined these believers to understand how the OT pointed to Christ. (Ac. 2:32-35) The Holy Spirit gave them the courage to speak about the same subject Jesus stymied the Pharisees with when He asked them, 'How could Jesus be David's son?' (Matt. 22:41-46) Now, the indwelling Holy Spirit was pouring into these believers truth with the power to declare it. They also knew that linking Jesus of Nazareth, crucified less than two months ago for blasphemy, to the fulfillment of OT scripture, might not be well-received.

Not A Language Miracle

Some argue that when the Galileans spoke their language, the crowd heard the message in their own language, consequently a 'speaking' miracle. One commentator writes that the phrase, 'the Spirit gave them utterance', "implies plainly that they were now endued with a faculty of speaking languages, which they had not before learned."[26] Rather, it implies that they needed to be informed by Holy Spirit to correctly prophesy in the languages they already knew.

Summary

Luke states that the Galileans spoke 'as the Spirit gave them utterance'. As they were impressed with the reality of God's grace in Christ, they shared it. Along with Spirit-given insight, came the joyful impetus to 'prophesy' Christ in a situation that might even endanger their lives.

WHAT LANGUAGE IS NOT 'OTHER'?

If we discover what language was not their own, then we will discover what language was not "other".

THE ONE-OF-A-KIND LANGUAGE

'They began to speak "other" languages'. This statement indicates that they had been listening to the service in a different language. "Other" also implies that this language, they had already been speaking, was unique. (*heteros*: 'other, of a different kind') It was in a different category than Aramaic, Greek or Latin. The languages they began speaking fell into one category: they were all Gentile. Therefore, there is only one language, which answers to all of the above as not 'other', and that is Hebrew.

HEBREW CEASED TO BE LANGUAGE OF BIRTH

Before their Assyrian and Babylonian captivities, the Jews knew Hebrew as their native language. But in time, they lost Hebrew as their native language, having assimilated the Aramaic language of their captors. Paul's reference to Isaiah's prophecy defines for us languages that were not "other" and which were.

> "In the law it is written, "With men of other tongues (languages) and other lips I will speak to this people; yet for all that they will not hear me," says the Lord." (1 Cor. 14:21 brackets added, NKJV)

When Isaiah prophesied this, they were still speaking their biblical Hebrew. Lack of proficiency required that Hebrew be translated into the Aramaic and explained! (Neh. 8:7,8) All "other" languages pertained to

---

[26] Albert Barnes, *Notes On The Whole Bible* on Acts 2:4

languages that were not Hebrew! The context indicates that the language that was not “other”, was Hebrew.

Since the Law and the Prophets were mostly written in Hebrew, it remained the language of advanced education for rabbis and the devout. Though parents raised their children in the common languages of the day, Hebrew continued to be the language of the Jewish religion. ‘Other’ languages had displaced Hebrew as the language of birth.

HEBREW WAS STILL SPOKEN

Though the languages of Assyria and later Babylon became dominant, the Hebrew text of the Law and the Prophets was still read in the synagogues. As devout Jews and proselytes, they would have been able to understand Hebrew, if not speak it. When Paul spoke Hebrew to a noisy and boisterous crowd, they became ‘even more silent’. They had a high regard for the ‘holy’ language. (Ac.21:40; 22:2)[27]

Some claim that the Hebrew was really Aramaic. During the captivities, the Hebrew text changed by accommodating place names peculiar to Aramaic. But the presence of Aramaic words in a language does not make the language Aramaic any more than the presence of Spanish words in English makes English Spanish. Yet, the linguistic integrity of the Hebrew OT remained intact, as it was originally written. It could still be read and heard and understood. Greek writers did not use the word ‘Hebrew’ to describe Aramaic.[28] Even extra-biblical scholarship demonstrates that the word ‘Hebrew’ cannot be translated as ‘Aramaic’ as it is, in some newer translations. The Bible states that people were speaking Hebrew, not Aramaic.[29]

---

[27] Lexicons state that ‘Hebrew’ refers to Aramaic spoken at the time. Translations have even substituted ‘Aramaic’ for ‘Hebrew’. The primary basis for this is that John has identified four Aramaic looking words as Hebrew: Bethzatha, 5:2; Gabbatha, 19:13; Golgotha, 19:17; Rabbouni, 20:16. He points out, as do others, that though these words have Aramaic roots, they are actually imported into Hebrew much as English has names that originated in other languages. *What Language Did Paul Speak in Acts 21-22?* by Ken Penner http://www.academia.edu/1669906/What_language_did_Paul_speak_in_Acts_21-22_Ancient_names_for_Hebrew_and_Aramaic

[28] *The Language Environment of First Century Judaea*, VOLUME TWO, Edited by Randall Buth & R. Steven Notley, P.67 http://www.biblicallanguagecenter.com/wp-content/uploads/2014/04/9789004263406_04-EBRAISTI.pdf

[29] E.A. Knapp, *Discovering the Old Testament*, Did the Messiah Speak Aramaic or Hebrew?, http://www.torahclass.com/archived-articles/413-did-the-messiah-speak-aramaic-or-hebrew-part-1-by-eaknapp

Some scholars have concluded that Jesus and His disciples knew Greek as well as Aramaic. Aaron Tresham writes, "it seems reasonable to conclude that Jesus could speak Hebrew, Aramaic and Greek."[30] Most or all at Pentecost would have understood either or both Greek and Aramaic, and as devout Jews they would have at least understood Hebrew. The view that Hebrew was not spoken or that 'Hebrew' means Aramaic are inferences inconsistent with Scripture.

Since the discovery of the Dead Sea Scrolls, evidence is overwhelming that many in Israel were fluent in Hebrew. The Samaritans preserved and spoke Hebrew, which is why Jesus was able to communicate easily with the woman at the well. (Jn. 4:4-26) When Jesus discussed the Torah in the temple with the experts in the Torah, He undoubtedly was speaking Hebrew. (Lk. 2:39-52) The title on the cross was also written in Hebrew. (not Aramaic, as it is incorrectly translated in Jn. 19:20; ESV) Hebrew was the sacred language because it was the language of Scripture.[31] God spoke Hebrew to Paul on the way to Damascus. (Ac. 26:14)

Though visiting Jews and proselytes were not as likely to be trained in rabbinical schools, their exposure to the reading of the Law and Prophets and sermons translated into the vernacular every Sabbath made them familiar with Hebrew. Recitation of prayers from the Hebrew scriptures during the sabbath day services would have given them the practice to speak it, though it was not the vernacular.

PETER PREACHED IN HEBREW

Perhaps one of the most erroneous beliefs about NT history is that the Septuagint was an authorized Greek translation approved and used for Jewish services.[32] Jesus preached that not one 'jot or tittle' shall pass from the Law and the Prophets till all is fulfilled. (Matt.5:17; Lk.22:44) Greek doesn't have 'jots or tittles'. Christ was referring to writings with Hebrew text! (Ac. 24:14)

Jesus highlighted the importance of the Law and the Prophets on numerous occasions. (Matt. 7:12; 11:13; 22:40; Lk. 16:16; 22:44) The

---

[30] Aaron Tresham, *The Languages Spoken By Jesus*, by p. 93
https://www.tms.edu/m/tmsj20e.pdf

[31] John J. Parsons, *Did Jesus Speak Hebrew*, fourth paragraph. Hebrew was 'sacrosanct'.
https://www.hebrew4christians.com/Articles/Jesus_Hebrew/jesus_hebrew.html

[32] *Did Jesus Quote From The Septuagint?*
http://0104.nccdn.net/1_5/1e0/2be/2f2/JesusQuoteSeptuagint.pdf
Also, please see 'Septuagint' in NOTES

disciples were familiar with the Law and the Prophets. (Jn. 1:45) The Law and the Prophets were read on the Sabbath day, which means that it was scripture, a writing with 'jots and tittles'. (Ac. 13:15)

Jesus asks the scribes and elders, 'Have you not read this scripture?' (Mk. 15:28) After He finished reading from the scroll, Jesus said, 'Today is this scripture fulfilled in your ears.' (Lk. 4:21) Jesus told his audience to believe as the scripture says. (Jn.7:38) Jesus and the Apostles made specific reference to the Scriptures, not translations.

Peter wrote that 'no prophecy of Scripture is a matter of private interpretation.' (2 Pe. 1:20,21) Translations of the Law and the Prophets were not regarded as Scripture.

"The Scripture"

The NT writers are very clear that 'Scripture' is not any writing. Mark writes that the scripture was fulfilled when Christ was numbered with the transgressors. (Mk.15:28) The disciples believed the word of Jesus and the Scriptures concerning His resurrection. (Jn. 2:22) Christ said the Scripture cannot be broken. (Jn. 13:18) Jesus was intent on fulfilling the Scripture. (Jn.17:12) Numerous other references with the definite article imply that Christ and the Apostles and indeed devout Jews, held to the Hebrew Scripture containing the Law and the Prophets. In the Bible, 'Scriptures' are not translations; they are copies of the original.

Peter's Sermon

The word 'Scripture' itself proves that during the apostolic period, Jews had access to 'jot and tittle' writings of the Law and the Prophets, that they could read and understand! When Peter stands before them to calm this crowd and explain why the Galileans were not drunken as they supposed, he quotes scripture, not a translation. Given the potential volatility of the crowd, Peter would preach in Hebrew. To hear quotations from the OT translated into 'other' languages likely would have aggravated an already unstable religious crowd. (Ac. 2:12,13)

DIGLOSSIA

For a further explanation of Jewish expectations in this regard, I urge the reader to explore the paper written by Robert Zerhusen.[33] He explains how societies have adapted high and low languages as they relate to

---

[33] Robert Zerhusen, *A New Look At Tongues*, p.9-14
http://www.onthewing.org/user/Tongues%20-%20Zerhusen.pdf

religious institution. One prominent example is the Roman Catholic Church use of Latin for liturgy such as the Mass in her services.[34] Similarly, the Jews expected that on special occasions, like Pentecost, only the sacred language of Hebrew be spoken.

THE 'OTHER' LANGUAGES

Perhaps the biggest stumbling block to discerning this event correctly, is the failure to appreciate the context of 'other' languages. Most commentators presume that 'other' must be a language that the Galileans did not speak. But is this what the text states and implies?

'THEY BEGAN TO SPEAK'

'Began' is in the middle voice in the Greek, which means that the subject both initiates and participates in the action. The subjects, in this case, the Galileans, initiated the response and participated in the response. Had this been a miracle of speaking unlearned languages, they would have been passive. The grammar precludes the miracle view.

However, 'as the Spirit was giving them utterance' the context permits the passive voice. The Galileans were receiving 'opinion' that did not originate from them. 'As the Spirit gave them utterance', they spoke in 'other' languages. It is implied that they were not articulate in the holy language of Pentecost and for that reason spoke 'other' languages.

WAS THE MULTITUDE MULTILINGUAL?

The language of birth of one from the East would naturally be Aramaic. The language of birth of one from the West would likely be Greek or Latin. Generally, immigrants learn the predominant language necessary for business while the language of their parents fade from use. In his letter to the church in Corinth, Paul alludes to the eastern Diaspora where Jews of the captivity had also lost their ability to speak Hebrew and even understand Hebrew. Aramaic had become their birth language. (1Cor.14:21) Though Jews and proselytes from various countries were represented at Pentecost, it is reasonably argued that there might have been only three or four native languages spoken.[35] Different region or ethnicity is not a basis to assume each to have had a different native

---

[34] *Catholic Culture*
https://www.catholicculture.org/culture/library/view.cfm?recnum=2786

[35] Robert Zerhusen, *A New Look At Tongues*, p. 4-7
http://www.onthewing.org/user/Tongues%20-%20Zerhusen.pdf

language. As stated above, jurisdictions listed are not equivalent to the number of languages represented.

Aramaic and Greek were the most commonly spoken languages in Israel. Scholars believe that many Jews would have been bilingual and even trilingual.[36] It is well attested that the majority in Israel spoke Aramaic, since it had become their vernacular during their captivities.

PURPOSE FOR MULTIPLE LANGUAGES

It is held that multiple languages were necessary for the spread of the Gospel. It should be noted however, that Peter preached to an agitated crowd in one language.[37] Secondly, Peter was preaching to mostly Jews. He addressed the crowd as 'men of Judea,' 'all who live in Jerusalem' and as 'men of Israel'. (Ac. 2:14,22) And thirdly, he reminded them of Jesus who performed miracles and wonders and signs, which He did among them, 'just as you yourselves know.'

Quoting Joel, Peter declares in Hebrew, that the words they were hearing was prophecy, despite the fact they were hearing it in Gentile languages and despite the fact that they were not hearing it from the Rabbis and teachers of the Law in Hebrew. The plurality of languages facilitated the proclamation of the good news of the long-awaited Messiah without the need of a translator. It was the means by which the Holy Spirit-given 'utterances' would be made known to all flesh.

WHAT ARE 'OTHER' LANGUAGES?

Miracle view advocates assume that 'other' languages were unknown to the Galileans or unknown to the multitude, hence either a speaking miracle or a hearing miracle. But ,they say nothing about the language for worship and ignore the context. 'Other' languages exclude Hebrew.

THE GRAMMAR

It is important to decipher what Luke writes about the speaking Galileans and the listening multitude.

---

[36] Ibid. p.3 Simon J Kistemaker and J.H. Marshall, both of the language miracle views indicate that Jews would know Aramaic and Greek.

[37] Robert Zerhusen, *A New Look At Tongues*, page 2. Zerhusen cites Robert Gundry, a language miracle advocate, who admits that Aramaic and Greek would have been sufficient to communicate to the hearers.
http://www.onthewing.org/user/Tongues%20-%20Zerhusen.pdf

The Speaking Galileans

Much of the interpretation difficulties have arisen from faulty translation. Note the following example,

> "And when this sound occurred, the crowd came together and were bewildered because each one of them was hearing them speak in his own language." (Ac. 2:6, NASB; Translators have added an extra 3rd person plural, pronoun, not in the Greek.)

This translation is typical in that it implies that the Galileans were either miraculously speaking the language of the crowd or the crowd was miraculously hearing their own language as the Galileans were speaking their own.

The following is an Interlinear translation of the Greek,

> "But the rumor of this having arisen, the multitude came together and were confounded because each one heard them speaking in his own language."[38] (emphasis added)

This translation still inclines the reader to infer that the antecedent of the personal pronoun 'his' is 'each one' of the multitude rather than 'them' of the Galileans, which is why many claim this to be a hearing miracle. But please note the following translation,

> 'The sound of [it] having occurred, the multitude, [it] came together and [it] was confounded, because [they] were hearing each one [man] of them speaking the own language.'[39]

The multitude were able to understand that each Galilean was speaking 'the own language'. This may imply that they were multilingual. But, more importantly, it implies that they were not speaking Hebrew. Hebrew was not anyone's "own language".

It states that 'they were hearing'. It does not state that they all heard the comparatively few Galileans speak their own languages. As they were hearing these Galileans speak, the crowd discovered who they were and were amazed. (2:7)

But there is another implication with the omission of the definite article in translations. "The" is indicative of a relevant point Luke already mentioned. He stated that they spoke in 'other' languages. (2:4) "The" 'other' languages, were 'the' 'own' language of each Galilean, therefore, it

[38] George Ricker Berry, *Interlinear Greek-English New Testament*, Baker Book House, 1985, p.314

[39] Interlinear Bible, biblehub.com (Acts 2:6)

could not have been unknown to them. Before they began speaking 'other' languages, they had been listening and/or speaking a language that was not favored for normal communication. It was not their 'own' language because it was Hebrew. Unusually enthralled with sudden new insight granted to them by the Holy Spirit, they deferred to the languages in which they were most proficient. The 'other' languages were those the Galileans normally spoke.

The Listening Multitude

Verse 8 is translated variously as 'our own language in which we were born', 'our own language to which we were born' and 'how is it that we hear, each of us in his own native language'.[40] Following is a literal translation,

> "And they were all amazed, and did wonder, saying one unto another, 'Lo, are not all these who are speaking Galileans? And how do we hear, each in our proper dialect, in which we were born?'" (Ac. 2:7,8; Young's Literal Translation)

Following is a literal translation from an interlinear,

> 'And then they were being amazed and marveling, saying, 'Behold, are not all these Galileans who are speaking? And how do we hear each the own language of us, in which we were born?' (2:7,8, biblehub.com)

From the grammar of verse 6 above, it is stated that the Galileans each spoke 'the own language', meaning one they knew and favored. Again, the notion that they had been supernaturally gifted to speak languages they had not learned would contradict the grammar and the meaning of "own". Since these Galileans were speaking languages they knew, there is to this point, no language 'speaking miracle'.

But, the narrative continues with another important fact. They heard the "own language <u>of us</u>." Now, if the Galileans were speaking their 'own' languages and the multitude were hearing their 'own' languages', it must be concluded that they knew each other's languages. How could there be a miracle if both speakers and listeners were communicating in their "own" languages? (2:11) How could there be a miracle if the languages of both the Galileans and the multitude were already known to one another? There was no 'hearing miracle.'

---

[40] NKJV, NASB and ESV, respectively, Acts 2:8

'In Which We Were Born'

Rather than providing a list of the languages of birth, Luke lists the ethnicity and places of birth. (2:9-11) Albert Barnes explains 'language in which we were born', as follows,

> "That is, as we say, in our native language; what is spoken where we were born."

The language preference of the multitude was determined by the region of birth. Luke implies that each person in the multitude "belonged to a particular place by birth."[41] They were 'natives' of different regions in the list. Secondly, Luke implies that the multitude was speaking languages "originating in a particular place".[42] One or more languages were spoken in each of the regions on the list. And thirdly, it is implied that there was cross-border language familiarity. The native language of a person from Pamphylia could be the same as a person from Cappadocia.

The 'native' language is not based on ethnicity. For example, children born in Canada to first generation Spanish speaking parents, have English or French as the language 'wherein they were born', though they may speak Spanish at home. An ethnic Spaniard in Canada could have English or French as his native language.

It is likely that many of the visitors also knew minority languages specific to the country from which they came. However, children of immigrants quickly assimilate the common language as their birth language, thus displacing their parents' language as their first. Likewise, children of the Jewish Dispersion would first learn the common language in use, which would then become their "own" or 'native' language. The Diaspora had, over centuries, assimilated the languages common to these listed provinces, thus sharing the same birth languages.

Greatly outnumbered, not all the many thousands would have been in close enough proximity to the 120 Galileans to hear them. The reference to 'multitude' should not be understood to be inclusive. For example, it may be truthfully stated that the 'congregation sang the closing hymn', without implying that everyone was singing. Certainly, the multitude quickly learned about the interruption, but not necessarily everyone in the multitude heard the Galileans.

---

[41] *Merriam-Webster online dictionary*. 'Native' definition #2

[42] Ibid. Definition # 6a

The Languages Of Birth Are The 'Other' Languages

Because of the definite article in the phrase 'the own language' in both verses 6 and 8, we are drawn to the specific matter of 'other' languages mentioned in verse 4. John Gill writes,

> "wherein we were born; our native language; for though these men were Jews by descent, yet were born and brought up in other countries, which language they spake; and not the Hebrew, or Syriac, or Chaldee."

In this context, both languages 'in which we were born' and 'other' language, exclude Hebrew, which everyone reading Acts at that time would know. No one had Hebrew as a 'birth' language or native language because it was not the vernacular of any region. Therefore, the language into which they were born was common to the places of birth.

The 'Birth' Languages Of Judea And Galilee

After listing the ethnicity and regions of the multitude, Luke writes,

> 'We hear them speaking in our own languages the wonderful works of God.' (2:11b)

Now, it is very important to focus on one region in Luke's list – Judea. As a majority in this multitude, Judeans also heard and understood the Galileans speaking the wonderful works of God. In all the interactions that Jesus and His Galilean disciples had with the Judeans, there was never any hint of a language barrier. Indeed, the Galileans had an unusual accent by which they were likely recognized, but they understood one another. (Matt. 26:73)

Since there was no language barrier between the Galileans and Judeans, the notion that the Galileans spoke unlearned languages miraculously is not credible. Why would a Galilean miraculously speak an unknown language when he already knew the language of the Judean?

Why then should the Judeans be amazed that they were speaking "our languages"? Since Galileans and Judeans knew the same languages, the apparent surprise among them therefore, could not be a suddenly acquired ability to speak an unlearned language. Given the fact that Galileans were multilingual, speaking the native languages of the visitors would also not have been a surprise. The Galileans were speaking languages common not only to the Judeans but all the visitors. They already spoke one another's native languages. **They were amazed that they spoke the 'other' languages, not different languages.**

If, as commonly believed, believers spoke <u>other languages than the ones they learned</u>, they would actually be speaking languages the Judeans and fellow Galileans <u>did not know</u> and were not their own! And, why would the entire multitude be astounded that the Galileans and Judeans, with common native languages, could understand one another?

SUMMARY

Judeans were surprised for the same reason as all visiting Jews and proselytes. As Judeans were hearing the languages into which they were born, so also were the visitors from the list hearing their languages into which they were born. Judea is on the <u>same</u> list as the visitors! (2:9) Since the multitude would have known that Galilee and Judea had common languages, they could not have been amazed by supposed miraculous linguistic abilities of the Galileans. The multitude first complained that the Galileans were speaking in common languages, then expressed amazement that they were speaking the wonderful works of God.

The passage does not teach that the Galileans were circulating among the multitude doing personal evangelism work. As any large international conference today, business might be conducted in English. But after the meeting is adjourned, people would break to discuss the issues raised, in a language familiar to them. In this case, the Holy Spirit adjourned the 'meeting' and the Galileans joyously proclaimed newly understood truth in languages they were proficient in.

The miracle view assumes that 'other' must be a reference to languages the Galileans didn't know. Nothing in this text suggests that anyone spoke unlearned languages.

ELEMENTS OF SURPRISE

Why was this 'worshipping' multitude startled and amazed? (Ac. 2:7) If reasons for this consternation are not rightly apprised, incorrect language miracle inferences are made. With a brief review of some underlying elements of this Pentecost, details emerge that preclude the notion that the crowd was amazed at the linguistic ability of the Galileans.

THE MIGHTY RUSHING WIND

The multitude was at the first bewildered at what was happening on this day of Pentecost. In the hush of the assembly for the third hour prayers, the multitude heard the sound of a mighty rushing wind. The crowd then became confused. They "ran and came together in a disorderly and tumultuous manner..." [43]

Galilean Notoriety

They were surprised to see that the ones who were speaking in languages were Galileans. (2:7) These devout Jews and proselytes knew that Galileans had played a part in other notorious events. They also knew that Jesus, a Galilean, had been crucified just 50 days before. Very likely, the crowd was amazed that these outnumbered Galileans would expose themselves to danger by proclaiming Christ.

'Other' Languages Could Agitate

On one occasion, Paul had been falsely accused of bring Greeks into the temple area and for that was dragged outside where the Romans arrested him. After identifying himself, the commander granted Paul permission to speak to this agitated crowd. But rather than speak to them in Greek, he spoke Hebrew. Luke writes that when they heard Hebrew, they became even more quiet. (Ac. 21:40; 22:2) Speaking Hebrew commanded attention.

It stands to reason that on the day of Pentecost, a high day in the Jewish religious calendar, the proceedings would have been in Hebrew. But rather than keeping quiet or joining in the recitation of prayers from the OT, exuberant Galileans interrupted the service by praising God in 'other languages'. This could only aggravate an already anxious, suspicious crowd of devout Jews and proselytes, and could have just as easily have turned into a mob. (Ac. 2:4-11) Contrary to tradition for this occasion, these Galilean believers were speaking inappropriate languages.

Galileans Were Actually Knowledgeable.

At this Pentecost, the Holy Spirit gave these believers the ability "to utter, or declare oneself, give one's opinion".[44] Unable to conceal their excitement of the Holy Spirit's pronouncements to them, even some of the multitude were amazed that these 'uneducated' Galileans were speaking the mighty works of God. (2:7,11,12) They understood that Jesus was indeed the subject of OT prophecy. (Ac.2:29-35)

---

[43] John Gill's commentary on Ac. 2:6. Also see Albert Barnes.

[44] *Thayer's Greek Lexicon*, biblehub.com, See 'Utterance'. https://biblehub.com/greek/669.htm

The Galileans Were Bold

Others, however, were dismissive. Who would deliberately speak to exalt this Messiah, crucified for blasphemy just 50 days prior? They tried to excuse this apparently reckless proclamation of this Messiah as a result of having too much wine. They were surprised at their courage.

Some Were Women

Women were publicly prophesying! (2:17) This was not in accord with customs and the culture of public assembly and worship.[45]

Summary

They were bewildered because these multilingual Galileans were all speaking 'other' languages inappropriately. (2:6) They were amazed that they spoke the mighty works of God. (2:11) Presumed uneducated, the multitude was amazed that the Galileans could speak boldly and with such authority. Women, also prophesying, likely contributed to their amazement. They were amazed that these unpopular Galileans had the courage and comprehension to talk about an unpopular Messiah.

THE CHARGES

Acquainted with Galilean notoriety, they asked, 'by what means' are we hearing them in our own language? Could this behavior be justified? 'By what means should we consider hearing these Galileans speak in our own language legitimate on this day?' (2:8) Peter answers this question by quoting Joel. The unexpected means was that the Holy Spirit was causing men and women to prophesy in languages other than Hebrew. (2:17)

Once fearful, Peter, now boldly and publicly confirmed Christ's identity as Lord and Savior to a potentially hostile crowd. (2:36) The memory of His crucifixion just 50 days earlier would have been fresh in the minds of all who attended this feast.

After hearing the mighty sound of the wind, a confused, disturbed, converging multitude asked how it is that they were each hearing the disciples speak in their own language. (2:8)

---

[45] Alfred Edersheim, *Sketches of Jewish Social Life*, Chapter 8

Rabbis did not encourage the same instruction for boys and girls. They believed that the woman's mind was not given for theological enquiry. However, the NT shows that women were part of public functions, attended the synagogue indicating that they were well-informed though not formally trained in the Law.

THEIR QUESTION IMPLIES INTENT

Surprised by the unconventional conduct of these believers some were asking, 'what does this mean?' Had they never heard 'other' languages spoken before? Certainly. But, why then, were they amazed?

'What wishes this to be?' more accurately expresses the apprehension of the crowd. (2:12) Amazed at the violation of the religious norms for an event such as this, they wondered what the underlying intent of these Galileans was. Men like Theudas and Judas of Galilee and their followers were killed and scattered but they were not drunk while they attempted their planned, attempted insurrections. (Ac.5:36,37) Questions arising from their identity, therefore, were not to be taken lightly! Why would they want to have any further association with this crucified Galilean? This exposed them to suspicions of sedition.

'THEY ARE DRUNK'

However, others mocked them for having as much intent in their actions as one would expect from someone 'filled with new wine.'

Wine Did Not Explain Their Joyful Speech.

It is common knowledge that the consumption of alcohol first loosens the tongue. Seeing their joyful proclamation of the wonderful works of God, they supposed that they had become talkative with 'new wine'. First, Peter defends his friends by saying that it is only the third hour of the day. After a night's rest, there wasn't enough time for all of them to experience the same elation by drinking wine.[46] Secondly, Peter explains from the prophet Joel that the source of their message and courage was the Holy Spirit, not wine. (Ac. 2:14, 17)

Wine Could Not Account For Miraculous Linguistic Abilities

But there is one other important point this charge raises. If, as supposed by miracle advocates, these Galileans were speaking unlearned languages, would they be charged with having too much wine? Of course, not. It is understandable that the crowd might accuse the Galileans of being drunken because of their excitement. But it is ludicrous that mockers would give wine as the reason for their multilingual ability. In reality, this accusation precludes a linguistic miracle.

---

[46] Wine of that day had a much lower alcohol content than today. So to be 'filled with new wine' would not necessarily imply slurred and incoherent speech, as it does today.

SUMMARY

To suggest that they were full of new wine is the less serious charge. If sober, staging a deliberately planned campaign in honor of the crucified Messiah would then have been deemed more likely. If they had 'just' had too much wine, they would not have had the capacity to stage a rebellion. They would then just be a nuisance. To be accused of having drunken with 'new wine', is evidence that the multitude had not observed any linguistic miracle.

THE MAIN ASSUMPTIONS

By way of review, the linguistic miracle theories are summarized as follows:

THE HEARING 'MIRACLE'

Some miracle advocates believe that "other" languages were known to the Galileans but not to the listeners. However, as they spoke, the Holy Spirit caused the crowd to hear the message in their own birth language.

THE SPEAKING 'MIRACLE'

Some miracle advocates believe that the Galileans miraculously spoke languages they had not previously known, but known to the listeners. (Ac. 2:4)

SUMMARY

These linguistic miracle theories presuppose many assumptions that cannot be supported by the text, context or the biblical history of the time. Miracle advocates <u>presume</u> that,

- 'other' languages were 'unknown' to the Galileans.
- Galileans spoke unknown languages that were understood by the multitude, hence a speaking miracle.
- the Galileans spoke their own 'known' languages unfamiliar to multitude, but were miraculously understood.
- 'language' and 'utterance' are synonyms.
- every one of many thousands heard the Galileans speaking.
- multilingualism was indicative of education.
- the multitude was surprised because of the multiple languages the supposed monolingual Galileans were speaking.
- languages of birth or native languages are familial, not regional.
- the Galileans were scattered among the multitude.

- the Galileans could not have known the languages of the multitude.
- the birth languages of the peoples and regions listed, mostly spoke different native languages than the Galileans.
- the Galilean language(s) were unknown to Judeans.
- the Jewish services were conducted in Aramaic or Greek.

These unproven assumptions have generated a language miracle narrative that has grossly distorted Luke's account of Pentecost.

CONCLUSIONS

The Galilean disciples did not speak unlearned languages; they spoke "other" languages. This implies that they knew 'other' languages than Hebrew. The Galileans knew different languages and could speak the same languages as the crowd, which were also their "own" languages.

Hearing different languages was not unusual because both the Galileans and the multitude were multilingual. It was however, unusual that 'other' languages be spoken on a solemn occasion such as Pentecost.

The Holy Spirit did not give them 'languages'. (2:4) The Holy Spirit impressed truth upon the minds of these believers, not understood before. As they were given "utterance", they spoke in "other" learned languages.

When they began to speak in "other" languages, the Galileans were glorifying God amongst themselves, <u>before</u> the crowd had arrived. (Ac. 2:8,11)

"Other" languages implies that one common language was spoken for Pentecost. (2:1,4) "Other" languages in verses 6,8,11 are native to the regions mentioned.

Language miracle advocates fail to show that the Galileans were linguistically challenged. Those from Luke's list of regions, heard and understood the Galileans speak their preferred language.

4. THE 'UTTERANCE' OF PROPHECY

The supposed linguistic 'miracle' views of Pentecost, have had a profound and deleterious effect upon the fellowship of believers. But, the Galileans were the recipients of a miracle, that united them in Gospel truth. It was not supernatural 'tongues'. This Pentecost was a miracle "utterance" event.

How would it be possible to keep any group of people on the same theological page? Despite their common ancestry, groups such as the Zealots, Pharisees, Sadducees and Essenes each had their own peculiar doctrines. Now, with the advent of Christ, there was yet another major factor that could expose believers to the ire of the authorities. It is therefore, noteworthy that the multitude observed that the Galileans spoke different languages, not different doctrines.

Beginning with a prophecy from Joel, Peter explains the essence of the Galileans' "utterance". Each believer was sharing the same message as a result of the outpouring of the Holy Spirit. "This is what was spoken by the prophet Joel:" (Ac. 2:16a) Since the entire quotation pertains to this event, it must be understood in this context, unless reason is given for another.

THE TERMS OF THE PROPHESIED 'UTTERANCE'

The Galileans prophesied an immanent and unified knowledge of the Person and finished work of Christ at the Passover that had occurred just 50 days prior. Supernaturally assured by the Holy Spirit that this Jesus had come to save them from their sins, these believers could not refrain from prophesying the Gospel of Christ in the language they knew best. Peter explained from the Prophet Joel, reasons why the Galileans had spoken in their own languages, namely, that the Holy Spirit had caused them to prophesy. (Ac.2:11,22-35)

LAST DAYS

The Jews knew that the end of Daniel's 70 weeks was upon them. (Da. 9:24) And, it is in this context that Peter references Joel. The writer of Hebrews indicated that Christ was the fulfillment of prophecy that would bring about a time of reformation, the end of offerings and sacrifices under the Levitical system. (Matt. 24:1,2; Heb. 8:13; 9:9-11) It meant that the Holy Spirit would enlighten the minds of a few Jewish believers that Jesus was both the High Priest and Sacrifice prophesied in the OT. This was the time for celebration because Jesus had fulfilled His Covenant to deliver His 'born again' people from Mt. Sinai to Mt. Zion. (Heb. 12:21,22) These were the "last days" in which God spoke by His Son. (Heb. 1:1,2) This Pentecost, according to Peter, was an event in the "last days". (Ac. 2:16,17)

ALL FLESH

God had promised that He would pour out **of** His Spirit upon all flesh, not just Jews. Up to this point, God had revealed His Word exclusively through Jewish prophets, primarily in the Hebrew language. At this Pentecost, the Gospel that Jesus was the prophesied Messiah, was proclaimed openly at a Jewish service for the first time, in 'other' languages, for all "flesh". Even truth proclaimed in the 'unholy' languages of the Gentiles like Latin, Greek and Aramaic is prophecy!

'SONS AND DAUGHTERS'

The subjects of the Spirit's outpouring were "your sons and daughters", that is, future descendants of Israel, who would prophesy in "other" languages, not just Hebrew. The Galileans were 'sons and daughters' because they were Jews.

'MY SERVANTS'

But Joel further qualifies who these 'sons and daughters' were. They were also God's servants. Most of Jewry, historically and then present, were not servants of God. Only Jews, who were His servants, would serve as the Spirit's channels of truth on this special occasion. (2:18)

VISIONS AND DREAMS

Some scholars believe visions and dreams in Joel's prophecy refer to the apostleship who heard from the Lord in this way, as did Paul and John. But the relevance of visions and dreams is still defined by Peter's introduction, 'This is what the Prophet Joel spoke about.' Peter quotes Joel to explain the Galilean outpouring, not how other Apostles received the truth. (Ac. 2:16) So, 'dreams and visions' must have a direct relevance to this special Pentecost.

Yet, there is no evidence that any of these Galileans were, even intermittently, suspended from reality, as you would be in a dream or vision. In fact, these believers were very articulate, prophesying in their own learned languages that Jesus was the prophesied Messiah they had been waiting for. It is pretty hard to prophesy when one is having a dream or a vision. Since they obviously not prophesying while they were asleep dreaming or having visions, the experience of 'dreams and visions' in Joel's context must be different.

Galilean Emotional Status

The believers were overcome with joy. Their critics tried to attribute their exultant state to wine. However, these followers of Christ had become excited about some very, very good news. They were exuberant for a reason and Joel prophesied what they would feel like. He predicted their joy with a figure of speech!

Figure Of Speech

The Prophet Joel did not say that 'dreams and visions' were a means by which they would prophesy. He prophesied, 'I will pour out of My Spirit upon all flesh'. How did He do that? The Spirit caused 'sons and daughters' to prophesy to 'all flesh'. Truth, so amazing, made them think they were having visions and dreams. (Ac. 2:17) 'Visions and dreams' is a figure of speech for immense joy.

Living In Dreams Of Spiritual Freedom

With Joel's prophecy, Peter explained that the Galilean believers were not drunk, but were beside themselves with joy as if they were living in a dream or vision.

Living In Dreams Of Physical Freedom

But centuries earlier, there was another time when Israel was so jubilant that they thought they were part of a dream,

> "In Jehovah's turning back [to] the captivity of Zion, **We have been as dreamers**. Then filled [with] laughter is our mouth, And our tongue [with] singing. Then do they say among nations,, 'Jehovah did great things with these' Jehovah did great things with us, <u>We have been joyful</u>." (Psa. 126:1-3; YLT, emphasis added)

Commentators are agreed that this pertains to the return of Jewish exiles after their physical captivity in Babylon of 70 years had ended and were permitted to return to Zion. One commentator explains that God "changed the captivity of Zion into freedom."[47] Hard to comprehend their good fortune, the returning remnant thought they were dreaming.

Note the following commentaries,

> "If this Psalm was written with a view to record the wonderful and gracious dealings of the Lord with his people, in delivering them from the Babylonish captivity, certain it is, that that event was as sudden and **unexpected as a dream**. For when Cyrus (as we read in the book of Ezra) gave commandment for the Jews to return to Jerusalem, and to rebuild the temple, it might well excite the astonishment of all that heard it."[48] (emphasis added)

> "When the Lord turned again the captivity of Zion, restoring His people to the Land of Promise after the long years of exile, **we were like them that dream**. Whether this is a prophecy or a statement of historical fact, it sets forth the **indescribable bliss** of those who were privileged to return to the Land of Promise."[49] (emphasis added)

> "**We were like them that dream**; we were so surprised and astonished with the report of such a favour, that we could not believe our eyes and ears, but **thought it to be but a dream or delusion of our own fancies**; as is usual in matters of **great joy**..."[50] (emphasis added)

> "Among the captives themselves the joy was so great, that they **scarcely knew whether it were a reality or a dream**. They were like Peter, when delivered from prison by an angel on the very night prior to his intended execution: "He went out and followed the angel; and wist not that it was true which was done by the angel; but **thought he saw a vision**." [Note: Acts 12:9.]"[51] (emphasis added)

Their release from captivity was prophesied. (De. 30:3) Now free to return to Zion according to prophecy, they thought they were living in a

---

[47] F. C. Cook, *Explanatory And Critical Commentary Of The Whole Bible*, 1875, Vol. IV, p. 462

[48] Robert Hawker, *Hawker's Poor Man's Commentary*, Psa. 126:1 https://www.studylight.org/commentaries.html

[49] Paul E. Kretzmann, *The Popular Commentary of the Bible*, 1924, Psa. 126:1 https://www.studylight.org/commentaries.html

[50] Matthew Poole, *Matthew Poole's English Annotations on the Holy Bible*, Psa. 126:1 https://www.studylight.org/commentaries.html

[51] Charles Simeon, *Charles Simeon's Horae Homileticae*, Psa. 126:1 https://www.studylight.org/commentaries.html

dream. This return of the Babylonian captivity appears to foreshadow the deliverance from another much more dangerous captivity. When Jesus read from Isaiah, He identified Himself as this prophesied anointed One to preach the gospel to the poor and to proclaim deliverances to captives. (Lk. 4:18, 19) Now, preaching to spiritual captives in Jerusalem, no less, Peter quotes Joel, "And it shall come to pass, that whosoever shall call on the name of the Lord shall be saved." (Ac. 2:21)

From Zion To Zion

There is another important 'captivity' that needed to be changed. More than just an earthly Zion, the final destination of His people was always the heavenly Zion. (Heb. 12:22,23) As the returning captivity thought they had been dreaming about being released from physical bondage when they returned to Israel, so also were the believing Jews, who also thought they had been dreaming and having visions, when it was confirmed to them that Jesus delivered them from spiritual bondage.

The return of the exiles to rebuild the Temple and Jerusalem under Ezra and Nehemiah foreshadowed the return of many exiles for this Pentecost, 3000 of whom would be delivered from spiritual bondage. (Ac. 2: 9-11; 41)

SUMMARY

Joel prophesied that the pouring out of the Spirit would cause these 'sons and daughters' to be overcome with joy to the point where they would wonder whether their experience was a dream or a vision. They were elated that Christ who died and rose just 50 days prior, delivered them from captivity so that they could be taken to the heavenly Zion.

This is not about personal dreams and visions to which Charismatics cling for 'divine' direction.

THE AWESOME 'DAY OF THE LORD' PROPHECY

At Pentecost, Galilean believers prophesied as the Spirit gave them utterance. (Ac. 2:4,18) The Holy Spirit enabled the Galileans to rightly understand the things they had already seen and heard concerning Christ. Thus, they were not just any witnesses; they had personally been witnesses of Christ and His ministry. (Ac. 1:8) (1:3, 9-11; 4:20; 1 Jn. 1:2,3) Peter affirmed the <u>identity</u> and <u>conduct</u> of these men and women as a fulfillment of a prophecy from Joel. But what were they talking about?

What was the subject of their prophecies? Peter quotes more from Joel to reveal what the Galileans were 'prophesying' about.

Commentators believe that Joel's prophecy predicted the 'pouring out of the Spirit', but the last half is yet to be fulfilled. However, Peter linked Joel's entire prophecy to an event that had already occurred: "This is what was spoken by the prophet Joel." (Ac. 2:16, 18b) It is therefore, especially important that this Scripture be read in the context of the Passover and our Savior's death just 50 days before. The Galileans were prophesying the truth about Christ. What did Joel say that truth was about?

The Signs in The Earth Beneath

Peter quotes Joel's prophecy, "I will show wonders in heaven above and signs in the earth beneath: Blood, fire and vapor of smoke." (Ac. 2:19; NKJ, emphasis added.) Other translations have it as 'I will grant' or 'I will give'. (i.e. NAS; YLT)

There are three signs: blood, fire and vapor of smoke. Familiar with Levitical sacerdotal worship, these devout Jews would have recognized the symbols of blood, fire and vapor of smoke, but would not have recognized who they represented. While following through with animal sacrifices on this Passover, they had not realized that these signs of the sacrifice were about the Priest and Sacrifice offered 50 days before.

Blood

Christ's work of the Passover was foreshadowed in the first Passover with the "sign" of blood,

> "Now the blood shall be a sign for you on the houses where you are. And when I see the blood, I will pass over you; and the plague shall not be on you to destroy you when I strike the land of Egypt." (Ex. 12:13; NKJV)

Peter reminds them of the first token of Passover – blood. The sign of blood at the Passover represented the blood of the Savior they had crucified. (2: 23:24)

Fire

Hebrews says that God is a consuming fire. (Heb. 12:29) The offerings to the Lord were to be made with fire. (Lev. 1:13) Not only must man have a suitable sacrifice, it must also be consumed by suitable fire. Nadab and Abihu offered strange fire before the Lord, consequently, fire went out from the Lord and killed them. (Lev. 10:1-3) The Levites were instructed that the fire for the altar was never to go out. (Lev. 6:12-14)

Ultimately the only fire that could satisfy the Lord would have to be His Fire. 'And there came a fire out from before the Lord, and consumed upon the altar the burnt offering and the fat, which when all the people saw, they shouted and fell on their faces.' (Lev. 9:24) When Elijah called upon the Lord to consume the drenched sacrifice, the Fire of the Lord fell and consumed the sacrifice. (1 Kg. 18:38,39) After Solomon had finished praying, fire came down from heaven and consumed the burnt offering and God's glory filled the temple. (2 Chr. 7:1-3)

The eternal Holy Spirit is represented by the fire. John prophesied that the one coming after him would baptize them with the Holy Spirit and with fire. (Matt. 3:11; Ac. 2:3) It is noteworthy that after the divided tongues of fire appeared to them, they were filled with the Holy Spirit, not consumed because their sins had already been consumed by God's fire in the Sacrifice of Christ.

Vapor of Smoke

There is yet another feature of the sacrifice. The Lord had given the priests a recipe of oil and frankincense that they were to burn upon the altar for a sweet-smelling savor. (Lev. 6:14,15) Naturally, this would mingle with the smoke of the burning of the offering itself, which also contributed to the sweet aroma with which God would be pleased. (Le. 1:13) Christ's sacrifice was a sweet smelling savor to God. (Eph. 5:2)

SUMMARY

Of course, animal blood, fire and incense could not satisfy the righteous demands of our Holy God. But they were emblems of how Christ, by the Holy Spirit, would expiate the wrath of God against our sin. Laden with man's guilt and sin, the 'fire' of the Holy Spirit forever purged the sin that Christ took upon Himself. However, because He was the perfect Son of God, His sacrifice was also a sweet-smelling savor to God and death could not hold Him. These were the three signs in the earth, representing the work of the Trinity for our salvation.

THE WONDERS OF HEAVEN

The Israelites promised God that they would keep His Laws. After three days of preparation, God made His presence known with thunder, lightning and a thick cloud on Mt. Sinai. (Ex. 19:9, 19) Israel was then given the Ten Commandments they promised to do, but never did. Of course, there was only One who could.

Christ was tried and pronounced guilty in the earthly Mt. Zion. He was crucified outside Jerusalem. From the sixth to the ninth hour there was darkness on the face of the land. Just as the darkness ended, Jesus cried out, 'My God, My God, why have You forsaken Me?' (Matt. 27:45, 46) Not only did God have to cloak Himself in darkness from the wicked Israelites at Sinai, He did the same as Christ hung on the cross near Mt. Zion. How could that be? Bearing our sins in His own body on the cross, he endured the wrath of God for His elect. (Jn. 3:36; Rom. 1:18; 1 Pe.2:24)

This was darkness, not a twilight. It lasted about 3 hours and therefore could not have been caused by an eclipse. Since no natural phenomena is known to have caused this, it may have been supernatural.

The 'darkness' was likely connected in some way to the affect of the moon appearing red. This, too, cannot be explained. These are the wonders of the heavens.

"The Day of The Lord"

At the beginning of this quotation, he noted what would happen in the "last days" and near the end what would happen in the "day of the Lord". It is vital that the context be kept in view. Pentecost, the Passover, Christ's death and resurrection are all part of the 'last days'.

'The day of the Lord' is a phrase that appears about 18 times in the OT and 5 in the NT. Many commentators believe that 'the day of the Lord' has not yet occurred. Unger defines it as a "protracted period commencing with the second advent of Christ in glory and ending with the cleansing of the heavens and the earth by fire preparatory to the new heavens and earth of the eternal state (Isa. 65:17-19; 66:22; II Pet. 3:13; Rev. 21:1)."[52] But, must all, if any of these 'days', refer to a future day?

Argument By Contrasting With Other Phrases

Moses is identified as 'the servant of the Lord', yet we know from other scripture that he was not the only servant. Joshua was also 'the servant of the Lord.' (Josh. 1:1,13; Jud. 2:8) Different temples under the administrations of David, Solomon and Ezra are each identified as 'the temple of the Lord'. (2 Kg. 11:10; 24:13; Ez. 3:6) As 'the servant' does not necessarily refer to the same person and 'the temple', the same building,

---

[52] Unger, Merrill F., *Unger's Bible Dictionary*, Moody Press, Chicago, 1976, P. 249

neither should it be assumed that 'the day of the Lord' refers to the same event. Only the context can elucidate each "day of the Lord".

Metaphors In Scripture

The prophet Isaiah describes "the day of the Lord" as a day of fierce anger against Babylon, a time of destruction. John Gill explains that the description of the stars and sun is figurative. (Isa. 13:1,9-11 Gill's Commentary) Despite Babylon's punishment, the sun, moon and stars still shone for Israel. The globe is not part of the 'world' in this context. (i.e., the 'world' of Augustus Caesar was the Roman Empire, Lk.2:1) The immediate context may indicate a metaphor.

When Would This Happen?

At the end of verse 18, Luke writes, 'And they shall prophesy:' The Galileans had been given insight by experience and understanding of the events described in Joel's prophecy. This would occur in the 'last days'. (2:17) But the subject of their prophecy pertained to the 'great and glorious' day of the Lord, which was part of the 'last days', in which they were living. (Ac. 2:20b)

Almost 490 years ago, Gabriel informed Daniel that 70 weeks are determined for Israel. (Da. 9:24) In these "last days", there was one great and glorious day.

Great and Glorious Day

What possibly could Peter have understood from Joel's prophecy? The signs discussed above have already given us the first clue. The sign of animal 'blood' is a reference to the blood of Christ. The sign of the fire is given as the Holy Spirit's active presence to show the righteousness of Christ and the vapor of smoke was the sign that showed that only Christ could satisfy the wrath of God for our sin.

While our Savior hung on the cross, the darkness from noon to midafternoon was a wonder in the sky that could not be explained by a simple eclipse. Since Christ was already on the cross, this 'great and glorious' day must still be future, that is, after the darkness passed.

After His death, the women who had prepared spices and ointments for the body of Jesus, returned to the tomb in which He was laid. There they found the stone rolled away from the tomb. Two men in shining garments asked them why they were searching for the living among the dead. (Lk. 24:1-12) Reporting the news to the Apostles, they thought the women were just telling tales. Someone rising from the dead? Even His disciples failed to remember and believe this essential truth that Jesus taught them.

What could be greater than this? What could be more glorious?

It is the greatest and most glorious news ever, because this Lord by whom people are saved, had risen from the dead. There is salvation in none other. By the time Peter finished his sermon, the people were moved to understand that the Man they had nailed to the cross was the Lord of glory was the risen, living Savior, who could save them from their sins! (Ac. 2:21-24; 37)

THE DREADFUL 'DAY OF THE LORD' PROPHECY

Malachi, also references 'the day of the Lord'. He prophesied that God would send them Elijah the prophet before the coming of the great and dreadful day of the Lord. (Mal. 4:5)

The following is a preview of events and prophecies pertaining to the dreadful day of the Lord.

- Malachi said that God would send Elijah.
- Jesus identified John the Baptist as the Elijah that was to come.
- The disciples understood Jesus identifying John the Baptist as Elijah.
- Elijah must come before the Messiah and had already come.
- John the Baptist will go before Christ in the spirit of Elijah.
- John did not see himself as Elijah. But he did see himself as a voice crying in the wilderness.
- Elijah was sent before the great and dreadful day of the Lord.

Does Scripture indicate that 'the day of the Lord' has already occurred?

The Time of 'Elijah's' Arrival

The people were exhorted to remember that He would send them Elijah before that great and terrible day of the Lord. (Mal. 4:5)

'Elijah' is a Metaphor

Jesus not only affirmed the disciples' expectation of the coming of Elijah, He informed them that he had already come. (Matt. 11:14; 17:10-13) The angel told Zacharias that John the Baptist will go before Christ in the spirit of Elijah. (Lk. 1:17) This explains why John only identified himself as the 'voice of one crying in the wilderness', not as Elijah. (Jn. 1:21-25) Jesus provided the right interpretation for us. John the Baptist was the prophetic Elijah, who was to come. He was not the person of Elijah. But he would be known by his prophetic calling, like Elijah.

'Elijah' Prepared The Way of The Lord

The coming Elijah would not be identified by this name, but rather by the work he was called to do. He would turn the hearts of the children to their fathers and the hearts of fathers to their children. (Mal. 4:6; Lk. 1:17) John the Baptist was the voice of one crying in the wilderness, calling upon people to repent, according to Isaiah and Malachi. (Isa. 40:3; Mal. 3:1-6) He pointed to Jesus as the Lamb of God, who would take away the sin of the world. (Lk. 1:36)

John's Message

In the scriptures, sin is punishable by death. (Rom. 6:23) Indeed, all those who die without the sprinkling of the Lamb's blood upon the doorposts of their heart, will have to bear the wrath of God for their own sin. But that is a deserved punishment. Each one bears his own guilt, unless Someone dies in his place. As the Lamb of God, Jesus would be the only acceptable Substitute.

No other person had ever been called the Lamb of God! Knowing that every lamb designated for an acceptable offering in the Levitical system must be perfect, John must have known that the Lamb of God would have to die as an offering for sin.

How Great and Dreadful?

Malachi calls this 'the great and dreadful Day of the Lord'.

After Jesus and His disciples had eaten the Passover, He went to pray alone in the Garden of Gethsemane. He prayed that, if possible, the Father would remove this cup from Him. Of course, willing to do the Father's will, He proceeded to drink the vile filth of our sin. He agonized. He sweat great drops of blood. He began to do His work as our High Priest. (Lk. 22:39-45) Betrayed by Judas, Jewish officials accompanied by soldiers armed with swords and clubs, found Him in the Garden. Arresting Him as they would a common robber, they brought our sinless Savior to the High Priest's house where his mock trial began. Beaten, then blindfolded, they scorned Him as they demanded of Him to say the name of the one who struck Him. This was the beginning of the most dreadful day – ever.

Herod and Pilate could find nothing worthy of death, but under the pressure of the Pharisees, they relented and sentenced this righteous Man to death. Even under normal human jursprudence, this was a gross miscarriage of justice. They led Him to Golgotha where He was nailed to a stake and lifted up before all to see.

He had done nothing wrong; but we had! Having taken man's sin upon Himself, the perfect Lamb of God would now pay and endure the penalty for our sin. Feeling the full force and power of the righteous wrath of His Father, he cried, 'My God, why have you forsaken Me?' Hanging on that cross, there just outside the city walls, He gave His life for the sins of the whole world, especially the elect. (1 Pe. 2:24) In all of history there was never any day as dreadful this. But, praise God, He finished His work and this dreadful day of the Lord finally came to an end!

SUMMARY

The 'day of the Lord' to which Joel pointed was His glorious resurrection! But before that, there was another 'day of the Lord', quite different than glorious. John the Baptist pointed to the 'great and dreadful' day of the Lord, when He paid the penalty for our sin. And, Peter showed how the great and glorious day of the Lord had been fulfilled in Christ's resurrection.

There is no more reason to expect another 'Elijah' in the flesh than there is to expect another 'David' in the flesh. (Hos. 3:5; Ezek. 34:23; 37:24; Jer. 30:9) King David, son of Jessie, will not occupy a future throne. Our 'David' is Jesus Christ. He is already on His throne. (Heb. 1:8; 8:1)

Peter disclosed to the crowd the content of the Galilean 'utterances'. As personal witnesses of the Person and work of Christ, the minds of Galilean believers had been supernaturally enlightened with the understanding that this was the prophesied Savior they had been waiting for. Moreover, these Galileans were enabled to accurately prophesy this truth about Christ in languages other than Hebrew, without contradicting the Scriptures.

The Galileans' utterances were prophecies that centered on the events that culminated at the great and glorious Day of the Lord.

5. THE SPIRIT'S CONTINUING MINISTRY

To grapple for a better understanding of the Holy Spirit's ministry before and after Pentecost, an appraisal of the events, means and effects of His work recorded in the NT is necessary. Has the essential work of the Spirit changed since Pentecost?

THE NT EVENTS OF THE SPIRIT'S MINISTRY

The following is a brief appraisal of specific occurrences of the ministry of the Holy Spirit in the NT.

THE GALILEANS

The ministry of the Holy Spirit to the Galileans was unique. These repentant "servants" were 'baptized' with the Holy Spirit, when He gave them 'utterance', they were enabled to understand and communicate in known languages that Jesus was the prophesied Messiah, without the aid of a preacher or teacher. (Ac. 1:6; 2:4,17) The baptism of the Holy Spirit took away their ignorance of who Christ was, according to the Scriptures.

THE MULTITUDE

When Peter preached Christ at Pentecost, about 3000 souls felt convicted for their part in the crucifixion. They had believed the Gospel, but were still not saved. Peter exhorted them to repent and be baptized for the remission of sins in order to receive the Holy Spirit as a gift. (Ac. 2:23, 36-38) Clearly, in this context, 'baptism' implies that sin is filthy and they needed to be cleansed from it. Washing the body with water could not clean the heart. This 'baptism' took away their sin.

THE SAMARITANS

Samaria fell away from God. Jeremiah censured the prophets of Samaria because they prophesied by Baal. (Jer. 23:13; 31:4,5) Hosea prophesied that Samaria would be cut off. (Hos. 10:5-7) They rejected Jerusalem and built their own temple at Mt. Gerizim. (Psa.102:21) The Samaritans accepted an edited version of the Pentateuch, but rejected all other OT Scripture. Jesus had incriminated the Samaritan religion when he told the woman in Sychar that salvation is of the Jews and that 'they that worship Him, must worship Him in spirit and in truth.' (Jn. 4:22, 24) This is a brief background for Philip's ministry in Samaria.

Receiving The Word

While Philip was preaching Christ, the paralyzed and the lame were healed, and the demon-possessed were set free. Many had believed the message concerning the kingdom of God and the name of Jesus. There was great joy in the city. Both men and women were baptized. (Ac. 8:4-8, 12) Like Peter at Pentecost, Philip convinced the Samaritans that Jesus was the Messiah. They received the Word. (Ac.8:5,12,14)

The Need For Repentance

Having heard that the Samaritans had received the Word, the Apostles and elders in Jerusalem sent Peter and John. But when the Apostles joined Philip, they immediately discerned that the Holy Spirit had not yet 'fallen' upon any of them; they had only been baptized in the name of Jesus. (Ac. 8:15,16) They had not yet been 'cut to the heart', like the multitude had at Pentecost. Still unsaved, like the multitude at Pentecost, the Samaritans had believed Philip's message, but had not yet personally repented of their sin, and had not yet 'received' the Spirit necessary for conversion. So, they prayed for them that they would receive the Holy Spirit. (The Greek for 'fallen' means 'to press upon'.) (Ac. 8:14-17)

Receiving The Spirit

How could Philip's converts be truly born again if they had not been convicted of their sin and repented of it? Could these 'converts' be called the children of God, if they had not received the Spirit? Of course, there was joy that many of their physical ailments and demonic possessions were healed, while they heard the Word. (Ac. 8: 14) But, it is possible to 'receive' the word and not be saved. (Lk.8:13) It is therefore a sobering evaluation of the Samaritans that they had received the word but the Spirit had 'embraced' none of them.

Jesus ministered to the woman at the well, not by performing yet another miracle, but by telling her of her sin. Amazed that Jesus knew the specifics about her adulteries, she left her water pot to tell others that she had met the Messiah, who could also quench their spiritual thirst. Under the ministry of Philip, they had not yet become aware of their dire need to admit their sin and be cleansed from it.

Conclusions Of The Spirit's Ministry In Samaria

Philip had done an excellent work preaching Christ. But the Samaritans had become preoccupied with miracles and consequently, had not yet been converted. They had not yet been 'cut to the heart' regarding their sin as the Pentecost multitude had been.

Purpose Of Miracles Was Not To Save People

Discerning his motives, the Apostle Peter, told him that because his heart was unrepentant, he had no part in the church. (Ac. 8:21,22) Had Simon Magnus truly repented of his sin, he would not have asked for a franchise to sell the Holy Spirit. Still, today, Simon's quest is the basis for charismatic deception. The Spirit is the gift of God, not a commodity for trade at the Pentecostalism Stock Exchange. The Samaritans had seen that Simon Magnus was no match for the power of God, however, they hadn't realized that miracles were only intended to authenticate Philip's message of salvation.

Though Lazarus rise from the dead to warn the rich man's brothers, Jesus said, they still would not repent. (Lk. 16:30,31) Jesus proved His power and His identity with many miracles, yet people rejected Him because they did not like His message. And, neither was Philip's healing ministry an incentive for true repentance. When Peter and John went to Samaria, the Holy Spirit moved upon the Samaritans without the need for miracles as He had at Pentecost.

The Ministry of The Spirit Is Essential

People may believe Christ, but themselves remain unrepentant. (Lk. 8:13) Not until they received the Spirit, were they born again. Then, the Holy Spirit bears witness with our spirit that we are the children of God. (Rom. 8:16) 'If any man have not the Spirit of God, he is none of his.' (Rom.8:9) He is the one who miraculously causes us to be born again.

CORNELIUS

Peter had an unusual call to go to Caesarea to minister to Gentiles, namely, Cornelius and his household. He told them that whoever believes in Jesus would receive the remission of sins. Evidently, while Peter was speaking these words, the Holy Spirit 'fell' upon all those who heard the word. Feeling the convicting pressure of the Holy Spirit through the spoken word, Cornelius, family and friends <u>received the Spirit</u>. They acknowledged their sin and repented of it. (10:43-48) Now, excited about their new-found hope in Christ, these 'unclean', uncircumcised Gentiles also glorified God by speaking in their own languages as the Galileans did at Pentecost. God could be glorified with languages other than Hebrew.

When Peter reported this to the assembly, they rejoiced that God also gave Gentiles repentance unto life. (Ac. 11:18)

TWELVE MEN

Paul met some disciples in Ephesus. It does not say whose disciples they were. It appears from their lack of knowledge that they may have been proselytes to Judaism. He asked them, 'Did you not receive the Spirit when you believed?' They replied that they had not heard of the Holy Spirit when they were baptized. Despite having been baptized into John's baptism, they apparently had not understood that John's baptism was unto repentance and that they should believe on Christ. When they heard this, they were baptized in the name of the Lord, Paul laid hands on about 12 men and the Holy Spirit came upon them and they spoke in languages they knew and prophesied. (Ac. 19:1-7) Again, it is important to note that the ministry of the Holy Spirit was not restricted to the language of OT Prophets. They could glorify God by speaking in Gentile languages.

THESE DISCIPLES WERE UNINFORMED

When these disciples stated that they had not so much as heard of the Spirit, they revealed their ignorance of the OT scriptures. The indwelling Spirit was just as essential to salvation before Christ as after.

Secondly, it is odd that these disciples of John had not heard about the Spirit of God descending on Christ like a dove, when he baptized Him.

Thirdly, they did not know what John the Baptist preached, "I indeed baptize you with water unto repentance, but He who is coming after me is mightier than I, whose sandals I am not worthy to carry. He will baptize you with the Holy Spirit and fire." (Matt. 3:11; NKJV) Despite John's clear reference to the Holy Spirit, they claimed they had not heard of Him.

Fourthly, they were unaware that John's baptism pertained to repentance, and that they should believe on Him who would come after him. They had not yet believed on Jesus to whom John pointed as the Lamb of God who takes away the sins of the world.

OTHER 'FILLING' MANIFESTATIONS OF THE SPIRIT

Following are another three instances of the 'filling' ministry of the Spirit.

PETER AND JOHN:

After Peter and John were released from prison, they reported what had happened to a few assembled believers. After prayer there was a shaking of the place in which they had gathered, they were filled with the Holy Spirit and they spoke the word with boldness. (Acts 4:23, 31) The Spirit gave them boldness to speak in a language they already knew, similar to Pentecost.

PAUL'S EXPERIENCE OF THE SPIRIT:

Having already repented for 'kicking' Christ, Saul was endowed with understanding by the Holy Spirit. Now converted, he humbly allowed himself to be anointed by someone who he would have arrested just three days prior. When Ananias laid hands on Saul, he was filled with the Holy Spirit and he regained his sight. He arose, was baptized, then preached the word in the synagogues. (Ac. 9:17-19)

DISCIPLES:

In Acts 13:52 disciples were filled with joy and the Holy Spirit, because of the word of the Lord that was proclaimed. (Ac. 13:49) This was a joy given by the Spirit. No speaking in multiple languages is indicated.

AN ANALYSIS OF THE SPIRIT'S MINISTRY

Though "filled" and "baptism" are used in connection with the pouring out of the Spirit at Pentecost, other contexts preclude universal association of the word 'baptism' with the "pouring out of the Spirit" experience of the Galileans at Pentecost. Secondly, 'filling' and 'baptism' is the supernatural work of the Spirit by which He causes man to understand the Scriptures.

PENTECOST:

The 'pouring' out of the Spirit was evidenced through the Galileans by an immanent and unified comprehension that Christ was the prophesied Messiah, and their bold proclamation of Christ.

The 'pouring out on all flesh' was evidenced when 3000 souls responded to the gospel the Galileans and Peter communicated. (2:37, 38)

SAMARIA

When Philip preached the gospel, it was received with joy because of the healings.

- Seeing miracles, they paid attention to the word.
- They had only been 'washed' (baptized) in the name of Jesus.

- The Apostles prayed for them to receive the Spirit.
- The Spirit 'pressed' upon them.
- They received the Spirit, for salvation. (Rom. 8:9)

The Apostles saw a problem. (8:14-17) Having not yet received the Spirit, the joy they had experienced occurred before they were converted. They rejoiced in physical relief, not spiritual relief.

CORNELIUS

Peter preached the gospel for the remission of sins through Christ. (10:43) He performed no miracles to convince this household.

- Learning about their sins, the Spirit 'fell' on them who heard the word. (10:44, 45)
- Jewish believers were amazed that the gift (divine truth) of the Spirit had also been poured out upon the Gentiles.
- This outpouring was evidenced by glorifying God in languages.

They spoke in the language they were most familiar with. Speaking in 'languages' implies multilingualism, excluding Hebrew.

TWELVE MEN

Paul found disciples who had not heard of the Holy Spirit, but had been baptized with John's baptism.

- These disciples had become moralists. (works salvation)
- They had not known that when John baptized Jesus, the Spirit descended upon Him.
- They had not known that John pointed to the Lamb of God who takes away the sin of the world.
- They had not yet received the Spirit.
- But when they believed that Jesus takes away sin, they were baptized with water.
- Paul, 'having laid' his hand upon them, the Spirit came to them. Like Pentecost, the disciples were given the right understanding of the Christ, as revealed in Scriptures in order to prophesy.
- They prophesied in the languages they knew.

Again, a language miracle is not implied. However, it is implied that it was not normal to prophesy in just any language.

PETER AND JOHN:

Peter and John were filled with the Spirit, as believers. Like the Galileans at Pentecost, they were given further insight into the things of

God. (Ac. 4:31) No mention is made of multiple languages, but it appears that they were granted greater boldness to speak.

PAUL'S EXPERIENCE OF THE SPIRIT:

Having already received the Spirit, Paul was later filled with the Spirit at the house of Ananias. This 'pouring out of the Spirit' gave Saul the necessary understanding to preach the word immediately. (Ac. 9:17-20)

DISCIPLES:

Not much is written about the disciples at Iconium. However, they were filled with the Spirit. Their new insight into the word of God filled them with joy. (Ac. 13:52)

THE MEANS OF THE SPIRIT'S MINISTRY

These incidents show the means by which the Holy Spirit ministers to mankind. He inspires, communicates in any language.

THE SPIRIT'S GIVING OF 'UTTERANCE' WAS EXCLUSIVE

The multitudes saved at Pentecost and Samaria, Cornelius and his household, the disciples in Ephesus were not given "utterance" by the Holy Spirit. Only the Galileans were given this unusual outpouring of the Holy Spirit by which they simultaneously recognized, understood and spoke the truth about Christ without hearing it from a Prophet first. In this way their experience of the Spirit's filling was exclusive.

THE SPIRIT'S GIVING OF UNDERSTANDING WAS/IS NOT EXCLUSIVE

Before He left, Jesus explained that the Galileans would be His personal witnesses._(Ac. 1:8) Having given them 'utterance' directly by the Holy Spirit, they prophesied to one another and the multitude. As per Joel's prophecy, 'all flesh' would learn the truth of the Gospel through the Apostles' teaching, receive it and rightly prophesy the Scriptures. (Ac. 2:38, 42)

THE SPIRIT GAVE THEM FREEDOM TO PROPHESY IN ANY LANGUAGE

Of the four prominent manifestations of the Spirit, only the Samaritans did not speak in languages. The Samaritan vernacular was Hebrew, not Aramaic.[53] Elsewhere in Judea and the Roman Empire, however, people were multilingual; in Samaria, they all spoke Hebrew.

---

[53] John J. Parsons, *Did Jesus Speak Hebrew?* P. 3
https://hebrew4christians.com/Articles/Jesus_Hebrew/JesusHebrew.pdf

Though Hebrew was not the common language among the Jews, it was still the language of OT scholarship and liturgy. (This is discussed in detail in chapter 18) With the exception of portions of Ezra and Daniel, God had delivered His Word in Hebrew. That was about to change.

The Galileans, Cornelius and his household, and the 12 disciples prophesied in languages common to them. Prophesying God's word in the languages they knew was just as valid as if it had been prophesied in Hebrew. No longer would it be necessary to hear the Hebrew read first, then explained as it was in the liturgy of Jewish synagogue and temple services. The Apostles wrote to the churches in the Greek most knew.

Multilingualism was a fact of life in post-exilic Israel, therefore, supernatural speaking in languages is not tenable. Unable to keep silent about their discovery, believers glorified God in the languages familiar to them, as the Galilean Jews had done. In the presence of the circumcision, the Holy Spirit validated even uncircumcised Gentiles to prophesy about Christ's saving work in their common languages. As they understood the truth, they also prophesied in a language familiar to them.

Though they did not speak in languages, the Samaritans were equally blessed by the Holy Spirit as those who did.

NT TERMS OF THE HOLY SPIRIT'S WORK

The meanings of the terms receiving, indwelling, baptism and filling of the Holy Spirit must be determined by context.

Receiving Of The Holy Spirit

As the Gospel of Christ was preached, the Spirit was 'pressing' upon the hearers, that is, convicting them of their sin. When they repented, they received the Holy Spirit. No one received the Spirit more than once.

In Samaria, the Apostles did not pray that they would receive the Spirit when they laid their hands on them. Peter and John only prayed that they would receive the Spirit. When they prayed, the Spirit 'fell' on them. Seeing God answering their prayer, they then began laying hands on them, thus affirming, not only their profession of faith, but their repentance of sin. (Ac.8:15-17) At Pentecost, 3000 souls received the Spirit without the laying on of hands. No one can be saved without receiving the Spirit.

Baptism of The Spirit

Because the Hebrew word for 'pour' means to shed, baptize can't mean 'submerge' in the context of Joel's prophecy. (Joel 2:28) John the Baptist prophesied that the One coming after Him would baptize with the Spirit and with fire. (Matt. 3:11) Before the day of Pentecost, Jesus explained to believers that they would be baptized with the Holy Spirit not many days later. (Ac. 1:4,5,8) Literally, they would be 'poured upon'. This baptism pertained to Jewish believers and is not an experience to be sought after. This 'baptism' was the sovereign work of God by the Holy Spirit.

Peter understood the experience of the baptism of the Holy Spirit at Pentecost as a 'gift'. Cornelius and his household received this gift after they had believed the message. (Ac. 11:15-17)

'Filling' Of The Holy Spirit

There are two words in Greek used for 'filled'. *Pietho* means to fill, imbue, influence, supply. (Ac. 2:4; 3:10; 4:8,31) *Pieroo* is to make replete or cram in a net. (Eph. 3:19; 5:18)

'Baptism' and 'Filling' Describe the Same Event

After His resurrection, Jesus promised that in a few days the Galileans would be 'baptized with the Holy Spirit'. (Ac.1:4, 5) According to Peter's sermon, the 'filling' at Pentecost was the fulfillment of a prophecy made by Joel. (Ac. 2:4, 16) The Spirit 'poured' out of Himself and the disciples were 'filled' or 'baptized' by the Spirit at Pentecost.

One Exclusive 'Filling'

Since the Galilean believers, no other group of believers were directed to wait at a specified location for the filling of the Spirit. Second, no Apostle initiated the Pentecost outpouring with a prayer or laying on of hands or any other means. Third, the Pentecost 'baptism' or 'filling' was specific to the fulfilment of prophecy by Joel and Jesus. Fourth, the Spirit's 'filling' at Pentecost revealed Christ as the fulfilment of the New Covenant. And, fifth, the 'filling' or 'baptism' of the Galileans was the direct influence of the Holy Spirit without the aid of a teacher.

The 'filling' ministry of the Holy Spirit upon the Galileans at Pentecost was unique. This is not a repeatable event!

Filling or Baptism Of The Spirit is Knowledge-Based

In every case where people were filled or baptized with the Holy Spirit, they had acquired greater knowledge and understanding of Scripture.

Believers Filled With The Spirit Were Bold And Joyful

Where there was every reason to be fearful, the filling of the Spirit caused believers to be bold and joyful. While Christ was on the cross, his followers lacked boldness as "witnesses", but that changed when the Holy Spirit empowered them as He had the prophets of old.

Believers Were Filled With The Spirit Again

Peter and John along with other believers experienced another 'filling of the Spirit' after prayer. The Holy Spirit reminds believers of truths already learned and enlightens them to comprehend more Scripture.

Another Greek verb also translated 'fill', is a command for believers. Rather than being filled with the empty thoughts and words that wine produces, Paul admonishes believers to be filled with the thoughts and words of the Spirit. (Eph. 5:18, 19)

Believers Filled With The Spirit Spoke Their own Language

Again, there is no reason to suppose that a language miracle occurred. Quite naturally, we would deduce that the vernacular might not be as well known by some, so they would revert to their favored dialect or language when conversing with one another of similar upbringing.

CONCLUSION

Unsaved believers can receive the Word; saved believers <u>also</u> receive the Spirit. The work of the Spirit is to convince people to believe on Christ and convict them of sin. The 'filling', 'baptism', or 'outpouring' is the necessary means by which the Holy Spirit influences the unbeliever to be saved and the believer to grow in the knowledge of Christ.

The Holy Spirit enables unbelievers to discern the truth. (1 Cor. 2:13, 14) Second, the Spirit convicts man of sin. Third, the Spirit abides in those who have received the remission of sin from Christ. Fourth, the Spirit enables believers to understand the written word of God. Fifth, the Spirit grants joy in the Gospel. Sixth, the Holy Spirit gives boldness to share the Gospel. And seventh, the Spirit enables believers to prophesy the truth from God's Word in other learned languages, not just Hebrew.

When the meanings of 'receiving the word', 'receiving the Spirit', 'filling of the Spirit', 'pouring out of the Spirit' and 'baptism' are understood, it becomes evident that the essential ministry of the Holy was the same before Pentecost, as it was after. His OT ministry was to point to the Savior, yet to come, and in the NT point to the Savior who has come.

6. THE REAL CHURCH IN CORINTH

It is alleged that the Corinthian church was a hub of supernatural miracles, healings, the speaking of unlearned languages and new revelations from God. To grapple with Paul's teaching on gifts, a review of the character of the Corinthian church is necessary for context. Much of the confusion, regarding Corinthian giftedness, centers on the false assumption that the Galileans spoke unlearned languages. Having noted the absence of supernatural linguistic abilities at Pentecost and subsequently, we begin an examination of the gifts of the Corinthians.

FOUNDING OF THE CORINTHIAN CHURCH

Paul found believers, Aquila and his wife, Priscilla, in Corinth. Hearing Paul teach in the synagogue, Crispus, a ruler of the synagogue, and his household, were converted. But this aggravated the Jews in Corinth, who tried unsuccessfully to get Gallio to make a judgment against him. God had told Paul in a dream that He had many people in this city. Despite Jewish opposition, through his ministry many in Corinth believed and were baptized. (Act.18:7-13)

THEIR SALVATION QUESTIONED

Paul expressed gratitude that they were enriched in Christ through the spoken word with all knowledge for a blameless appearing before the Lord. But this affirmation of their testimony in Christ is not based on giftedness. But, there was the sense among them that lack of ability gifts was a barometer of the reality of faith. (1:4-7)

Though he writes to "those who are called to be saints", Paul is under no illusion that everyone in the assembly was converted. (1Cor. 1:2-8) In 5:11, Paul exhorts the church not to associate with a certain so-called brother. He lists sinful practices that would deny entry into the kingdom. (6:9,10) He warned the church about the possibility of believing in vain. (15:2) Though addressed to believers, Paul is concerned for some among them, who did not have a credible profession of faith. Even in his second letter, Paul told them to test themselves to see if they were in the faith. (2 Cor. 13:5) Speaking to them as infants in Christ, stunted in growth, and walking as mere men, he wonders if some had been saved. (1 Cor. 3:1-3)

ATTITUDE

At the beginning of his letter, Paul exposes their divisiveness. (1 Cor. 1:10-13) Had this church truly been of the same mind and judgment, they would have recognized that doctrines necessary for salvation and sanctification were identical to the teachings of Jesus, Cephas, Paul and Apollos. Dismayed, that some were saying they were 'of Paul', he reminds them that only Christ was crucified for them. So, he wants them all to say the same thing: 'I am of Jesus'.

Unity of mind is impossible without the knowledge revealed to us through the Apostles and Prophets. (1:10-16; 3:3; 14:37) Unlike the noble Bereans, the Corinthians had a dismissive attitude to the revealed word of God. They boasted in men. (3:21; 4:18-21) Some thought themselves to be wise. (1:20-25; 2:6) And, others depended on gifts as necessary to confirm their testimony, rather than the Word. (1:6,7; 12:21-23) They were competitive and arrogant.

KNOWLEDGE

Their inability to agree on the same thing was symptomatic of their ignorance, which Paul repeatedly draws to their attention by asking, 'do you not know?'

- "Do you not <u>know</u> that you are the temple of God?" 3:16
- "Do you not know that a little leaven leavens the whole lump?" 5:6
- "Do you not know that the saints will judge the world?" 6:2
- "Do you not know that we shall judge angels?" 6:3
- "Do you not know that the unrighteous will not inherit the kingdom of God?" 6:9
- "Do you not know that your bodies are members of Christ?" 6:15
- "Or do you not know that the one who is joined to a harlot is one body with her?" 6:16
- "Or do you not know that your body is the temple of the Holy Spirit?" 6:19
- "Do you not know that those who minister the holy things, eat of the things of the temple...?" 9:13a
- "Do you not know that those who run in a race all run, but one receives the prize?" 9:2

Their obvious lack of knowledge is evidence that they needed to be filled with the Spirit Himself, that is, learn not to exceed what is written. (2:13; 4:6)

Conduct

Their conduct proved to be the evidence of sinful attitudes.

Leadership Discrimination

They were divisive. Here the church aligned themselves with a preferred leader saying, 'I am of Paul' ... etc. Rather than each speaking for his favored leader, they were to be of the same mind with leadership who were true to the Word on vital matters of faith and practice. (1Cor. 1:10-13)

Grievances Taken To Secular Courts

Among them were professing believers who took one another to the secular law courts. The wisdom craze continued to affect their thinking on law. They wondered how the church could provide fair judgment when the 'wisdom' established in Greek jurisprudence was centuries old. Yet, Paul candidly asks them if there is a wise man among them. (6:1-8) The just and moral principles of His word predate anything the 'wise' Greeks could offer. The scriptures are perfect and timeless, never needing any statutory revisions, yet the Corinthians brought their cases before unbelieving judges who had no knowledge of the Scriptures.

Sectarianism

The Lord's table had become a party where many were left ignored and unfed. (11:17-22) Some were excluded because of their apparent lack of ability, being weak, impotent, and without strength. (feeble) The 'less honorable' were excluded because of embarrassment. (12:22-25)

Inappropriate use of minority languages in assembly was just one example of Corinthian immaturity. (14:18-20)

Cultural Influences Of Wisdom And Signs

Worldly philosophies in the church elicited a quest for wisdom contrary to Christ. (1 Cor. 1:20-31) So, Paul addressed their special regard for 'intellectual' abilities with a quote from Isaiah that God will destroy the wisdom of the wise. (Isa. 29:14) Gentile devices to make the gospel appear intellectual and wise, were foolish. (1 Cor. 1:18-22)

Paul also noted the Jewish obsession with signs. (1 Cor. 1:22; Acts 18:1-12) They would not accept a sign unless it aligned with their own contrived theology, so Christ remained a stumbling block to them. Jesus spoke of the sign-seeking Jews as an evil generation. (Mt. 16:4)

SUMMARY

Doctrinally illiterate and immature, Christian witness and God-honoring use of Spirit-given abilities were seriously compromised. Yet, teachers today infer that these Corinthians were endowed with supernatural abilities to speak unlearned languages and receive new revelations from God.[54]

Had they been truly inspired by the Holy Spirit to receive and prophesy new divine revelation, Paul would not have admonished them for their ignorance. (1Cor. 3:16; 5:6; 6:2,3,9,15,16,19; 9:13,24) Rather, the church, including these 'prophets', had already been enriched in the knowledge of Christ by the preaching of this message, not by these 'prophets'. (1 Cor. 1:5,21) They were not to exceed what is written and Paul's writings were the Lord's commandments. (1 Cor. 4:6; 14:37) They already had all the revelation they needed for faith and godliness. Paul's letter shows that these 'prophets' had not faithfully revealed what the Prophets and Apostles had already revealed. Their conduct indicated that they hadn't even lived according to OT and apostolic teachings.

The evidence is clear that the Corinthians were generally immature and uninformed. And, some may not have been truly saved. This gives us pause, when it is claimed that they had supernatural abilities to reveal the unknown, to speak in unknown languages and heal sickness.

---

[54]Robert L. Thomas *Understanding Spiritual Gifts,* (p.61) This author believes that for the first 70 years of church history, the "Holy Spirit chose to use direct revelation to communicate previously unrevealed truths to the body of Christ."
Larry D. Pettegrew, *The New Covenant Ministry of the Holy Spirit,* p.163 Since prophecy is directly from God, "the gift of prophecy can be defined as *the supernatural ability to receive revelation from God and to communicate to others in the people's language.*" He was referring to the Corinthian gifts.
John MacArthur, *The Truth About Tongues,* Part 4, GTY.org., Regarding 14:29a, The prophets "spoke direct revelation from God that had never been given before for the life of the church."

7. THE MEANINGS OF 'GIFT(S)'

New Testament writers use three Greek words that are translated as 'gift'. As always, meaning and context must be known if 'miracles', 'healing', 'tongues', etc. have any supernatural implications. So, before the meanings of each of the gifts is examined, a review the word 'gift' in its various contexts is necessary.

Is there a difference between "gift" (dorea) in Acts and "gift(s)" (charisma) in 1 Corinthians? Do the 'gifts' in Acts have any connection with the 'gifts' in Corinth? Do 'gifts' signal a completely new ministry of the Holy Spirit? Does 'gift' indicate a physical or spiritual application?

LUKE'S REFERENCES TO GIFTS

Luke uses the word 'gift' (dorea), meaning gratuity, four times: Acts 2:38; 8:20; 10:45; 11:17. Do these 'gift' references indicate or imply that the Galileans had received supernatural ability gifts?

THE GIFT OF THE HOLY SPIRIT AT PENTECOST

Christ had assured Galilean believers before He left, that they would receive the promise of the Father. (Lk. 24:49; Ac. 1:4-8) As promised to His disciples at the Passover meal before He left, Christ would dispatch the Holy Spirit when he departed. They had received the promise of the Holy Spirit from the Father. (Ac. 2:17) The Holy Spirit 'baptized' these waiting believers to boldly, joyfully prophesy the truth about Christ. This is what the multitude was hearing and seeing. (Ac. 2:33) Luke's Pentecost narrative is clear that the Holy Spirit had not granted the Galileans any supernatural abilities. (Chapter 3) The promise belonging to the Spirit was delivered according Joel's prophecy.

As Peter preached, 3000 souls were convicted for their approval of Christ's death and wanted to know what to do. He told them if anyone repents and is washed[55] in the name of Christ for the remission of sin, he

---

[55] 'Baptized' should be understood as 'washed' or 'cleansed'. It was vital that Peter's audience understand that this Christ, who they rejected, needed to wash their sins away. Secondly, water baptism doesn't save anyone. If Peter had meant water baptism, he would have exhorted them to be baptized in the name of the Father, Son and Holy Spirit as Christ had instructed His disciples.

will receive "the gift of the Holy Spirit"[56] (Ac. 2:38,39) 'The Holy Spirit' is in the genitive, meaning that He is possession of 'the gift'. Furthermore, the context indicates that ***the*** should be translated 'this': 'You shall receive this gift of the Holy Spirit'.[57] If they would repent, they would receive **this** 'gift' of the Holy Spirit: the remission of sins. According to the promise in the prophecy, this gift of the remission of sins by the Spirit, is now formally extended to all who are 'far off', as many as the Lord will call. (Ac. 2:37-39; Eph.2:13)

In this context, the 'gift' is not the Holy Spirit.

THE GIFT OF GOD (AC. 8:14-20)

Simon Magnus had tried to buy the power to confer the Holy Spirit upon others by the laying on of hands, as he thought the Apostles were doing. He wanted to buy the authority that he perceived the Apostles had to bestow the Spirit at will. (Acts 8:18,19) But the Holy Spirit was not subject to the authority of the Apostles, as Simon thought. He failed to notice that the Apostles appealed to God in prayer that the Samaritans might receive the Spirit. Even the Apostles had no authority to demand salvation for others by the Spirit. The Holy Spirit wasn't subject to the authority of anyone, therefore He was the gift of God, not man.

Under Philip's preaching, many had heard the gospel and believed in Christ and were even baptized. But, since their joy was founded upon God's power to deliver them from physical illnesses, they had not received the Holy Spirit. Not until He 'pressed' them to understand the gravity of their sin and the necessity for personal repentance, could they receive the Spirit. This essential spiritual healing occurred when they received the 'gift of God', the Holy Spirit.

THE GIFT OF THE HOLY SPIRIT - CORNELIUS (AC. 10:45,47; 11:17)

When Cornelius and his household responded the gospel message, Gentiles also received the 'gift of the Holy Spirit.'

---

[56] Translation of "the" varies. In Acts 1:16, KJV and NKJV translate 'this Scripture'; NAS and ESV translate it as 'the'. In 2:6, *tes* is translated as 'this sound' or 'this was noised'. In Ac.2:37 the KJV, NKJ and NAS, translate 'the' as heard 'this' but it is italicized. The ESV does recognize the definite article and translates it as 'heard this'. In Ac.2:40, these four translations have translated 'the' as 'this', crooked, perverse or untoward generation. These are just a few examples of how Strong's 3588 isn't always translated as 'the'. Sometimes, it is ignored altogether.

[57] The Greek definite article *ho, he, to* is translated as 'this' in Acts 9:2; 10:17; 17:30; 27:10.

The Spirit 'Fell' On Those He Received

While Peter was preaching to Cornelius and his household, that the one who believes on Christ receives the forgiveness of sins, the Spirit 'fell' on them. Peter explains that the Holy Spirit received them. The text should read, "...who the Holy Spirit did receive - even as also we." (Ac.10:47b; YLT)

The Spirit Gave The Gift To Those He Received

Peter and those who accompanied him were astonished that these Gentiles were magnifying God in their own learned languages. God had poured out the gift of the Holy Spirit. Recalling the Galileans' experience at Pentecost, Peter informed the assembly, that the Spirit had 'fallen upon them as on us at the beginning.' Like the Galileans on the Day of Pentecost, these Gentiles also rejoiced in their salvation in their own languages. (Ac. 10:44-46; 11:15-17, '*dorea*')

In this case however, 'the Spirit fell on them as on us at the beginning', when the Galileans praised God in their own languages at Pentecost. (Ac. 11:17) The ministry or 'embrace' of the Holy Spirit was evident when they exalted Christ in the languages they knew. Not only had they received the forgiveness of sins, they were emboldened to joyfully prophesy Christ in their own languages. This baptism or 'pouring out' of the Spirit was the 'gift' that also made these Gentile believers united in the Gospel.

SUMMARY OF LUKE'S 'GIFTS':

The gift of the Spirit received by the multitude at Pentecost was the remission of sins as evidenced by repentance.

In Samaria, Peter and John had noticed that the Spirit had not 'fallen' upon any of the professing believers. When they trusted Christ for the remission of their own sins, they received the Spirit.

No doubt, Cornelius and his household, also received the forgiveness of sins, but the gift of the Holy Spirit, in this context, pertains to the outpouring of truth into the hearts and minds of new Gentile believers as evidenced by their exuberant declaration of the wonders of God through Christ.

'Gift' and 'Gifts'

In each of these cases, 'gift' ('*dorea*') is singular, but the 'gifts' of Corinth (*charisma*) were diverse. (1 Cor. 12-14) In one context, the 'gift' of the Spirit is the remission of sin and in another context, the 'gift' of the Spirit is to understand and prophesy of the Person and work of Christ.

PAUL'S REFERENCE TO 'GIFTS'

Paul's word for 'gift(s)' in 1 Corinthians is different than Luke's. Again, different Greek words translated as 'gift' do not carry the same meaning. Following are some examples from Paul's writings.

GIFTS OF RIGHTEOUSNESS AND LIFE

The righteousness of Christ is an exclusive gift. (Rom.5:15-17) In this passage both 'charisma' and 'dorea' are used to convey the idea of a gratuity. One gift not in everyone's possession is eternal life. (Rom.6:23, charisma) The grace of Christ is our "unspeakable gift", not abilities. (2 Cor. 9:15, *dorea*)

GIFTS OF ABILITIES

Paul teaches that abilities are not self-generated and that the source of them is the Holy Spirit. (1 Cor. 12:4-11, *charisma*) The Spirit of God distributed diverse abilities. However, He didn't 'pour' them.

The members of the body of Christ are members of one another, each possessing a gift(s) differing according to God's grace to serve one another. (Rom. 12:3-9, charismata) "Having then gifts differing according to the grace that is given to us..." (Rom12:6a, NKJV) His grace is manifested in the members of His body, with the supply of all the necessary differing abilities for the proper function of the body.

The body of Christ stands in sharp contrast to organizations and institutions. The fire department needs trained men who are also physically strong; the physically weak are excluded. Hospitals need physicians, not morticians. The courts practice jurisprudence with judges, lawyers and witnesses. Depending on the purpose of the institution, its membership is selectively based on specific abilities, therefore exclusive.

In the body of Christ, all these differing gifts are placed according to His grace where the focus is the Person of Christ, not expertise. No ability is excluded. All ability gifts are part of one body. All abilities are important. In this body analogy no ability member has authority over another. Christ, the Head, alone is the direct authority over each.

Different abilities are necessary to meet all the needs of body. Though baptized into this body, believers still struggle with the fact that they no longer need to strive for what they perceive to be the best gift. There is no need to be competitive in the body of Christ. It's only in this 'body' that our distinctive abilities can be profitably employed.

But, there is nothing in Paul's words to suggest that abilities were given at conversion. This is explained more fully in chapters 11 and 12.

Gift of Material Support

Paul commends the afflicted Macedonians for their joy and provision of a gift for the Corinthians. (2 Cor. 8:4, *charis*)

Gift of Desire of Marriage

The same Greek word for 'gifts' is also used in 1 Cor.7:7 to identify preference to marry. Appropriate sexual desire in marriage is not only a gift from God to the believer, but to the unbeliever also. (charisma)

Gift of Prayer

Paul expressed appreciation for the "gift" of prayer for him in his ministry. (2 Cor. 1:11, charisma)

Christ's Gift (Eph. 4:7)

Paul states that each believer was given grace, but then suddenly changes the subject to 'Christ's gift'. (dorea; Eph. 4:7) Believers who have received grace are identified as Christ's gift. Christ's gift is the saints; it is His body; it's His purchased possession.[58] (Psa. 68:9; Eph. 1:14, 23) The saints are the Lord's inheritance. (Eph. 1:18) Christ's gift is us, His people, a limited, measured portion of people according to divine choice. Christ's gift is one body, one church, one bride, His saints. (Eph.4:7,8,12) Christ actually became our necessary righteousness in order that we then could become a gift for Him – faultless! (Eph. 5:27; Col.1:22; Jude 24) This is a gift from the Father to Christ. (Jn.6:37)

By His descension to inferior domains of earth and His ascension to the throne, He has ultimately prevailed to retrieve us from enemy territory. (Eph. 1:21; 4:9,10) Thus, we are Christ's gift. (Eph. 4:7)

Gifts Unto Men (Eph. 4:8,9)

Paul alludes to Christ as King, who took His chosen captivity of helpless, rebellious, yet chosen, slaves captive, by bringing them out of Egypt, the land of sin, to Mt Sinai, then Zion. (Psa. 68:17-19) When the Israelites escaped on that first Passover, they plundered Egypt of silver, gold, clothing and other items depicting how God had taken[59] 'gifts' for

---

[58] Paul is clear that as there is one God and one faith, so also, there is only one body. He nowhere teaches that OT believers belong in a different class. (Eph.4:4-6) See also, Heb. 12:22-23.

[59] The Heb. 'laqach' primarily means 'to take'. 'Accept', 'bring', 'buy', 'fetch' along with 'receive' are also appropriate meanings for this word but the context does not allow for 'receive'.

men. Israel's work as slaves had not been paid for. (Ex.11:2,3) On Israel's behalf, God recovered from the Egyptians, the payment due.

These 'Gifts' Are Rewards

The word 'gifts' in Ep. 4:8 is 'doma', not the 'charisma' used for 'gifts' in 1 Corinthians. This word means 'gift' or 'present', a reward for work done. Moses 'suffered affliction with the people of God, esteeming the reproach of Christ greater than the treasures of Egypt. He looked forward to his reward.' (Heb. 11:24,25) Jesus said that our reward would be great if we suffer for Him. (Matt. 5:12) The life of every believer is a spiritual battle. Because our King has conquered our enemies, He will 'deliver up rewards to men.'[60]

Israel Represents All Saints Before And After Christ

Israel symbolizes all God's chosen spiritual people before and after Christ, Jew and Gentile. For this spiritual deliverance, there must be another Passover! King David prays that the salvation would come out of Zion when the Lord would bring back the captivity of His people. (Psa. 14:7; 53:6) To this end, David's prayer has been answered in Christ's death and resurrection. (Rom. 11:26; Heb. 12:22; 1 Pe. 2:6) This Passover occurred when Christ offered Himself as the sacrificial Lamb of God.

Since all OT saints went to heaven, there was no need to lead them to heaven as is supposed by some commentators. (2 Kg. 2:1) OT saints were born into Zion, the same as NT saints. (Psa. 87:5,6) So, Christ's descent to the 'lower parts of the earth' cannot be a reference to freeing OT saints from Hades.[61] He did not go 'under the earth'.

He First Descended Into The Lower Parts Of The Earth

The perfect incarnated Son of God descended from the dazzling heights of heaven to the dismal lower regions of the earth. Paul would have been acquainted with Isaiah, who commanded both the mountains and the 'lower parts of the earth' to sing. This context indicates that the lower parts of the earth are the valleys, and the open prairies. (Isa. 44:23) The Dead Sea is over 1300 feet below sea level and is the lowest land

---

[60] The word for 'gave' allows for a number of meanings depending on context. In my opinion, it should be God 'delivered up gifts to men' in Eph. 4:8 as in Lk. 7:25. Unlike ability gifts, in this context 'gifts' are material, which God recovers for us, as a king would distribute the spoils of war.

[61] Hades is an invention of the Jews found in the Talmud. As the other parables, Jesus used a fictitious story with a beggar named Lazarus meaning 'favored one', to show the Pharisees that at the end of days, wealth does indicate the favor of God.

elevation on earth. Jericho, at the north end of the Dead Sea, is about 800 feet below sea level. As Jesus passed through Jericho on His way up to Jerusalem, he healed two blind men and called out Zacchaeus to repent. (Matt. 20:29; Lk. 19:1-10) Quite literally, Jesus descended to the lower parts of the earth! (Eph. 4:8-10)

He Ascended Far Above The Heavens

From Jericho, Jesus ascended the earthly Mt. Zion in Jerusalem, which was 2400 feet above sea level. The total ascent was about 3200 feet over a distance of about 15 miles. Aware of the change in elevation, Paul writes that Christ, who descended, is also the One who ascended, not only to the earthly Jerusalem, but also far above the heavens, to finish all things. (Eph. 4:9, 10) God took His chosen captivity in Egypt captive. Like the captivity of Israel in Egypt, God's elect throughout the world, before and after Christ, also needed deliverance from their enemy, Satan. Christ liberated us when He made His elect His captives by His death and resurrection.[62] Now fulfilled according to the oath of His covenant, He had 'captured His captivity'. (Heb.6:17,18) All believers are citizens of this heavenly Zion to which Christ ascended! (Heb. 12:22,23; Psa. 87)

Paul states that when he Christ ascended, He gave gifts to men. Therefore, 'gifts' cannot be a reference to gifts such as 'discernment' or 'helps' because we know that OT saints had these abilities before He ascended. Rather, Paul illustrates how our conquering King secured every believer's reward, before and after Christ. When He comes again, His rewards are with Him. (Rev. 22:12) Thus, He gave gifts unto men. (Eph. 4:8)

'SPIRITUAL GIFT' OF TRUTH:

The only mention of 'spiritual gift' in the Greek is in Romans. Paul anticipates the opportunity to impart to the church in Rome something previously unknown to them. "Spiritual gift", in this context, is truth, not ability. (Rom. 1:11,12, charisma) Having taught that the Holy Spirit imparted ability gifts, he knew that he himself could not give anyone ability gifts, but as an Apostle could impart to them truth from the Spirit. This spiritual gift of truth is available to everyone.

---

[62] Paul quotes Psa. 68:18 where it actually states that He **takes** captivity captive, not led. Similarly, in Eph. 4:8, it should be translated, 'He took captivity captive'.

GIFT OF FAITH

Timothy was given divine truth by prophecy, through the teachings of his grandmother Lois, his mother Eunice and the apostle Paul. With the laying on of hands, he was confirmed as one having sufficient biblical understanding to lead and teach others. (1 Tim. 4: 13-15, charisma) He reminded Timothy of the faith of his grandmother and mother and called upon him to "stir up the gift" of faith (teachings) he had already received. (2 Tim. 1:5,6, charisma)

SUMMARY:

Gifts such as truth, marriage, material possessions and abilities are given to believers and unbelievers. The Holy Spirit's gifts such as faith and repentance and rewards, are given only to His elect. We, who belong to Christ, is His gift. But, it is noteworthy that unbelievers also share in some of God's blessings, though temporal.

HEBREWS REFERENCE TO 'GIFTS'

The Greek word 'merismos' meaning division or separation is translated as 'gifts'. The meaning and context precludes any application to Paul's ability gifts. Please see '*Gifts' In Hebrews* in the Notes, page 207.

8. HOW PAUL APPLIES "SPIRITUAL"

The word 'gift' is wrongly inserted by the translators in 1 Cor. 12:1; 14:1,12. So, it is also important to show that the association of the word 'spiritual' with the word 'gift' is artificial in most translations.

VARIOUS USES OF 'SPIRITUAL'

Used in a variety of ways, 'spiritual' must be examined in each context.

'SPIRITUAL' TEACHING AND ITS SOURCE

Paul shows how 'spiritual' is essential in two ways. Despite man's claims to wisdom, he has proven himself incapable of discerning the wisdom of God. (1 Cor. 2:1-9) Since all man's knowledge is limited to his own spirit, a true knowledge of God is precluded unless another Spirit with God's knowledge intervenes. To rightly know the thoughts of God, man must receive another Spirit, His Spirit. Only then, does he have the capacity to know "things" that have been freely given by God. (2:10-12) Not in the words taught by man's wisdom, God's wisdom must be taught by the Holy Spirit. All knowledge (things) of God is communicated to man's spirit, and was spoken by Paul, Apollos and Cephas. (1:12; 2:12,13)

The word 'spirituals' refers to specific knowledge or teachings not known to man naturally. Secondly, the Spirit is the source of this 'spiritual' divine communication.

SOME PEOPLE ARE 'SPIRITUAL'

Since the natural man does not accept the knowledge and wisdom of the Spirit, he cannot understand them. Only those who have the Spirit of God are able to spiritually discern the Apostle's teaching. (2:14-16) Paul writes, "If any one thinks himself to be a prophet or spiritual, let him acknowledge that the things which I write unto you are the commandments of the Lord." (1 Cor. 14:37, emphasis added, NKJV) Anyone who does not accept the writings of Paul as from the Lord, is evidence that he is not spiritual, therefore still a natural man. (1 Cor. 3:1) With these teachings, the spiritual man has the potential to discern the deficiencies of human wisdom, and be dissuaded from taking a brother to a secular court. (6:1-7) In this context, 'spiritual' describes a person.

SPIRITUAL AND MATERIAL:

Paul also uses the word 'spiritual' to differentiate the gospel from the material. (1 Cor. 9:11) In return for dispensing the words of spiritual truth, material sustenance should be provided for the teacher.

FOOD AND DRINK ARE SPIRITUAL:

In his brief reference to Israel's belligerent history in the wilderness, Paul applies the word 'spiritual' to material items. All Israel drank of the same spiritual drink and ate from the same spiritual food, yet with most of them, God was not well pleased. Though they ingested God's 'spiritual' provisions, they remained immoral and idolatrous. (1 Cor. 10:1-10) Those who died in the wilderness represented a lost generation of unbelievers. Despite their direct contact with God's 'spiritual' material provisions, it did them no good. (Heb.3:16-4:2)

OUR FUTURE BODY IS 'SPIRITUAL':

In yet another application, 'spiritual' describes a body that we will one day acquire. (15:44-49) It is a body that cannot die.

SUMMARY

Paul explains that God's teachings are 'spiritual'. Some people are 'spiritual'; some are not. The means by which teachings are communicated is 'spiritual'. Knowledge from God is spiritual, the means of assimilating His teachings is spiritual, nonphysical personhood is spiritual and our future body is spiritual. God's material provisions of food and water are also 'spiritual', given to believers and unbelievers alike.

Whether seen or unseen, whether material or not, whether given to unbelievers and believers, "spiritual" denotes something that comes from God.

"SPIRITUALS" IS PARTLY ABOUT 'GIFTS'

In 1 Cor. chapters 12 and 14, where the word 'spirituals' is used, 'gifts' has been added by translators to read 'spiritual gifts'.[63] (1 Cor. 12:1; 14:1,12) Young's translates, 'and concerning the spiritual things, brethren' in 12:1. An interlinear Greek translates this as "but concerning spirituals". When the noun 'gifts' in 12:1 and 14:1 is inserted after the

---

[63] The insertion of another word after 'spirituals' here, changes the meaning of his statement by introducing a different noun. Dynamic equivalence is appropriate to aid the reader in a right understanding of the Greek, even when that word does not appear in the original. But care must be taken not to editorialize.

plural adjective *pneumatikon* (spirituals), Paul's overarching concern for their knowledge of the thoughts and words from God in his entire letter, is obscured and even changed. The context does not permit 'gifts'.

'SPIRITUALS' INCLUDE TEACHINGS ABOUT GIFTS.

Still needing to give them more advice, he states that the rest he will set in order when he comes to Corinth. (11:34b) With this letter, he sets in order certain matters of immediate concern. The context for 'spirituals' must **not** exclude how he had applied this word to truth he had already taught. All his teachings are 'spirituals'. But, not all his teachings are about 'gifts'. The insertion of 'gifts' is erroneous because it restricts the meaning of the word 'spiritual'.

'SPIRITUALS' PROVIDES ESSENTIAL KNOWLEDGE TO MAN

From the start of the letter, he has been relating to them 'spirituals' of knowledge originating from the Holy Spirit, necessary for 'spiritual' growth. Knowledge about carnality, stewardship, immorality, marriage, the Lord's supper, conscience, etc., is spiritual. But, 'spirituals' in 12:1 and 14:1 pertain to the teachings of the entire letter. They are teachings of God, given by the Spirit, of which teachings on gifts is only a part.

Not wanting them to remain ignorant, he puts the urgent 'spirituals' in writing without delay. (11:34b -12:1) Repeatedly, throughout this letter Paul asks, 'do you not know?' Spiritual knowledge in this letter was the means to address the pervading ignorance of everyone. That the man is the head of the woman, that their behavior at the Lord's Table [64] was unacceptable, that we are to become weak to win the weak, were just some of the 'spirituals' he wanted them to know before he came. (11:2,3, 23) 'Spirituals' were given to alleviate ignorance.

Concerned for their growth and the salvation of some, it is important to keep in mind that Paul is addressing the entire assembly, both believers and unbelievers. The teachings of the written and spoken word are the 'spirituals' essential for man's deliverance from spiritual slavery and for his growth after he has been set free.

[64] The majority holds that people got sick and died for eating 'unworthily'. This view however, contradicts the context and sound doctrine. See The Lord's Table in NOTES, page 217.

'SPIRITUALS' ABOUT CHRIST

Before Paul informs them concerning the 'spirituals' of abilities, he wants them to be clear regarding Christ's identity. He is not accursed! He is Lord!

Paul reminds the Gentile converts of their past idolatry. Their objects of worship, being dumb, were incapable of imparting knowledge. Only by obeying the 'spirituals' of divine truth of the Holy Spirit were they able to escape the clutches of their idolatrous bondage. (12:1,2) This is not about demons who have taken control of an individual to impart knowledge. Paul confronts those claiming Jesus to be accursed with knowledge about who Christ really is.

CESSATIONIST INFERENCES

Here the Cessationist is distracted with some incorrect extrapolations. [65] Cessationists argue that professing Christians, in Christian surroundings, called Jesus accursed. Secondly, Cessationists claim they were in a state of 'uncontrolled emotionalism' ecstasy, beside themselves with emotion, frenzied. Yet, this is deemed to be evidence of the Spirit's presence and activity for inspired prophecy. Thirdly, Cessationists teach that Jews were attempting to influence Gentiles to call Jesus accursed, when they got up to speak in their assemblies. Fourthly, the Cessationist is puzzled why this was tolerated in their assemblies. To answer this apparent dilemma they suggest that Corinthians were falling for an early form of Gnosticism where some said that the body of Christ was accursed but His spirit wasn't. Fifthly, one Cessationist, explains that outright demonic control of unbelievers had an affect on the Christian state of some of Paul's acquaintances. Corinthian believers had "confused demonic leading in their lives with that of the Holy Spirit." But, really what is the context?

THE CORINTHIAN CONTEXT

The Gentiles, on the other hand, had been carried away with dumb idols. Incapable of saying anything, everything written and believed about idols was contrived by man. Therefore, the paths in which they were "led", were of their own making. These lifeless Gentile idols communicated nothing about the solution for man's sin. In contrast to their former pantheism, Gentile believers were reminded that there is only one source

[65] Robert L. Thomas, *Understanding Spiritual Gifts*, Kregel Publications, 1999, p. 19-22

for truth: the Spirit of God. (12:2,3) Moreover, they are warned that some will attribute wrong words to the one living, speaking God, which He never said. Paul wanted them to know that anyone who said that 'Jesus is accursed' does not have the Holy Spirit, as the Jews claimed. In fact, the Jews had worshiped idols long before the Greeks had. (1 Cor. 10:7) The Jews had to be rescued from idolatry as did the Greeks and Romans.

The Jewish Context

Paul had reasoned with the Jews that Christ did not stay on the cross or in the tomb. (1 Cor. 15:4) Yet, most of the Jews continued to blaspheme Him. (Acts 18:5,6) However, Crispus, the leader of the synagogue in Corinth was converted. Sosthenes, who had replaced him, and other blaspheming Jews, brought Paul to Gallio's judgment seat, alleging that he was teaching contrary to the Law. (Ac. 18:12-17) Having inflicted persecution upon fellow Jewish believers himself, Paul understood the reaction of Sosthenes to the conversion of many Jews in Corinth. He, likewise, had believed that 'Jesus is accursed'. (1 Tim. 1:13) To blaspheme Christ is to curse Him. Paul explained to the Galatians that we were redeemed because Christ took upon Himself the curse of the law, which we could not bear. Since Christ had not sinned, neither could He sin, He was <u>made</u> a curse for us. (Ga. 3:13) The Jews failed to see that because of their failure to keep the Law God gave them, they were cursed, not Christ. Instead, they cursed Christ for claiming to be God. And, likewise, anyone who taught that 'Jesus is Lord' was also accused of blasphemy and harassed. But, Paul made it clear that anyone who preached a different gospel, was accursed. (Ga. 1:8,9)

There were Jews in Corinth who in the name of Jehovah God, called Jesus accursed. Paul stuns the unbelieving Corinthian Jew that no one can call Jesus accursed by the Spirit of God. (1 Cor. 12:3) Furthermore, he indicts these Jews, "If anyone does not love the Lord Jesus Christ, let him be accursed. O Lord come." (1 Cor. 16:22) Jesus remained a stumbling block to the Jews, consequently curse Him. (1 Cor. 1:22,23) This is the Jewish context.

Summary

There is no hint that demonically controlled professing believers were ecstatically declaring Jesus accursed. There is no call for exorcism. Anyone exhibiting demonic behavior would have been ostracized, as Paul had censured the man committing adultery. (1Cor.5)

Though the unregenerate Jew was likely to pronounce Jesus accursed as those who crucified Him did, neither Jew or Gentile could say 'Jesus is Lord', except by the Holy Spirit. Anyone who calls Jesus accursed does not speak by the Holy Spirit, and anyone who testifies that 'Jesus is Lord' does so by the Holy Spirit. Refraining from declaring Jesus to be accursed is not enough either. There must be a heartfelt acknowledgement that He is Lord, indeed.

The Gentiles among them were duly warned that even devout Jews who do not worship idols, who claim the same scriptures as do true believers, are just as lost without Christ, as were idolatrous Gentiles.

Spirituals

Paul introduced the subject of 'spirituals' in verse one. These 'spirituals' pertain to information that can be known. More specifically, this information is about God and man's relation to Him. Again, 'spirituals' is not limited to the topic of gifts. Spirituals are true teachings or knowledge that does not originate with man. (12:1-3)

'SPIRITUAL' WORDS ABOUT THE TRINITY

Paul provides more 'spiritual' words about the work of the Trinity. To this point he has informed them that Jesus is Lord and that this truth cannot be known apart from the Holy Spirit. Before Crispus was converted, he was also of the opinion that Jesus was cursed. As the Holy Spirit changed Jews who cursed Christ when they were saved, so, He also changed idol-worshipping Gentiles, when they were converted.

Paul corrects lingering suppositions about the source of their abilities and service.

DIVERSITY OF ABILITY GIFTS BUT THE SAME SPIRIT

In addition to the gift of knowledge, that Jesus is Lord, the Holy Spirit also provided other diverse gifts. (1 Cor. 12:4) It seems that some recent pagan converts still believed that abilities came from different 'spirits' or good 'daimons', as they were called, not directly from God.

> "Among the ancient Greeks, the concept of the daimon led a dual existence as it progressed along two distinct but related strands. On the one hand, daimons were conceived in typically animistic terms as spirits that inhabited or haunted certain places, affected the weather and other natural occurrences, and so on. Some were associated with the spirits of the dead. On the

> other hand, a spiritualized or psychologized view placed the daimons in a position of deep intertwinement with human subjectivity. Essentially, the Greeks regarded daimons as objectively real presences that made themselves known through their influence upon and within the human psyche. The objective, animistic beliefs about them were thus matched and accompanied by a more subtle and psychologically oriented view that framed them as inner influences upon human thoughts and emotions, and even as the keepers and emblems of individual character and destiny. This second view gradually became dominant over time."[66]

The Greek pagans thought that each good demon (daimon) had a specialty gift, such as healing, prophecy, etc.[67]

Pagan Greeks petitioned different gods for private and social desires. They would ask Poseidon for a safe voyage and women would ask Artemis or Hera for childbirth.[68] (12:2)

Paul encountered a slave-girl, who was possessed with a spirit of divination or 'prophecy' from which her masters gained a profit. (Ac. 16:16) This girl was obviously 'gifted' with the true knowledge that 'these men are the servants of the most High God'. But her 'gift of prophecy' did not come from the Spirit of God.

Summary

As true believers, the Corinthians certainly would have renounced their former worship, but may not have shed some of the faulty philosophies from their pagan past. False, lingering notions among professing Gentile believers, that abilities came from multiple spirits, as Greek mythology taught, needed correction. Paul wants them to be clear that all normal ability gifts come from the same Spirit. These gifts all come from one Spirit.

DIFFERENCES OF SERVICE, BUT THE SAME LORD (12:5)

The Lord governs. He is Lord of unbelievers as well as believers. Everyone is given opportunity for service and is ultimately accountable to

---

[66] Matt Cardin, *The Teeming Brain, Possession, Exorcism,, and the Daimon: A Brief History* https://www.teemingbrain.com/2018/02/22/possession-exorcism-and-the-daimon-a-brief-history/

[67] *F.B. Hole's Old And New Testament Commentary*, 1 Cor. 12:4

[68] Cara Leigh Sailors, *The Function and Mythology and Religion in Ancient Greek Society*, page 38 https://dc.etsu.edu/cgi/viewcontent.cgi?referer=https://duckduckgo.com/&httpsredir=1&article=3471&context=etd

this same Lord. Abilities exercised in different kinds of service are under the governance of Christ. The same Lord presides over everyone's service.

Even unregenerate man serves man when calamities such as earthquakes, floods and hurricanes strike. This inclination to serve could hardly be credited to man or the devil.

Differences of Activities but the Same God. (12:6)

And there are differences of activities or operations but the same God. 'Activities' is defined as 'effects'. The same sovereign God also expedites all outcomes by uniting abilities and service for meaningful outcome. (1 Cor. 12:6)

Summary

Paul reminds and informs believers that the same Spirit gives all beneficial ability gifts, that the same Lord governs all service and that the same God expedites all outcomes. This countered pagan mythology that spirits (daimons) were the source of gifts, that idols controlled events. God, the Father, the Son and the Holy Spirit alone expedite, govern and gift each person for necessary for beneficial communal human existence.

The Holy Spirit is not the sole source of all things spiritual. The manifestation given to every man is evidence that the Lord governs and the Father expedites. However, there is a reason for gifts,

> "But the manifestation of the Spirit is given to every man to profit withal." (1 Cor. 12:7)

With this statement Paul introduces the 'spiritual' or teaching of ability gifts. He discloses the reason for the gifts. Though everyone is gifted, not everyone has employed his gifts to please God. Desiring these gifts be used to profit others, the Apostle graphically depicts what this should look like with his analogy to the body. It is this aspect of giftedness that is not universally present or visible.

Importantly, Paul's use of 'spiritual' at the beginning of chapters 12 and 14 includes all inspired truth, the Word of God. Information concerning gifts forms a small part of these revealed 'spirituals'.

9. MEMBERS OF THE BODY

From Paul's body analogy, it is assumed that members are gifted only at conversion. (1 Cor. 12:12-27) Having specifically named some endowments of the Holy Spirit, Paul elaborates by showing how gifted members ought to function in the body of Christ.

WHY DID THE HOLY SPIRIT DISTRIBUTE GIFTS?

Although the Holy Spirit gives abilities to everyone, they are not intended for personal aggrandizement. They were given for everyone's benefit. (1 Cor. 12:6,7)

WERE THE GIFTS EXCLUSIVE?

The manifestation of the Holy Spirit is the distribution of ability gifts to everyone, however, He does not manifest Himself to everyone with 'baptism'. Only the "we" are baptized. (1 Cor. 12:5-7,11,13) Cessationists claim that gifts were 'graciously given to believers by God' at conversion.[69] But is that so?

Just prior to Paul's body analogy, he listed multilingual and interpretation skills as gifts distributed by the Holy Spirit. We know that unsaved and saved alike possess various degrees of aptitude in linguistic skills. Therefore, the different abilities distributed by the Holy Spirit to each one "individually as He wills", must occur before being baptized into His body. (1 Cor. 12:11) Already variously gifted, it is neither stated or implied that these gifts would be replaced with the same abilities after conversion. Having the gift of languages before conversion is the same gift of languages after conversion. There was no gift exchange.

THE BODY COMPARISON

After making the point that the Spirit distributes gifts according to His will, Paul compares the human body to the body of Christ. (1 Cor. 12:12) The human body is one, yet it has many members. Christ's body is one and this body also has many person members. Secondly, Paul points out that though the members of the body are many, every member is necessary

---

[69] Larry D. Pettegrew, *The New Covenant Ministry of the Holy Spirit*, Kress Biblical Resources, 1993,P. 160

to make up one body. The body would be incomplete with even one less member, as insignificant as that member would appear to be. Thirdly, only all the members of that one body are members. There are members (persons) not part of that one body.

What Are Members?

This body of people is composed of many members with a variety of gifts or abilities. These person members are depicted as eyes, feet, hands, ears, smelling etc. but there is only one place for the proper function of these members – in a body.

Why The Body Analogy?

The human body illustrates coordination. With Christ as the Head of His body, Paul depicts how the members, each with his gift, support the Head.

What Then Was Paul's Concern?

Paul's concern centered on how and where abilities were employed, not their acquisition. His was not a psychological diagnosis for members to pursue another more suitable gift or a campaign to recruit better gifted members. Lack of abilities was not Paul's concern. Even in the body of Christ, Paul shows how self-esteem might interfere with a God-honoring use of Spirit-given abilities.

Who Were the Members?

Paul had been inclusive regarding the possession of ability gifts, but exclusive on being a member of the body. Having an ability does not make one a member of a body. Speaking as a member of this body, Paul states, "we were all baptized into one body". Jews, Greeks, slaves or free, all without distinction are part of this body. Paul says that all of "we", that is believers, were baptized into His body. (1 Cor. 12:13) Jews, Greeks, slaves and free were identified as being members of the body. However, not all Jews, Greeks, slaves and free are members of the body.

What Motivated The Members of The Body?

Indeed, everyone has at least one gift, which must be used not only for the purpose it was intended, but also with the right motivation. Still ignorant of the fact that the Holy Spirit distributes abilities according to His will, they believed that abilities were personally selected. (1 Cor. 12:16,17) They clamored for the prominence that another gift offered.

WHAT IS UNIQUE ABOUT "ALL" MEMBERS IN THIS BODY?

There is only one Head, therefore only one body. (1 Cor. 3:4,5; Eph. 4:4) Numbers are important, even the number 'one'. This body is unique because it's one of a kind.

> "For, even as the body is one, and hath many members, and all the members of the one body, being many, are one body, so also [is] the Christ." (1 Cor. 12:12, YLT)

"All" the members of that one body are the members of that one body regardless of ethnicity or status. Who would think that Jew and Gentile, slave and free could be united in one body? This body is unique because it unites people who normally clash. (12:13) Gentiles are fellow heirs and members of the same body as Jews. (Eph. 3:6) The Jewish fellowship of believers had not been replaced; the Gentile believers have been incorporated into the same commonwealth, being built together with Jewish believers. (Eph.2:12,13,18,22)

And "all" the members of that one body are the members of that one body, indicates that if the most 'insignificant' member would be missing, His body would not be complete. The 'slave' is as important as the most learned Jew or Gentile. This body is unique because it has no insignificant member.

Like the natural body, members of this body can't be split into separate bodies, as they wanted to do under Paul, Apollos or Peter. No one has the authority to remove any member from this body. (1 Cor. 12:21) Comprised of every ethnicity or class, this is Christ's indivisible Body.

HOW DO PEOPLE BECOME MEMBERS?

Paul states that "we were all", baptized into Christ's body. (1 Cor. 12:13,14) Jews, Greeks, slaves and free are all eligible to become part of the body. "We" (members) were "all" baptized. Members, that is, gifted people already in existence were 'poured' into His body, made to drink of one Spirit. The Holy Spirit had come to dwell within. (1 Cor. 6:19)

Gifts are not baptized into people, but people must be baptized into the body to become members of the body. Abilities are distributed, not 'baptized', to every man. People do not receive an ability gift when they become members; they receive the gift of salvation from sin and made to drink of one Spirit. We become members when the Holy Spirit connects us to the Head who is Christ. The Holy Spirit's distribution of abilities is not synonymous with the baptism into the body of Christ. (1 Cor.

12:11,13,18,24) Since no one is naturally part of this body, God has ordained that all His people become part of this one body by the baptism of one Spirit.

How Is The Usefulness Of The Member NOT Determined?

Usefulness is not determined by individual aspirations to be other than what he is. Desires to be a 'hand' instead of a 'foot' cannot improve the potential usefulness of a member. He still remains the "foot" or "ear" God supplied for Christ's body. All members are important. (1 Cor. 12:15,16) The perceived status of a gift does not determine its value or its usefulness.

Members who had considered themselves inferior, erroneously perceived the abilities of others superior to theirs. Others who considered themselves to be superior members in Christ's body, were assertive, thus denying others opportunity for service. (12:22-24) Usefulness is not determined by the opinion of other members. Prominence based on human standards of excellence is not the standard God uses.

How Is The Usefulness of The Member Determined?

Before we can become useful members, we must be baptized by the Spirit into the body of Christ. (1 Cor. 12:12,13) Secondly, God sovereignly places us where He wants us. (1 Cor. 12:18, 24) The maturing believer recognizes that his profitable place in the body has not been the result of his own achievements or contrivances. Thirdly, like the human body, the usefulness of the member is determined by coordination under the Head. Therefore, each member should know that unsuitable service results from the lack of submission to the Head. In this body, there is decreasing divisiveness and increasing care for one another. It is a maturing process in which each member increasingly compliments the others as they submit to the Head. (1 Cor. 12:15-19,24,25)

Why Did God Place The Members?

God has composed His body in such a way that divisions need not occur. Imagine a hand reaching out to bring food to the mouth and the other hand being jealous, slaps it? If the 'hand' knows that there is a cut on the 'foot', it naturally reaches down to attend to it with antiseptic and a bandage to stop infection and facilitate recovery. It is most unnatural for the members of a natural body to fight one another, so should it also be in the body of Christ. Paul exhorts every member to have the same care for one another. Naturally, the differing functions of each member will express their care differently. As individual members of this body, Christ our Head, directs us to serve others. Again, lack of abilities from the Holy Spirit was not Paul's concern; the appropriate use of abilities was. (1 Cor. 12:24-26)

Placement Of Members According To His Will

God has set or placed the members; He does not create a 'gift' at baptism, at our conversion. Having already distributed the gifts according to His will, the Holy Spirit baptizes people into the body to become members. God places each member in the body according to His will. (1 Cor. 12:11,18) 'Distributing' and 'placing' are different operations. God places members according to what the Spirit has already distributed.

Whom did the Spirit baptize into Christ? People with their giftedness were baptized into the body. (1 Cor. 12:12-13) It is by this work that the Holy Spirit cleanses us with the blood of Jesus Christ. Having given us the faith and repentance necessary for this transaction, He clothes us with the righteousness of Christ and makes us members of Christ's body.

Not only is Paul's analogy of the body symbolic of believers' relation to Christ, it also highlights the reality of the interdependence of each believer. As it is ludicrous to say that certain parts of the human body are not needed, so it is with Christ's body. (1 Cor. 12:21-25) Each member is placed by God where he is needed for God-honoring service.

Believers are members individually. (1 Cor. 12:27) Like the human body, each member of Christ's body is expected perform its unique and different function as directed by the head. The Head of the spiritual body is Christ, not one another.

Credibility Of Membership

Despite being favored with Spirit-given abilities, mankind inevitably fails to profit from them. (1 Cor. 12:6,7) When a professing member continues to use his abilities for self-promotion, legitimate concerns are raised whether the 'member' is truly connected to the Head. So, abilities given by the Holy Spirit do not provide evidence of a credible profession of faith. Only, when connected to the Head in this body can we be in possession of the only credible evidence there is. That evidence pertains to how we use the abilities the Spirit has given to us, not the presence or number of gifts.

People Before And After Baptism

Well then, is there no difference between the gifts of the unbeliever and believer? Paul regarded himself as one who was not clever with words, or superior in speech as Apollos might have been. (1 Cor. 1:17; 2:1,4; 2 Cor. 10:10; 11:6) The difference of skill isn't judged by outward appearance. Paul's concern was not the presence of ability. In the body every member ultimately has a defined, though different purpose for the exercise of his ability, than one outside the body. Every believer has the capacity to glorify God with even the most 'ordinary' ability. Outside the 'body' of Christ the rich young ruler discerned exactly what Jesus was saying about how to inherit eternal life. His love of riches precluded the love for Christ necessary to profit from the gift of discernment the Spirit had given him. (Mt. 19:22) His gifts weren't the issue; his attitude was. Outside the Body, the motivation is to serve self; inside the Body it is to serve Christ and one another.

SUMMARY

This illustration of the body graphically depicts what the believers' relationship with Christ and each other ought to be. Some members did not behave like they were part of the body.

The Members Are Natural

Perhaps the most prominent aspect of Paul's analogy is that the body is natural. This body analogy serves to sift out behaviors contrary to nature. Erratic behavior is indicative of malfunction, not an ability or gift. Claims to various mystical experiences are nothing but charismatic contrivances that are confused with abilities. The body parts function naturally because they are natural. Likewise, no part of the spiritual body can be coordinated with invented abilities such as 'ecstatic utterances', simply because they aren't natural. With this body analogy, pseudo gifts like gibberish are easily recognized, and dismissed.

The same coordination expected from a healthy human body is also expected of the members within Christ's spiritual body. (1 Cor. 12:12) Unlike an aging human body, this spiritual body continues to grow to inevitable perfection because the Head is perfect. (Col.2:19; Eph. 5:26,27)

Failure to understand that the gifts of the Holy Spirit were never considered supernatural has contributed to the surge of charismatic contortions. Gifts of the Holy Spirit not only have a natural function within the body, they also look normal and behave naturally.

The Body Of Christ Is Supernatural

If there is a supernatural element to this analogy, it is that unity of mind and purpose can be achieved where it had not been impossible.

With the human body, Paul illustrates the sinful foolishness of competition based on abilities. (1 Cor. 12:15-21) Without Christ, the exercise of each one's abilities to complement one another is impossible. (1 Cor. 12:22-26) This indeed is supernatural, unlike the Charismatic movement, which has caused injury to many members of the Body and prevented many others from being baptized into His body.

There is one mystical element of Paul's illustration that applies to every member of the Body. It is simply that every member is connected directly to the Head, who is Christ. None have a special connection that surpasses other members of the Body. And, neither does this connection with the Head produce behavior contrary to the nature of Christ.

Every Member Is Important.

Every part of the body is necessary; no one in the body is useless. Invisible functions of the 'body' are necessary to support the visible and conversely, the visible supports the obscure. (1 Cor. 12:22-24) Both the inconspicuous and apparently unimportant are necessary. (1 Cor. 12:22)

Gifts Do Not Certify Conversion.

Ability gifts. such as generosity. to not confirm membership in the body of Christ. (1 Cor. 13:3) In chapter two, I had referenced some OT personalities, both believers and unbelievers, who were gifted by the Holy Spirit. Paul's analogy should serve to alert believers that when professing believers continually use their gifts for selfish and conflicting purposes, they might actually not be part of Christ's body. Their giftedness is real, but their profession of faith is not.

However, not everyone who is not part of the Body uses his gifts in an inordinate fashion. Despite the apparent natural exercise of one's gifts, they are of no avail because they do not honor the Head as part of His body.

God Has Placed Members That Already Function.

With this analogy, Paul illustrates how our desires may interfere with our abilities. Jealous of others, we want to have someone else's ability.

Varying emphasis has been placed on knowing what one's 'gift' is. In this analogy it is not implied that the 'eye' should search for its gift. The 'eye' member, along with all the other members is already functioning. Therefore, we are not exhorted to search for a gift; we are exhorted to use the gift we always had for the benefit of the body.

Having explained how ability gifts were expected to function together, with his 'body' analogy, Paul highlights the fact that gifts are diverse and limited. No one in this special body receives new ability gifts. But, in order to be part of this body, one must receive a new character. (discussed in chapter 15). Only then can a person be awakened to new opportunities, where abilities he always had can now be employed for lasting and eternal advantage.

10. THE THREE PERSON GIFTS

The leadership-based divisions of some Corinthian believers were evidence that they did not understand God's means of revealing His word. (1 Cor. 1:12,13; 3:3,4) Desire for prominence, generated conflicts that compromised their spiritual growth and witness. Paul's 'body' analogy illustrates the expected unity of believers under Christ's headship. And, how do unbelievers learn how to become part of this body under the Headship of Christ? The solution to this dilemma is three person gifts.

THE PERENNIAL PRESENT TENSE (1 COR. 12:29-30)

Ability gifts existed from the time of Adam. God gave Adam the gift of government or administration. (Gen. 1:28; 12:28) The Levites had the gift of speaking in languages.[70] (12:30) Throughout history, God caused already gifted people to repent of their sin and set them in the assembly of believers. In the aorist tense, 'God had set', implies a one-time action, unfolding in time. (12:28) The principles of giftedness are true before and after Christ. In this context, the present tense indicates a reality that does not expire. (12:27, 29, 30)

THE GIFTS ARE NUMBERED

Paul classified his list of gifts. There are three categories of gifts: person gifts, ability gifts and character gifts. We begin this study with *person gifts*.

The members of Christ's body are set by God. (12:18) Whether the foot, hand, ear, eye or nose, each is necessary for the body to function properly. The total number of these member-gifts is not specified. However, there is another category of gifts that is.

THREE NUMBERED PERSON GIFTS IN 1 CORINTHIANS

There are three person gifts established in the church: Apostles, Prophets and Teachers. (12:28) Numerically distinguished from the ability gifts, Paul cites three categories of person gifts: "first" Apostles, "secondly"

[70] Jamieson, Fausset & Brown, *Commentary on The Whole Bible*, P. 350 See comments on Neh. 8:7,8. Whether the Hebrew Scripture was translated into Chaldee, which every Jew understood, or the meaning explained in Chaldee, without translating text, the gift of languages was evident.

Prophets and "thirdly" Teachers. (1 Cor. 12:28) Though all believers are gifted members of the body individually, God has distinguished the Apostles, Prophets and Teachers by numbering them. Are the numbers important? Richard Mayhue says,

> "...it is commonly understood as a basic rule of hermeneutics that numbers should be accepted at face value, that is, they convey a mathematical quantity unless there is substantial evidence to warrant otherwise."[71]

They are numbered because they are deemed to be of special significance. Though distinct, they are one cohesive delegation, each complimenting the other with the same authoritative revelation of Spirit-given truth.

Classifying The Unnumbered Person Gifts In Ephesians

However, in his letter to the Ephesians, Paul references four unnumbered persons gifts: Apostles, Prophets, evangelists and shepherd-teachers, instead of just three. Does Paul contradict himself?

Following is a literal translation for Eph. 4:11,

> And (*de*)[72] He himself gave the Apostles indeed, yet the Prophets, yet the evangelists, yet the shepherds, namely teachers.[73]

The Greek for 'and' [*kai*], is translated 'also', 'even', 'then' and 'namely'. In this instance, it is obvious that Paul does not intend literal shepherds to 'guide' believers, so 'shepherds <u>and</u> teachers' is erroneous. However, with the phrase, 'namely teachers', Paul explains who these metaphoric shepherds really are.[74]

The following is a summary of Eph. 4:11,

---

[71] Richard L. Mayhue, *How To Study The Bible*, by Christian Focus Publications c. 2009, p. 137

[72] The adversative conjunction *de*, is translated as 'now', 25 times as 'yet' in the NAS. Translating it as 'and', doesn't fit the context.

[73] This quotation was partly derived from the Interlinear on the following website. Scripture4all.org/ Online interlinear.

[74] Thayer's shows that *kai* can be epexegetical. (No. 3, *Thayer's Greek Lexicon*, 2532) It is the addition of a phrase for further explanation. For example, Paul "cried out in the council, 'Men **and** brethren, I am a Pharisee..." (Acts 23:6, emphasis added) Brethren are men, so NAS leaves out 'men and'. It should be translated, 'Men, namely brethren...'. Paul more specifically calls attention to his Jewish brethren. Another example: "...Jesus began to preach, **and** to say, 'Repent for the kingdom of heaven is at hand.'" (Matt. 4:17) Is Jesus doing two things: preaching and saying? Again, it should be translated, 'Jesus began to preach, namely, 'Repent...', which would explain what he was preaching.

- Paul is emphatic that Christ is the source of the Apostles' ministry. He ordained twelve men 'to be' Apostles. These men saw the Lord. (Ac. 1:21,22; 1 Cor. 9:1)
- 'Gave' is aorist/indicative/active, meaning that death cannot terminate what He gave. (Eph. 1:1; 2:20; 3:5)
- Paul affirms the new apostleship, with the word 'indeed'. Most certainly, Christ gave 'Apostles'. (Jn. 14:26; Ac. 2:42,43)
- Though Paul affirmed the Apostles, he said, 'yet the Prophets'. With the word 'yet', Paul implies that Prophets, evangelists and teachers already exist. (Ac. 17:11; 1 Cor. 4:6) Therefore, it is implied, 'yet the Prophets...' He gave, remain. It doesn't make sense to say, 'yet He gave the Prophets'.
- The ministry of Prophets, evangelists and teachers already existed and were not replaced. He had given them long before 'Apostles'.
- 'Evangelist' means the bearer of good news. The Prophets Jonah and John the Baptist were also evangelists. (Isa. 52:7) Philip is an example of a NT evangelist. They 'teach' the lost.
- Paul also says, 'yet the Shepherds' remain. Of course, believers don't need literal shepherds, so this is a metaphor for the kind of 'teachers' He still gives to His people.

Since Paul numerically specified only three person gifts, the four mentioned to the Ephesians must be explanatory. Apostles and Prophets are common to both lists. Evangelists and shepherd-teachers in Ephesians, both describe teachers as per 1 Cor. 12:28.

It is evident that these Person gifts perform a unique and essential function for the members of the Body of Christ.

FIRST, APOSTLES

Paul identified himself with "us Apostles" the <u>last</u> to be displayed as men condemned to death along with the Prophets who preceded them, John the Baptist being the last. (1 Cor. 4:9-13; 9:1,2) He places the Apostles first. The Jewish component of the church could not ignore apostolic teachings as they did in Galatia. The teaching of the Apostles was as important as the Prophets. Given by Christ's authority through one of His chosen Apostles, Paul, all future authorities were precluded from introducing another 'apostle' or 'prophet' or 'teacher' in the first position.

Two Kinds of Apostles

An apostle is one who is commissioned to convey a message. There are two kinds of apostles: delegated apostles, and God-appointed Apostles.[75] Though Epaphroditus is identified as 'your apostle', and Titus is named an apostle of the churches, they are clearly distinguished from the twelve Apostles. (2 Cor. 8:23; Phil. 2:25) Barnabas is also recognized as an apostle with Paul because of the gospel they were teaching. (Ac. 14:14) However, the majority of the 80 times *apostolos* appears, it denotes the disciples that Jesus had chosen. So, "God has appointed these in the church: first apostles..." (1 Cor. 12:28a) Since every other use of *apostolos* in this letter to the Corinthians is a reference to the twelve, 'Apostles' cannot be interpreted as delegated church officials. These were God-appointed Apostles. (1 Cor. 12:28)

The Apostles Were Personally Appointed By Christ

Jesus was the Prophet, Moses predicted. (De.18:15; Ac.3:22) This Prophet Christ, called 12 disciples, who then became His Apostles. His primary focus in His teaching ministry had been His personally chosen disciples, who after His death confirmed the Gospel to others, as personal witnesses of His life, death and resurrection. No other group of men had been so privileged to be in close contact with God incarnate.

Since Apostles were appointed, and Paul declared that he was called to be an Apostle by the will of God, the numeric description of 'apostles' in 1 Cor. 12:28 must exclude unappointed apostles. (1 Cor. 15:9; 2 Cor. 1:1; Eph.1:1; Col.1:1; 1 Tim.1:1; 2 Tim. 1:1)

Apostolic Appointment Is Exclusive

The twelve apostles are the foundation stones of the New Jerusalem and the gates of the city are the twelve tribes of Israel. (Rev.21:12-14) By casting lots to replace Judas, the eleven apostles confirmed that a full compliment of the apostleship needed to be twelve, not eleven and not thirteen. (Eph. 2:20; Rev. 21:14) Man chose Mathias; God chose Paul. The only legitimate replacement for Judas was Paul. Many references clearly indicate only twelve Apostles were directly chosen by the Lord. (Acts. 2:37, 43; 4:33; 5:12; 15:2,4,6,22; 1 Cor. 15:9) Since the number of the apostles had been appointed; there were no more to come.

---

[75] Some think that 'apostles' is an indefinite number citing Andronicus and Junia as apostles. (Rom.16:7) But this verse states that they were of note only among the apostles. God-appointed apostles are known by every believer.

Besides the twelve Apostles, other apostles like Barnabas were commissioned to assist in the preaching of the gospel. (Ac. 14:14) However, the number of God-appointed Apostles was only 12. They could not quit. God appointed them for His people; they were not self-appointed or church-appointed.

Christ promised that He would dispatch another Comforter of the same kind as He only to the Eleven. This 'Comforter' (parakletos) would be an advocate for the truth, bringing to remembrance the things Christ had taught them. With Paul as the replacement for Judas, only twelve Apostles were to receive and bear record of the truth as given by Christ. This calling is exclusive. (1 Cor. 9:1,2; 15:9)

APOSTOLIC AUTHORITY

Paul claimed that the Holy Spirit has now disclosed the meaning of mysteries not known in previous ages to "His holy apostles and prophets". The question arises, 'if the age of prophets had passed, how can Paul say that more revelation had then been given to both the apostles and prophets, since the Prophets were dead?' (Eph. 3:5)

The 'apostles' and 'prophets' may be seen as the same person.[76] (Eph. 3:2-6) Apostolic authority was to be regarded with the same status and as the Prophets of the OT. (Rom. 1:2; 16:26) The apostleship is 'holy', that is, specifically set apart by God and therefore not inferior to the prophetic office that preceded them. (1 Cor.14:37; 2 Thes.3:14) Jewish converts were to regard Jesus' Apostles with the same authority as OT Prophets, hence, "apostles and prophets". As Christ's appointed Apostles, they were commissioned to herald good news that Jesus had come as prophesied, and as prophets, they spoke on behalf of Christ. Moved by the Holy Spirit, the Apostles received and revealed the unedited word of God. (2 Pe.1:20-21) The Apostles spoke with the same authority as did the OT Prophets.

APOSTOLIC CREDIBILITY

The Apostles performed **signs and wonders**. (Acts 2:43; 2 Cor. 12:12) They confirmed the Apostles' authority to speak from God to the saints and the lost. (Ac. 4:7-11; 1 Cor. 14:37; 2 Cor. 12:12) The Apostles, Peter and John, healed a man. (Acts 6:3-9) But, these were signs and wonders,

---

[76] Ephesians 3:5: The use of the word 'and' does not mandate two different people. In Col.1:2 Paul addresses the "saints and faithful brethren". Here the 'saints' and 'faithful brothers' are the same persons. In Col. 3:17 "God and the Father" are not intended to be two different Persons. (KJV, in other translations 'kai' has been removed)

not 'gifts' of the Spirit. No expectation exists in Scripture, written or implied, that believers other than the Apostles, or those they approved, were to perform signs and wonders.

SECOND, PROPHETS

God also set Prophets in the assembly. The basic meaning of 'prophet' is 'one who announces'. The classical meaning of *prophetes* is 'one who speaks for another.'[77]

THE UNINSPIRED PROPHETS

Throughout Scripture God also used uninspired prophets to make His will known. There were prophets prophesying with Samuel, who he was 'standing and presiding over.' (1 Sa.19:20) When Paul states the OT principle that 'the spirits of the prophets are subject to the prophets', he implies two kinds of prophets. (1 Cor. 14:29-33) The 'prophets' in the Corinthian church could not contradict the Apostle Paul's teaching. Uninspired prophets were knowledgeable believers who were delegated to teach what had already been revealed by inspired OT Prophets, like Elijah, and inspired Apostles like Paul. (1 Kg. 18:4-20; 1 Cor. 14:29-32) Accurate teaching required that uninspired prophets must submit to the inspired Prophets. Inspired Prophets heard directly from the Lord; uninspired prophets 'hear' from the Lord through inspired Prophets. Before Christ, the prophets were subject to the Prophets; after Christ the prophets were subject to the Prophets and the Apostles. NT prophets were to be evaluated by one another. (1 Cor. 14:32,37)

THE INSPIRED PROPHETS

Only God-appointed 'Prophets' spoke His word without error. Jesus revealed that John the Baptist was the last of the Law and the Prophets. (Matt. 11:13; Lk. 16:16) God 'set' Prophets in the church to communicate the truth.[78]

PROPHETS WERE CHOSEN

Prophets appointed in the church must be chosen and called to that office, as John the Baptist was and as those who preceded him were. (Lk.16:16) With the phrase 'law and the prophets', Jesus identified the

[77] Merrill F. Unger, *Unger's Bible Dictionary*, Moody Press, 1976, p. 890

[78] Please reference, Did The Church Start at Pentecost? p. 19-22

class of prophet John the Baptist belonged to. This position was not assigned to prophets who wanted a career. When the word of the Lord came to the Prophets, it wasn't perceived as an opportunity for career advancement and fulfillment. Moses and Jonah didn't even want the job. We know about Jonah's detour to Nineveh. God's compliment of Prophets was completed with John the Baptist - and we also know what happened to him.

The Prophet Received Knowledge From God

In the OT, a 'prophet of God' is one chosen to receive knowledge from God to reveal to man. (Lk. 11:49) Zacharias, himself a chosen Prophet, prophesied that God spoke by the mouth of His holy Prophets since the world began. (Lk. 1:70) The message of the Prophets is informative, prescriptive and predictive. Through the Prophets, God revealed to man who God is and His works, and who man is and his works. The Prophets, informed mankind about who God is, who man is, future events in this life and in the life to come, and how to escape the wrath of God.

The Prophets' Message Is Still Relevant

The Prophets foretold of Christ. (Ac.3:22-26; 10:42,43) Jesus told his disciples that He did not contradict the message of the prophets. They were expected to believe the Prophets. (Lk. 16:31; 24:25) The Bereans checked the OT prophets to verify Paul's message. (Ac.17:10-11 They knew that God spoke by the Prophets. (Hos.12:10; Heb.1:1) By drawing some important lessons from the life and writing of the Prophet Moses, the Apostle Paul shows how OT prescriptions for sin have not expired. (1 Cor. 10:1-22) The predicted fulfillment of many prophesied events serves as evidence that the Prophets did, indeed, speak for God. (Acts 7:42; 13:15; 15:15; Rom.1:2; 16:26) Still relevant today, the word of the Prophets remain with us in writing to confirm the Apostles' teaching.

Christ Quoted The Prophets.

Jesus cited the Prophets as a source for His teaching. (Matt. 7:12) Jesus quoted from Deuteronomy to Satan. Jesus identified one of those Prophets as Abel. (Matt. 22:31-36) Jesus' reference to 'prophets' were two kinds: the Prophets and false-prophets. Except for false prophets, everyone of Jesus' references to 'Prophets' were chosen by God, not man. Christ did not quote from prophets delegated by man. Jesus exhorted His listeners to hear Moses and the Prophets concerning Himself. (Lk. 16:29; 24:25-27)

THE APOSTLES AND ASSOCIATES QUOTED THE PROPHETS

Jude states that Enoch prophesied the coming of the Lord, who would also execute judgment. (Jude 14,15) Philip explained the Prophet Isaiah to the Ethiopian. (Jn.12:38; Ac. 8:30) Paul referred to the Prophets when he preached to Gentiles. (Ac. 26:27,28; 28:23,24) They did not quote from man's 'delegated' prophets.

SUMMARY

Though God's revelation of His word through the Law and the Prophets was finished, Prophets remained **appointed** person gifts for His people after Christ. (Matt. 11:13; Lk. 16:16; 1 Cor. 12:27,28) They had been personally sent by God to reveal His will to man in spoken and written word. John the Baptist, was the last one specifically appointed to this office. (Lk. 24:44)

God's sent the Prophets He appointed. (Jer. 7:24-26; 26:5-9; Zech. 7:12) God spoke by His appointed Prophets. (Hos. 12:10,13) God's Prophets warned His people of the lying prophets. (Jer. 27:12-15) Despite God's gracious warnings through the Prophets, they were mostly rejected. (Zech. 1:4; 7:12; Matt. 5:12; 23:31, 37)

The inspired writings of the Prophets do not expire. The Prophets remained an integral part of the Apostles' teaching and ministry, therefore remain as person gifts to the people of God. Numbered in the second position, Paul had in mind the inspired Prophets to whom 'prophet' preachers must be subject. The Prophets God had set in the church were and are credible, authoritative and exclusive. God-appointed Prophets heard directly from the Lord. Their ministry of the word needed no editing or revision.

THIRD, TEACHERS

God also chose a third category of person ministers as a 'gift' to God's people - teachers. A teacher is one who instructs. The Apostles and Prophets had a <u>special</u> calling to be revelators of God's word, and as such were teachers. But the Bible also refers to other teachers of God's word.

THE ORDINATION OF TEACHERS

As the last of his numbered person gifts, Teachers were delegated to teach the word of God. Parents were instructed to teach the law and the statutes to their children. (De. 4:10) Israel was commanded to keep the commandments God would teach them, to fear and love God. (De. 6:1-7; 11:19) But, how was Israel to know what God told the Prophets? The Lord had commanded Moses to teach, but he certainly couldn't fulfill that task alone. (De. 4:14; 5:31; 6:1; 31:19)

THE TEACHING PERSON GIFT BEGAN UNDER MOSES

Aaron was the first official uninspired prophet. God told Moses that he had made his brother Aaron, his prophet. Whatever God told Moses, he would tell Aaron, who would then 'teach' Pharaoh. (Ex. 7:1,2) In both the OT and NT, these prophets are uninspired Teachers.

After God brought His people out of Egypt the teaching of God's word was organized as an official profession. The Lord had instructed Moses that Aaron and his sons would occupy the office of the priesthood. (Nu. 3:10) Commissioned under Moses through the budding rod, only Aaron's sons inherited the duties of the tabernacle sacrifices. Others from their tribe of Levi could assist in the maintenance of the temple, but only Aaron's progeny were delegated to serve as the priests. (Nu. 17,18:1-8)

After the corpses of Nadab and Abihu, two of Aaron's sons, had been carried outside of the camp, the Lord commanded Aaron to teach the sons of Israel. (Lev. 10:9-11) The priests were the messengers (angels) or teachers, delegated to teach Israel the Law, to 'preserve knowledge'. (De. 33:8,10; 2 Chr. 15:3; Mal. 2:7)

The organized teaching administration began with the person gift of Teachers in the OT under Moses. Specifically chosen by God for this ministry, only Levites descended from Aaron's sons, were born into the teaching (messenger) position. They were to teach what had already been revealed through the Prophet Moses and the Prophets to follow. The Person Teacher gift was set among believers under Moses.

THE TEACHER PERSON GIFT CONTINUED UNDER CHRIST

God's people did not remain under the appointed teaching administration of Levitical priests. The Levitical priesthood, along with its ceremonies, was officially terminated at Christ's death, but the office of the priest was transposed from the tribe of Levi to Judah. (Heb. 7:11,12) While on earth, Jesus, our High Priest and Apostle from the tribe of Judah, called twelve disciples to be His inspired Apostles. Through them He supplemented OT truth about Himself for the continuing ministry of Teachers He had already set in place for His people. He commanded His followers to teach observe all things He had commanded. (Matt. 28:20) All believers are ordained to be teachers.

SUMMARY

Under the Levites only the descendants of Aaron had the responsibility to teach the Law and the Prophets, most of whom were never truly saved. (i.e. Scribes and Pharisees) Despite the teaching failures of the OT priesthood, God had not abandoned the means by which revealed truth would be dispensed. The new teaching administration under Christ was no longer under the mandated jurisdiction of a Levitical physical progeny. Having personally commissioned all believers to teach the world, Jesus granted official status as potential teachers of the Law and the gospel to Gentiles as well as Jews. (Matt. 28:18-20) The Person gift of Teacher was transferred from the physical priesthood of Aaron to the spiritual priesthood of Christ.

THE IDENTITY OF TEACHERS

The third numerical person gift is unique in status and function because of its relation to the Apostles and Prophets. Though Teachers are also communicators, their teaching mandate is restricted to the revelations of the Apostles and Prophets.

TEACHERS ARE UNINSPIRED

Not all prophets prophesied as they were moved by the Holy Spirit. (2 Pe. 1:20,21) In fact, most prophets and indeed apostles, were uninspired. Yet, uninspired prophets, who loved God, also functioned as teachers of the word of God that had already been revealed to them by God-appointed Prophets and Apostles.

Teachers Are Subject To Critique

The notion that Corinthian 'prophets' were announcing new revelations or making new predictions from God in the church is without foundation.[79] If that were so, it would not have been necessary for Paul to advise 'prophets' to critique one another and not speak contrary to his letters. (1 Cor. 14:29, 32 37) These prophets were Teachers.

Paul also wrote that anyone who thought himself to be a prophet or spiritual, must submit to the instructions of the Lord given through Paul,

[79] John Calvin, *Calvin's Commentary On The Bible*, See Acts 13:1 Calvin does not see how 'prophets and teachers' can 'hang together', if 'prophets' were those endowed with the gift of foretelling things.

an Apostle. Only the scriptures of the Apostles and Prophets qualified to adjudicate the teachings of other uninspired prophets. (1 Cor. 11:23; 14:37,38; 2 Thess. 3:14) The inspired Apostles' and Prophets' message needed no correction. (2 Cor. 11:13) In the absence of the Apostles, prophet-teachers were subject to each other's critique based on the Prophets and the Apostles. (Ac.18:26; 1 Cor. 14:29)

Teachers May Misinterpret

One teacher 'prophesies' pre-trib. rapture, another, post-trib. another post millennial and still another no millennium. One Bible teacher believes that the 'rapture' is not synonymous with the second coming, while another does. Yet, only one eschatological system will prevail as the correct one. Despite the importance of eschatology, teaching a wrong view does not always indicate a 'false prophet', or teacher.

Agabus was an uninspired prophet who also got his 'eschatology' wrong. Though Agabus' prophecies pertaining to Paul's arrest in Jerusalem were partly incorrect, Charismatics and Continuationists still think that an authentic gift of predictive prophecy does not have to be exact. (Please see **Prophecy**, page 123 and **Agabus**, page 210) They assume that he had the so-called 'gift of prophecy', by which he had special insight into Paul's future, should he go to Jerusalem. His inaccurate predictions also compromised his claim: 'thus says the Holy Spirit.' This uninspired prophet provides absolutely no support for the damaging doctrines of the charismatic and the continuationist.

Teachers Appeal To Scripture

The teachings of these 'prophets' in the church are of no benefit unless they speak on behalf of a trustworthy source. Passing judgment on what another prophet said must therefore be based on a propositional record of the Prophets and Apostles. OT and NT 'prophets' were "subject" to Prophets, not each other's opinions. The 'prophets' of Corinth were to 'reveal' what had already been revealed by OT prophets and the Apostles.

As teachers, the Corinthian prophets were subject to error and therefore had no inherent authority. (1 Cor. 14:29,31, 32)

'PROPHETS AND TEACHERS'

Luke states that there were 'prophets and teachers' in the Antioch church. (Ac. 13:1,2) Scholars think that 'prophets' and 'teachers' are synonymous. Again, by definition, a prophet is one who speaks on behalf of another. This implies that these uninspired 'prophets' were familiar with the teachings of the inspired Apostles on whose behalf they would speak to the church.

EXAMPLES OF TEACHER PERSON GIFTS

Numerically third, the Teacher person gift would have included uninspired prophets, evangelists and shepherd-teachers before and after Christ.

PHILIP'S DAUGHTERS

Philip, the evangelist, had four daughters who were prophetesses. They were acquainted with scripture to edify, exhort and comfort others with truth revealed through the Prophets and Apostles. (Ac.21:9) Biblically knowledgeable, they were most certainly teachers of women, as was Miriam the Prophetess. (Ex. 15:20,21)

THE EVANGELIST

Philip is called an evangelist and Timothy is exhorted to do the work of an evangelist. (Ac. 21:8; 2 Tim. 4:5)

SHEPHERD-TEACHERS

As an appointed Prophet, Jeremiah himself was also a shepherd of God's people. (Jer. 17:16) Yet, he and other Prophets lamented the lack of shepherds to rightly lead God's people. (Jer. 25:34,35; Ez. 34:2) Paul was appointed to be both an Apostle and teacher. (2 Tim. 1:11) Jesus challenged Peter to be a shepherd-teacher. (Jn. 21:15-17)

AQUILA AND PRISCILLA

This couple taught Apollos how to teach the Scripture more accurately. (Ac. 18:26) All three are examples of the Teacher person gift.

SUMMARY OF PERSON GIFTS

The many unappointed persons that have ignored the truth and introduced false teachings into the believer's assembly, highlights the importance of knowing who Paul's numbered person gifts are.

PERSON GIFTS COMMUNICATE TRUTH FROM GOD

Since the gospel was not self-evident to man, God ordained that it be made known through Apostles, Prophets and Teachers. The Prophets, Apostles and Teachers were given to the body of believers for the perfecting of the saints, for the work of ministry and the building up of the body of Christ. (Eph. 4:12)

Thus, Paul informed believers that a numbered list of three person gifts to the believers' assembly are the only channels by which God would make His Word known to mankind. With the inevitable death of the Prophets and later the Apostles, the ministry of 'Teacher' continues as the means by which His word would continue to be made known. These three person ministers were and remain essential to the proper function of the body. To that end, God inspired Prophets and Apostles to reveal His will and illumines Teachers to correctly discern His revelation.

Person Gifts Were Appointed

These three person types were "set" or "appointed" for His people, perhaps better translated as 'some indeed God did set in the assembly'. Therefore, they cannot be self-appointed.

Person Gifts Are Permanent

Time does not diminish the value and effect of their ministry. The Apostles and Prophets left a timeless written record of God's revelation as a legacy for Teachers to communicate to each succeeding generation.

Person Gifts Are Foundational

The whole household of God, including OT believers, is built upon the Apostles and Prophets. (Eph. 2:19,20; Rom. 1:2; 3:21; 11:3; 16:26)

Person Gifts Are Complimentary

OT prophets also served in the same body by one Spirit as the Apostles did. (Eph. 4:4) The Apostles did not replace the ministry of the Prophets. The ministry of the Apostles and Prophets continues through their inspired writings. The Teacher is dependent upon these writings.

Person Gifts Expose False Doctrine

Jesus warned the crowds to beware of false prophets who come to you dressed in sheep's clothing. (Matt. 7:15) The Apostle John warned that false prophets are known by their doctrines about Christ. (1 Jn. 4:1-3)

Paul's statement that spirits of prophets are subject to Prophets is based in the OT. Ezekiel warned the foolish prophets of Israel that they were following their own spirits, really have seen nothing. (1 Cor. 14:32; Ez. 13:3) Many false prophets before Christ rebelled against God's Prophets. They boasted about the vain visions of their own heart. (Jer. 23:16) They were people-pleasers. (2 Chr. 18:11-27) They prophesy lies in God's name. (Jer. 14:13,14) Not subject to the evaluation of other prophets, they become an authority unto themselves. (Jer. 28:5-11) Like Balaam, they lead people into sin. (Mic. 3:5)

Note Jeremiah's warning of charismatic prophets of his day:

> "Your prophets have seen for you false and deceptive visions; they have not uncovered your iniquity, to bring back your captives, but envisioned for you false prophecies and delusions." (Lam. 2:14, NKJV)

God did not set these person gifts in His church.

Indeed teachers may have incorrect views on matters such as eschatology and baptism, as did Apollos, and still not be false teacher. If, however, anyone's teaching interfere with who God is, who man is, how man is to be saved or sanctified, that person must be censured.

The doctrines of the Charismatic and the Continuationist are just two that do.

Person Gifts Essential For Ministry

Through the Spirit, the Apostles and Prophets communicated truth to the world. Every believer is also commanded to preach this truth to every creature and to speak Scripture to one another (Mk. 16:15; Rom. 10:15; 15:20; Eph. 5:18) To a greater or lesser degree, every believer has been placed in the body as a teacher of the God-appointed Prophets and Apostles. Teachers are the legacy of the Apostles and Prophets.

From creation to Christ, Prophets were appointed to reveal God's grace and mercy to mankind with the aid of Teachers. After Christ's ascension, the Apostles claimed their appointed role as His personally appointed messengers, commensurate with the same function and authority as OT prophets.

Though the Teacher has no inherent authority or credibility, he has the authority of the Word of God, revealed to us through the Apostles and Prophets. (1 Tim.6:3) As the Prophets and Apostles, Teachers continue as a God-fixed, essential and permanent reality in God's assembly.

11. ABILITY GIFTS

Paul had interrupted his teaching on ability gifts with a brief but contrasting reference to appointed persons, but then continues to listing a few ability gifts, repeating the gifts of healing, miracles, languages and interpretation from earlier in the chapter. He does not add more person gifts such as 'healers', 'administrators' and 'linguists' to his list. (1 Cor.12:28) These *charismata* 'gifts' are not persons; they are listed as abilities and are manifestations of the Spirit.

Despite the fact that each had been uniquely gifted, some thought they could do it all and boasted about their abilities. So, Paul asks them some embarrassing rhetorical questions. (1 Cor. 12:29,30; 13:4)

Abilities Are Dependent

'After that' and 'then', implies that ability gifts are set in place as a separate category from person gifts. (1 Cor. 12:28)

Gifts Are Granted According To God's Choice

All ability gifts are granted by the will of the Holy Spirit. Divinely appointed Prophets and Apostles "spoke as they were moved by the Holy Spirit." (1 Cor. 12:28; Eph. 4:11; 2 Pe. 1:21b) Likewise, ability gifts are not self-initiated. (1 Cor. 12:7, 11)

Purpose Of Gifts

God ordained that Apostles, Prophets and Teachers be messengers of His Word. Though different than these 'person gifts', abilities were also given by the Holy Spirit to everyone. While abilities are often misused, in Christ's body they are to edify others. (1 Cor. 13:4) When exercised in love, ability gifts are certain to generate a profit, as God intended. (1 Cor.12:4-7; 14:12) Peter states that each one has received a gift, but believers are to be good stewards of that gift. (1 Pe. 4:10)

Who Are The Ones Who Make A Profit?

Only believers who have been baptized by one Spirit into one body whose head is Christ are gainfully employed. (1 Cor. 12:12-14) Paul is specific about who the members of this body are: "For also in one Spirit we all to one body were baptized..." (1 Cor. 12:13; YLT) He doesn't say 'you all', or 'everyone' or 'each'. Paul says 'we all', meaning anyone, who, like himself, has turned to Christ, is baptized into this membership.

Profit from ability giftedness is not possible outside the body of Christ. God composes the body of Christ by personal appointment of each member, thereby making a profit certain. (1 Cor. 12:12-28)

DIVERSITY OF GIFTS

The first category is the person gifts: Apostles, Prophets and Teachers were divinely appointed for special revelation and communication. The second category is abilities. They are diverse, and as such minister to the physical and spiritual needs of people. (1 Cor. 12:4, 27-31) Though all do not have all the gifts, everyone will have a gift. Paul did not mean that everyone had all the gifts he listed,

> "Everyone of you...That is, all the things which are specified would be found among them. It is, evidently, not meant that all these things would be found in the same person, but would all exist at the same time; and thus confusion and disorder would be inevitable."[80]

GIFTS ARE NOT EXCLUSIVE TO BELIEVERS.

Paul does not imply that an unbeliever is not 'gifted' by the Holy Spirit. In fact, all gifts are from the "same Spirit." Whether Christ is claimed as Lord or not, the same God works all in all.[81] The Holy Spirit did not exclude the world from having abilities. In chapter two, we discussed the Spirit's involvement in the lives of OT unbelievers and believers. If we believe that God is truly sovereign, then why would we think that it was impossible for the Holy Spirit to gift the unregenerate?

All governments have been ordained and sent by God, having judicial abilities to punish evildoers. (Rom.13:1-6; 1 Pe.2:13-17) Rulers are actually ministers of God! Judges, lawyers, though tainted by sin, have abilities given by the Holy Spirit. Peter says everyone is required to minister according to a gift he has received. (1 Pe. 4:10) If one is able to "minister" as a worldly government does, then he must also possess a gift.

---

[80] *Albert Barnes Notes on The Whole Bible*, for 1 Cor. 14:26

[81] Paul's use of the word "all" does not refer exclusively to believers. Paul is a servant to all men. (9:22) Whether believers or not, 'all' passed through the sea, ate and drank of the same spiritual food. (10:1-5) Paul's intent not to please 'all' men includes everyone. (10:33) Paul spoke with languages more than 'all' included any unbelievers among them. (14:18) In Adam we 'all' die. (15:22) There is no context that limits the phrase 'all in all' to believers. (12:6)

Never does Paul distinguish the unsaved and the saved by ability giftedness, but he does distinguish the saved and unsaved sinner by unrepentant sin. (1 Cor. 5:11-13; 6:9,10) Many will rightly claim that they have prophesied in His name, but will be cast out, not because they didn't have the gift of prophesy, but because they practiced lawlessness. (Matt. 7:21-23; NKJV) People have even been saved through the ministry of the unsaved, but this is not the essential quality of what makes a gift profitable, which will be shown later.

Unbelievers are as adept at administration, as are believers. Among unbelievers are teachers, who are equally gifted as are believers. Some unbelievers have contributed greatly to the wellbeing of society. In every field of endeavor there are unbelievers who are superbly talented. Unconverted multilingual speakers and interpreters are as skilled as believers. Everyone has abilities.

The manifestation of the Spirit is given to "each"; baptism is not. Diversities of activities are the work of God who works "all things in all." (1 Cor. 12:5,6,11) Despite the sins of this church, Paul made no exceptions for giftedness. Along with other delinquencies, their divisiveness certainly made him wonder if some were true believers, but he never questioned their abilities. In his entire discussion on the abilities given by the Spirit, there is no class of people excluded from ability giftedness. (1 Cor. 4:7; 12:7)

If Paul had intended to exclude the unbeliever from giftedness, he would certainly have been specific. Regarding the adulterous relationship of the man living with his father's wife, Paul very explicitly directed that this so-called brother be excluded from fellowship. He was concerned for his salvation. (1 Cor. 5:11) Never in Paul's exhortations is there the slightest hint that the immoral are not gifted. At the Lord's Supper, Paul states that some who were drinking damnation to themselves, had discernment enough to assess their spiritual condition. (1 Cor. 11:31-32)

But Aren't The Gifts Supernatural?

From the list of abilities, some infer that some are visibly supernatural. They are called 'sign gifts', discussed in greater detail in a later chapter. But for now we refer again to the 'ability gifts' of languages and interpretations. (1 Cor. 12:10) Are we to understand that only the believer has the ability to interpret when we know that unbelievers are also able to interpret? Whether believer or unbeliever, the ability to interpret is given by the Holy Spirit. But charismatics claim that they speak supernaturally in 'tongues' and another can interpret it supernaturally. Really, these 'interpreters', so-called, feigns supernatural discernment and language. Sadly, people still believe it.

SATAN DOES NOT GIVE ABILITY GIFTS

The devil never gave anyone a gift of any kind. Satan hasn't given anyone the ability to learn music, design and build a skyscraper, rocket, or develop vaccines. He never gave man the ability to communicate truth, accumulate knowledge, and acquire wisdom. Only God has given man skills necessary to invent and build. OT examples show that the Holy Spirit has also given unbelievers abilities. However, Satan does lead people to squander their God-given gifts.

With the proliferation of various cults, there has been a corresponding increase in 'testimonies' of healing and miracles. Along with professing evangelicals, Catholics, Christian Scientists, Mormons and other cults, all claim healings of various kinds. Astrological testimonials are filled with 'word of knowledge' claims. Satan, the expert deceiver, distorts Spirit-given abilities into something visibly miraculous, which they never were.

ALL GIFTS ARE UNEARNED

Writing to everyone, Paul asks, 'who makes you to differ from another?' No one is short a gift or has a deficient gift. They were boasting about their abilities as if they had created them. But they had earned nothing; all of it was received. (1 Cor. 4:6-8)

SUMMARY

Even Paul, as an appointed 'person gift' to the church, recognized that the ability gifts he had in prophecy, languages, etc., were given to him. He would rather boast about his weaknesses, that the given strength (gift of miracles) of Christ's power would be evident. (2 Cor. 12:9,10) Everyone possesses ability gifts. Ability gifts are not acquired by personal effort. Though gifts of the Holy Spirit were misused, there is no record of one being withdrawn.

12. EXAMPLES OF REAL ABILITY GIFTS

Paul's list of ability gifts has been distorted beyond recognition. Knowing the actual 'spiritual' condition of this church, it is incredulous that among them were those who could heal, perform miracles, and speak unlearned languages at will. Supposed supernatural abilities are errantly deemed to be 'sign gifts'.

God warned His people that even a prophet's fulfilled prediction does not validate him as a prophet of God. (De. 13:1-5) Claims to the supernatural are means by which false teachers gain a following and make idols of themselves. It should be emphasized that 'supernatural' stories are not confined to Christianity.

> "There is no alleged miracle being performed today by Pentecostals, or those of a similar "Christian" persuasion, that cannot be duplicated by various cults and non-Christian sects."[82]

As these 'gifts' are examined in their textual and cultural contexts, it becomes impossible to believe that any of them were supernatural. In the Greek they are normal words used to describe un-supernatural **abilities**.

'ANOTHER'

Near the beginning of chapter 12, Paul states that each one is given the manifestation of the Spirit, as evidenced by the reality of different gifts given to different people. (1 Cor.12:7-10) In this context, the use of either *allos* or *heteros,* broadens the scope of giftedness. Whether the possessors of ability gifts are another **of the same kind** or another **of a different kind**, giftedness is not limited to status or ethnicity. Everyone has been given a gift, and every person, depending on perspective, is either of the same sort or of a different sort. A Jew with the gift of languages shares this gift with other Jews (people of the same sort), as well as other Gentiles (people of a different sort) Troubled with their claims to superior status, Paul emphasized that all the gifts come from one Spirit; therefore, they had nothing of which to boast.

---

[82] *What Does the Bible Say About Miracles?* By Wayne Jackson https://www.christiancourier.com/articles/5-

'WORD OF WISDOM' AND 'WORD OF KNOWLEDGE'

Some professing believers falsely infer that the 'word of wisdom' and 'word of knowledge' are supernatural gifts that enable a person to declare an unknown present or future reality about someone's situation by inspiration of the Spirit.[83] Stories abound in Pentecostalism of people who have allegedly declared something that they did not know or could not have known. But, lacking witnesses, these accounts cannot be verified.

Having limited His revelation through the Person gifts of Apostles and Prophets, new messages from God are precluded. The Teacher proclaims the message of the Apostles and Prophets, not his own dreams, visions, sensation or any other experience. The only 'supernatural' communications that we are required to believe, are found in the pages of Scripture. So, Paul's meaning for these two gifts must lie elsewhere.

Revelation By Un-Chosen Apostles Contradicts Scripture

Cessationists teach that this is a gift restricted to "a certain group in the body of Christ for the communication of special revelation. First generation Christians were the divine mouthpieces of God's wisdom."[84] This is problematic because Peter states that only 'holy men of God' spoke as they were moved by the Holy Spirit, thereby excluding other un-chosen 'apostles' and 'prophets'. (2 Pe. 1:20-21) Set apart for the revelatory offices and ministry of Apostles and Prophets, these men claimed exclusive authority to speak from God. (1 Cor.14:37; 1 Thes.3:14)

What Is The Meaning Of These Gifts?

What is meant by "a word of wisdom" and "a word of knowledge?" The right understanding of 'logos' (word) in this context is pivotal to a right understanding of this gift. [85] (1 Cor. 12:8) Not having the gift of 'a word of wisdom', does not imply that everyone else is foolish, and likewise, not having 'a word of knowledge' does not imply everyone else ignorant.

---

[83] John White, *Accessible Prophecy*, This opines 'word of knowledge' from a charismatic perspective. The Bible is not exegeted and consequently misinterpreted.
https://accessibleprophecy.com/tag/words-of-knowledge/
Joel R. Beeke, *Pastoral Concern About Evangelical Prophecy*,
https://www.crossway.org/articles/pastoral-concern-about-evangelical-prophecy/

[84] R.L.Thomas, *Understanding Spiritual Gift*, Kregel Publications, c.1999, P.28,29

[85] There is no definite article before 'word'. It should be translated 'a word of knowledge' and 'a word of wisdom'. (12:8 YLT) What is meant by "word"? This is the Greek word 'logos', but context may vary its meaning. For example, in Mt. 5:37, Eph.4:29 and Lk. 24:17, 'logos' is translated as 'communication'. In Mk. 11:29 it is translated as 'question', and in 1 Cor.1:18 it is translated as 'preaching'.

Therefore, if everyone has some wisdom and knowledge, the meaning of these gifts must be embedded in the definition of "word", which is translated elsewhere as 'communicate'. These gifts refer to the ability to articulate knowledge or wisdom as it relates to a specific trial or problem or blessing in another's life. For believers, this gift is especially useful to help apply scriptural knowledge and wisdom for the benefit of others, but in no case is this gift mental or spiritual telepathy.

Biblical Examples Of These Gifts

In the case of the Pharisee, Gamaliel, the Holy Spirit's gifting enabled him to provide wise counsel. (Ac. 5:33-40) The Apostles had defied the Council by preaching Christ. Based on recent events pertaining to the demise of the insurgents Theudas and Judas, Gamaliel stood before the Council and wisely advised them on a course of action. This is God-given ability where one is enabled to evaluate his knowledge in order to provide wise counsel for a specific circumstance.

After hearing Apollos preach in the synagogue, Aquila and Priscilla took him aside and explained the way of God more accurately. They had the knowledge and communicated it. This is the ability of a 'word of knowledge' given to Aquila and Priscilla. (Ac. 18:26)

But there is no statement or implication that the Holy Spirit gifts people to supernaturally sense someone's problem and solution. Both the 'word of knowledge' and 'word of wisdom' are gifts that facilitate counsel, based on one's own knowledge and evaluation of the circumstances. Certainly, believers receive assistance in the counsel they give with the word of God, but nothing in these gifts suggests a sense of feeling a special communication from God. These gifts must be distinguished from emotions. Men and women gifted with 'word of knowledge' and 'word of wisdom' have the ability to communicate necessary knowledge and wisdom in a way that is easily understood, better than others who are equally knowledgeable and wise. These ability gifts have not expired.

FAITH: (12:9; 13:2)

This gift is misunderstood to be the ability to get very specific answers to prayer. For this reason George Mueller is often cited as one having the gift of faith, which he himself denied.[86] Are specific answers to prayer the gift of faith? Certainly, men and women who walk by faith also prayed for

---

[86] Desiring God, *George Mueller's Strategy for Showing God*, http://www.desiringgod.org/biographies/george-muellers-strategy-for-showing-god

things they did not receive. Does this then suggest that men like Jeremiah did not have the gift of 'faith'?

The Greek word for faith ('pistis') is defined variously as credence, persuasion, truthfulness, trust in God for salvation, constancy in a profession, assurance, belief, believe, faith fidelity. (Strong's 4102) Vine's states that 'pistis' has "the secondary meaning of assurance or guarantee." Referring to Acts 17:31, Vine's states that "by raising Christ from the dead, God has given 'assurance' that the world will be judged by Him..."[87]

It is unanimously held that this gift of faith could not refer to trusting God for salvation. What then is this faith? This gift of faith is simply the inward persuasion that it is possible to overcome a huge obstacle. Jeremiah describes mountains as an obstacle for stumbling in the dark. (Jer.13:16) A mountain is a metaphor for a huge difficulty. He, and other prophets demonstrated this faith ability by overcoming great difficulties. But do the unsaved have the faith ability? Consider Herod who had the inward persuasion that a great temple could be built. Before we discount Herod's gift, note that Christ taught at the temple Herod was building and drove the moneychangers out from this temple. Though still incomplete in Christ's day, without the Spirit-given inward persuasion that a difficult job could be done, nothing would be done. Of course, Herod profited nothing because his aim was to glorify himself. Another secular example might be the enterprising brothers, Wilbur and Orville Wright. Convinced that it was possible to fly, despite no one ever having done it before, they invented an airplane that could.

But how was this gift evident in the NT church? The leadership of Peter and James are examples of this 'faith to move the mountain' of division between Jew and Gentile believers. Major conflict arose regarding receiving uncircumcised Gentiles into fellowship. After considerable debate the Apostles proposed that the ceremonial Law of Moses and circumcision should no longer be imposed, especially on Gentiles. A letter was drafted and sent by designated men to the church in Antioch. (Ac.15:1-30) They were inwardly persuaded that to overcome this problem it was necessary to move in a new direction, though it might not be well received with many Jewish believers. Not knowing if their decision might exacerbate the problem at first, it "seemed good to them", then confirmed to them by the Holy Spirit. (Ac. 15:22, 25, 28) Certainly "a word of

---

[87] *Vine's Expository Dictionary of New Testament Words*, p. 84

wisdom" was also needed, but prior to the debate and counsel that followed, they had the inward conviction that this 'mountain' could indeed be moved. Motivated by love for both Jew and Gentile believers, despite the possible loss of popularity among the Jews, this was an example of the gift of faith.

Paul writes, 'if I have all faith.' Why not just write 'faith'? Faith is faith, is it not? The removal of large obstacles like a 'mountain' suggests that this faith persists even when it runs into an unforeseen obstacle. To have 'all faith' is to possess the continuing conviction that even when another unexpected difficulty looms, it can be overcome. Many have 'faith,' to begin a difficult project, but when unexpected circumstances disrupt their plans, faith to overcome huge intermediate stages dissipates and the project is abandoned. They lacked 'all faith'. This is simply the tenacity to persevere through much hardship with specific difficult tasks, convinced that they are achievable.

George Mueller tried to help others to take God at His word, believing that trusting Him was not a special ability. But, contrary to Mueller's humble opinion of himself, he did indeed have the 'ability gift' of faith, not because of specific answers to prayer, but because he had the enduring conviction that certain 'mountains' could be moved.

The removal of a huge difficulty, even among unbelievers, does not happen without an inward conviction that it might be possible. The 'faith' to move mountains is a reality in both the presence and absence of love. However, in the absence of love for God and man, this 'faith' amounts to nothing. (1 Cor. 13:2)

HEALING:

Two Greek words are translated as 'healing'. The Greek word 'therapeuo' is sometimes used to describe the supernatural relief from physical sickness and calamity. On the other hand, '*iama*' means 'cure'. Vine's defines this as a <u>means</u> of healing. Not found elsewhere in the NT, it is this word that is used in 1 Cor. 12:9, 28, 30. '*Iama*' gifts of healings do not presuppose the supernatural. 'Gifts' is plural, indicating that various means are employed to promote the physical well-being and care for another's affliction.

God has gifted people to attend to the physical needs of others, to diagnose a medical problem and apply the remedy. Charismatics have twisted the gifts of healings into a 'signs and wonders' movement, thereby depleting the financial and emotional resources of the poor, sick and the hopeful. But this healing gift is not to be conflated with 'signs and wonders' as even cessationists do.[88]

Apostolic Signs And Wonders Were Not "Gifts".

The Apostles Peter and John healed a man lame from birth. (Ac. 3:1-10) Philip, a close associate of the Apostles, did signs and wonders. (Ac. 8:13) Paul healed the father of Publius. (Ac.28: 8-10) Peter brought Tabitha back to life. (Ac. 9:36-40) Others were healed. (Ac. 5:16; 8:7) But the Apostles did not heal everyone who was sick. Paul supernaturally healed others, but did not heal himself or seek healing from another Apostle. (2 Cor. 12:7-10) Paul did not supernaturally heal Trophimus. (2 Tim. 4:20) Instead of healing Timothy, Paul gave him medical advice, thus depicting an actual example of the 'gift' of healing Paul writes about to the Corinthians. (1 Tim. 5:23)

Other signs and wonders caused physical injury and even death. After Ananias and Sapphira died for lying, Luke again records that through the Apostles many signs and wonders were taking place. (Ac. 5:12) Paul struck Elymas with blindness. (Ac. 13:8-11)

Both supernatural physical recovery and physical judgment came through the Apostles. (Ac.2:43; 4:30) Both supernatural physical healing and even death did indeed take place as signs and wonders, but they were exclusive to the Apostolic ministry. (2 Cor. 12:12) On the other hand, none of the ability gifts listed were exclusive to the Apostles and none of them were stated to be 'signs and wonders'. 'Signs and wonders' were not ability "gifts". 'Sign', associated with the plurality of languages in 1 Cor. 14:22, does not convey a supernatural context, as shown in chapter 17.

Where is the evidence of people with the 'gift of supernatural healings' in the Corinthian church? No one in the Corinthian church had the unfailing capacity to say the word or pray for someone to be healed.

MIRACLES:

Similarly, the gift of miracles is presumed to be an endowment conferred on a believer by the Holy Spirit to perform supernatural phenomena. The English word 'miracle' may steer the reader in the wrong direction, if the context is ignored. Like 'healings' there is no evidence that the Holy Spirit directed any visible physical supernatural miracles in

---

88 Robert L. Thomas, *Understanding Spiritual Gifts*, Kregel Publications, c. 1999, p. 32

Corinth in the absence of the Apostles. How then are we to understand 'miracle'? The Greek word for 'miracle' pertains to strength. A supernatural event is necessarily implied.

Examples of 'miracle' (dunamis)

The Greek word *dunamis* is translated as 'miracles'. (1 Cor. 12:10,29) It is also translated elsewhere as power, ability, strength and abundance. While it is helpful to search other lexicons, the Bible often serves as its own lexicon. Note the variations of *dunamis* in the following references:

- "And to one He gave five talents, to another two, and to another one, to each according to his own **ability**; and immediately he went on a journey." (Matt. 25:15 NKJV emphasis added) In this verse '*dunamis*' is translated 'ability'. Talents were distributed, each according to their own power or ability.
- In the NKJV, '*dunamis*' is translated 'abundance', in the ESV, it is 'power'. (Rev. 18:3) The nations possessed their own 'power'; they weren't working supernatural miracles.
- "Therefore, if I do not know the **meaning (miracle)** of the language, I shall be a foreigner to him who speaks, and he who speaks will be a foreigner to me." (1Cor.14:11, NKJV, emphasis added.)
- In Col. 1:11 *dunamis* is 'might', being "strengthened with all <u>might</u> according to His glorious power." In Eph. 1:21, Christ is "far above all principality and power and <u>might</u> and dominion." In Eph. 3:16 we are "strengthened with <u>might</u> through His Spirit." Peter talks about angels who are greater in power and might. (2 Pe.2:11)
- In 1 Cor. 15:56 *dunamis* is translated as 'strength'. 'The strength of sin is the law.' In 2 Cor. 1:8 Paul was burdened beyond strength. (miracle) In 2 Cor.12:9, Christ's <u>strength</u> is made perfect in weakness. In Heb.11:11, Sarah received strength to receive seed.

Since the normal meaning of the word *dunamis* does not imply a supernatural occurrence, only context can determine if it does.

The Gift Of Miracles Was Not Supernatural.

Believer and unbeliever alike possess 'miracle' (*dunamis*), power. 'Miracle' has to do with personal ability, not a supernatural event, unlike "signs and wonders", which were supernatural events, not gifts. *Dunamis* should therefore, be translated as 'power', 'strength' or 'abundance', not 'miracle'. Again, the context must determine whether the event was supernatural.

Why does Paul refer to the 'effecting of miracles' or effecting of strengths? (1 Cor. 12:10) God's demonstration of power is not limited to an instant in time. It can also be a process as when God gave strength and power to Sarah to bear a child in old age. (Heb.11:11)

Most believers know individuals who have endured great trials over long periods of time. Plentiful examples show how God has given believers the gift of strength, power and ability to endure their struggles with the love of Christ. Unbelievers have also endured with strength, but without love, their struggle profits nothing. The gift of miracles or strength becomes evident in times of trial and weakness.

Discerning Of Spirits

'Spirits' means 'breath', 'wind' or 'spirit'. (1 Cor. 12:10) As a force in the natural world, wind or 'spirit' is a metaphor for the good and bad movements in a non-material world. Mankind is vulnerable to the winds of philosophy, secularism, feminism, cults, euthanasia, racism, and for that reason needs the ability to discern how devastating these 'winds' are.

The Corinthians needed to discern between the 'winds' of the Lord's wisdom and the world's wisdom. (1:20,21; 2:5, 12) They hadn't discerned the 'wind' of favoritism that was causing divisions and seemed oblivious to the 'wind' of immorality among them. (1:13; 5:11) Rather than exercise their own God-given ability to discern, matters of right and wrong they took one another to the courts. (6:4-7) Paul was concerned that believers would not jeopardize their witness by appealing to secular courts that were not aligned with Scripture.

Non-Christians are often able to discern some harmful cults, racism, many disagree with abortion, etc. However, when believers are familiar with the Scriptures, they have the greater potential to rightly discern between the destructive and beneficial 'winds' around them.

Helps

Paul himself had personal, physical needs. (1 Cor. 9:8-11) Should not the one who teaches the gospel, not receive sustenance and lodging from the believers he serves? Paul was grateful for helpers such as Priscilla and Aquila. (Rom. 13:3) Pagan Roman soldiers protected Paul from the Jewish crowd. (Ac. 21:34-36) A Roman centurion built the Jews a synagogue. (Lk. 7:5) The gift of 'helps' is the ability to recognize and meet a physical need. However, in the absence of God-given love, the gift of 'helps' is also of no avail. (13:3)

PROPHECY:

Charismatics mistakenly understand 'prophecy' to be a gift still given whereby one is able to proclaim new truth authoritatively like the Apostles and Prophets, 'thus says the Lord.' Charismatics claim visions and dreams as a means by which they hear directly from God. They believe this gift to be a function of the 'word of knowledge' and the 'word of wisdom'. Continuationists say this gift is the Holy Spirit brings useful advice or information to a believer's mind, about a situation unknown to him, for the benefit of another person.[89]

However, in Paul's context, the gift of 'prophecy' is not equivalent to being a 'Prophet'. He is not exhorting believers to prophesy so they can write more prescriptions and predictions for 'Scripture'. Listed in the second position, no more applications for Prophets were available.

The gift of 'prophecy' was not achieved or recognized by an anointing. Neither does Paul exhort believers to pray for it. (1 Cor. 14:1,5)

Definitions Of Prophecy And Prophesy

Paul exhorts the church in Rome to prophesy according to <u>the</u> faith, meaning the written word of God. (Rom 12:4-8) Prophecy pertains to propositionally revealed truth, the revealed word of God. Peter defines prophecy as Scripture. (2 Pe. 1:20,21) The Greek word for prophecy may be predictive as well as prescriptive.

To prophesy is the ability to make prophecy known. An ability to prophesy is not a license to make personal prognostications: 'the Lord told me'. It is not having 'a word from the Lord' that portends an event. By ignoring the definitions and contexts of 'prophecy' and 'prophesy', these words are forced to fit the subjective perceptions of a charismatic paradigm. (Please see Agabus in Notes, page 212)

Prophecy Is Both Predictive And Prescriptive

Biblical prophecy accurately predicts future events for the church and the world. Any predictive element of biblical prophecy must also be prescriptive. When people are edified with the gift of prophecy, sanctification becomes a reality. Failure to comply with prescribed exhortations in prophecy will result in predicted judgment. Believers are comforted with prophecy that trials and tribulations will come to an end, and a future in heaven with Christ awaits them.

---

89 Please see interview Wayne Grudem and Ian Hamilton, (times: 13:20, 13:40, 30:00) https://vimeo.com/37169587

Biblical prophecy consists of objective, assessment of the conditions of church and society with appropriate exhortations to repent. With that comes the unfailing prediction that if man does not repent, he will go to hell. Conversely, we can confidently assert or prophesy God's eternal blessing to those who truly repent.

Prophecy Is Not Limited To The Believer

It is a fact that Balaam prophesied truth; it is also a fact that he was a false prophet; it is also a fact that God instructed Balaam what to say to Balak. King Saul and Caiaphas are examples of how God does gift even the unconverted to declare truth. As Paul explains in chapter 13, they failed to profit from them because they had no love. Balaam had no concern for the edification, exhortation and comfort of Israel. Yet, he prophesied what God wanted, not because he wanted to, but because his life depended on it. Ministers have testified of how they had been preaching the gospel, yet not been truly converted. So, the unsaved can also have the gift of prophecy.

Though the believer most certainly has a better understanding of truth, God has not withheld His word from the lost, though most do 'exchange the truth of God for a lie'. (Rom. 1:24,25)

Timothy's Gift

It is important to note that when Paul refers to Timothy's 'gift', it is singular. Despite mentioning ability gifts such as the reading of scripture, exhortation and teaching, Paul admonishes him not to neglect "the gift", one gift. Affirmed as a believer, as one who trusted God and belonged to the fellowship of believers, every indication appears to point to Timothy's gift of faith. (1 Tim. 4:10-14)

In his second letter to Timothy, Paul remembered the genuine faith that was in him and expressed his hope that he might see Timothy again. Perhaps not hearing from him for a considerable period of time, and concerned that his faith not fail, as did that of Hymenaeus and Alexander, Paul exhorted him to stir up "the gift of God" that was given him through the laying on of my hands. (1 Tim.1:19,20; 2 Tim. 1:5-7)

Of course, the laying on of hands could not be a means by which faith or any other gift was mystically conferred. Laying hands on the scapegoat did not initiate God's forgiveness; it just depicted it. Though Isaac unwittingly blessed Jacob, he pronounced a blessing upon him that God had already made through his mother Rebekah. (Gen. 25:23) Likewise,

Timothy was also blessed with the laying on of hands, that depicted an already existing reality in his life.

Timothy was exhorted to continue in the things he had learned, specifically the Holy Scriptures. (1 Tim.4:14) As his mother and grandmother taught the Scriptures to Timothy, they functioned as prophetesses. Timothy received this gift of truth by learning the prophecy of the Law and the Prophets. (2 Tim.3:14-17)

This gift was received over a period of time. As a man of God, Timothy was exhorted not to neglect this gift, to have the character and ministry that honors God. (1 Tim. 4:13,14) Timothy was exhorted to 'stir' his gift of God in him. By following what he knew to be God's word, he would be an example to the believers in word, in love and purity. (1 Tim. 1:18; 1 Tim. 4:12,14; 2 Tim.1:6) Timothy's 'gift' was not exclusive. Timothy's gift was His Word, the Gospel, the Scriptures, truth, that is, God's inspired propositional revelation to man. Prophecy is not an ability gift.

SUMMARY

Both the meaning of the words and evidence in the church, show that supposed supernatural 'gifts' of 'faith', 'healing', 'miracles' and languages were non-existent in the Corinthian church. Had there been supernatural healings and miracles, given the immaturity of the church, they would certainly have boasted about that too. They would have been admonished for it as he did their behavior at the Lord's Table. It is therefore not credible to deduce that this church was speaking unlearned languages at will or performing any other supernatural phenomena.

Everyone has abilities. They are natural abilities. The Holy Spirit distributes all abilities. Whether we are unilingual, multilingual, whether we like to help, give sound advice, or interpret languages, God, by the Holy Spirit has given them all. Even unbelievers can prophesy (exhort) biblical principles into the lives of their children. Unbelievers also show strength in weakness. Unbelievers can also communicate prophecy, that is, they can also exhort, edify and comfort others. They can even communicate their knowledge of scripture. Both believers and unbelievers can gain skill in languages and interpretation. Believers fail, as do unbelievers, in the exercise of their abilities. Human sinfulness does not negate the reality of these 'manifestations' or expressions of the Holy Spirit. The manifestation of ability gifts is not limited to believers.

These are all gifts of abilities, not signs. (The gift of languages is addressed in chapters 16 and 17.) There is a big difference between 'signs and wonders' granted to the apostles and 'gifts' given to everyone. 'Sign-gift' is a misnomer.

But, does lack of skill play a role in making a profit from one's ability gifts?

13. THE INADEQUACY OF ABILITIES

The Corinthian pursuit for prominence really centered on the misuse of the abilities they had. Paul had encouraged those who thought their abilities to be inferior and exhorted others who thought theirs to be superior. Inordinate quest for preeminence, with abilities they had not even earned or caused, evidenced their carnality. Having abused their ability gifts with arrogance, unkindness, jealousies and inappropriate behavior, they needed another "way". So, Paul is about to adjust their abilities perspective by directing their ambitions elsewhere. (1 Cor. 12:31)

WERE THEY TO DESIRE ABILITY GIFTS?

To these professing believers Paul writes, "And desire earnestly the better gifts; and yet a far excelling way do I show you". (12:31; YLT)[90] He instructs the church to desire "**the** greater gifts". After having just explained that the 'ability gifts' are given by the will of the Spirit and that everyone is not gifted the same, it is not tenable that Paul now instructs them to desire greater 'ability gifts'. If that was his purpose, we would expect Paul to give us a specific example of a 'better' ability gift such as teaching, but he doesn't. Paul changes the subject.

IS THERE ANY GIFT THEY SHOULD PURSUE?

So, it is puzzling that commentators teach this to be a command to desire 'greater' ability gifts, despite the fact that the Holy Spirit determines who gets what. (1 Cor. 12:6) He had just concluded his argument that everyone is not in possession of all the ability gifts. Desiring the 'best' ability gift was what some were already doing, so to issue a command that everyone should do the same, would only exacerbate the very competition he is trying to quell. Concerned for restored fellowship, Paul is not about to aggravate the issue with commands to earnestly desire the best gifts from the list he had just discussed. However, another kind of gift was needed.

Who determines what the best gift is? Is the best gift determined by popular opinion? Still not identified by name, the evidence of this gift had

---

[90] Some have claimed that this verse is indicative and not a command because it is deemed that Paul is instructing them to seek ability gifts. The Interlinear has it, 'be emulous of the better gifts.' (Vine's, p.458)

been depicted in an allegory, where members of the body care for one another, bear with the suffering of another and rejoice with the honor of another. (1 Cor. 12:16-17, 25-26) As members of this special body, this gift facilitates believers' independence and coordination. What could that be?

After another brief list of specified ability gifts, Paul states that there is still a more excellent way. (1 Cor. 12:29-31)

Are The Best Gifts Available To Everyone?

After asking rhetorical questions, to which the answer to each is 'no', he doesn't tell them to try harder to interpret, to heal, to speak in languages, etc., so that everybody will finally claim the ability they would really like. Instead, he diverts his focus away from abilities, which are not available to everyone, to gifts which are. Though he had not yet named these gifts, Paul had already shown them what these gifts were like by the way members of the body submit to the Head and relate to one another. He is about to unveil these gifts by name.

There is another "way", a more excellent way essential to Christ's body. And this way must be desired! It's almost as if the Apostle can't contain himself any longer and consequently bursts forth with nine mentions of the word 'love' in a few verses,

> "Though I speak with the tongues (languages) of men and of angels (messengers), but have not love, I have become sounding brass or a clanging cymbal. And though I have the *gift* of prophecy, and understand all mysteries and all knowledge, and though I have all faith, so that I could remove mountains, but have not love, I am nothing. And though I bestow all my goods to feed the poor and though I give my body to be burned, but have not love, it profits me nothing." (1 Cor.13:1-3, NKJV, brackets added)

Paul shows how the other 'ways' of prophecies, languages and knowledge, faith, etc. could not guarantee any profit or status.

'Heavenly' Messengers With Language Ability?

When *glossolalia* is properly translated as languages and *aggelos* as messengers, it is easier to grasp the meaning of the passage.

When heavenly messengers spoke to men they always spoke in languages men understood. Gabriel spoke to Daniel. Gabriel announced the birth of Christ to Mary in human language. (Dan. 8:16; Luke 1:26)

The shepherds heard the heavenly hosts announcing Christ's birth. (Lk.2:14) Quite rightly, we infer that the heavenly messengers spoke in the language already known to the audience. Paul knew that heavenly messenger did not speak 'gibberish'. The languages of 'messengers' were understood and spoken by men.

But, why the distinction between 'men' and 'messengers'? The messengers are God's Prophets and the language by which His will was communicated was primarily Hebrew. (Heb. 1:1) It was considered by Jews to be the holy language because it was the language in which God spoke to them; the others were the 'languages of men'. But even as God's ambassadors, the ability to speak the language of Scripture amounted to nothing without love for God and man. Balaam is an example of this.

Ability Without Status

Since apparent success in the use of God-given abilities could not be considered evidence of being part of Christ's body, he noted in greater detail what that evidence actually is. Self-deceived, many thought they had accomplished much, but Paul shows that all is not what it appears to be.

Without love "I am nothing". Paul did not say, 'I have become nothing'. One must be in possession of love before all his goods are given to feed the poor. It is a dangerous misconception to think that if we just start to feed the poor that we will suddenly learn to love them. Many sympathize with the poor, but that isn't love. Indeed, a person can be motivated to do good things without love, but abilities are not the cause of love. If I am not in possession of love, I am nothing. I may have a whole bunch of ability gifts and even given to the poor, but without love my status is still nothing as far as God is concerned!

Ability Without Profit

There is another sad and ultimately terrifying consequence of the absence of love. Without love, I profit nothing.

What distinguishes the believer from the unbeliever is not their giftedness, but how they profit with their giftedness. (1 Cor. 13:3) John wrote concerning Caiaphas, "Now this he did not say on his own authority; but being high priest that year he prophesied that Jesus would die for the nation." (Jn.11:51) God even used a blasphemer to prophesy truth but he profited nothing. (Matt.26:3,4)

The profit principle stands out in Jesus' parable of the talents. Three slaves were entrusted with the Master's assets in the form of talents, each according to his ability. None complained when they received their talents, but when the moment arrived to give an account, the slave who hid his talent, sued his Master for being a marauder. Despite his ability, he realized zero profit, consequently thrown into outer darkness. (Matt. 25:14-30) All three slaves had abilities, but just two distinguished themselves with proper and profitable use of the assets entrusted to them.

Profitability is directly linked to the preservation or loss of the soul. What profit is there if one is even able to gain the world but lose his soul in this quest? (Matt. 16:24-27)

MAN NEEDS A BETTER WAY

Aware of the condescending behavior of 'elitists' in the church, he wrote to affirm all believers that in their anticipation of the Lord's return, that they were not deficient with any ability gift they possessed. Paul thanks God for the grace given to the saints through Christ. (1 Cor. 1:2,4) They had been enriched by Him in speech and knowledge of His word and their testimony of Christ was confirmed in some of them. Yet, ability gifts could never make them spiritually rich. More than just abilities are needed for a 'better way'.

14. PROPHECIES AND KNOWLEDGE

Still on the topic of love, Paul contrasts it with prophecies and knowledge to add proof that without love, 'I am nothing.' (13:3) If I am nothing without love, then love cannot fail. Literally, 'love never falls prostrate.' It never descends from a higher to a lower status.[91] (13:8-10)

LITERAL TRANSLATION

To minimize incorrect inferences, I have used an on line interlinear to help me with a more literal translation of the following text,

> 8'Love not even at any time fails. But, whether prophecies, they will elapse, whether languages, they will be ceasing, whether knowledge, it will elapse.[92] 9For, from a part we know and from a part we prophesy. 10But, whenever the complete does come, then this from a part will pass away.'
>
> 11 'At which time I was a child, I was speaking like a child, I was thinking like a child, I was reasoning like a child, when I became a man, I have ended the ways of the childhood. 12'Indeed, we now see through a mirror, in obscurity; then, however face to face. At this moment, I know from a part, then, however, I also will fully discern just like I have been fully known.'[93]

DEFINING KEY TERMS

Though this Scripture is relatively well-known, rightly understanding it is compromised, if we fail to define some of the key words.

WHAT IS MEANT BY 'KNOWLEDGE'?

The Greek *gnosis* means, 'knowledge', 'wisdom' or doctrine. Any or all of these definitions describe one who is knowledgeable about the circumstances of life, physically or spiritually.

---

[91] *Thayer's Greek Lexicon*, Please not definition #1 for 'fails'.

[92] 'Vanish away' and 'done away' are translated with same Gr. word:- 'katargeo':- to be entirely idle (useless) Compare with how a different Gr. word is also translated 'vanish away' in Heb. 8:13, vanish here means disappear, abrogate, Strong's 854)

[93] Please see biblehub.com for interlinear Greek.

What Is Meant By 'Prophecies'?

The Greek for 'prophecy' or 'prophesy' is often presumed to only mean 'foretell'. But the Bible must serve as the lexicon of choice. Someone who is a 'prophet' speaks on behalf of another. God spoke to Moses as His prophet; Moses spoke to Aaron as his prophet, and Aaron spoke to Pharoah as his prophet. (Ex. 7:1) While Paul implied that 'prophesies' originated from God, he did not imply that each person heard directly from God. All prophecies of Scripture are informative, prescriptive or predictive. Anyone who passes on the Prophets' or Apostles' doctrine are prophets, as Aaron was. Therefore, the Corinthians were not receiving 'prophecies' directly from God! **If they had, Paul would not have needed to exhort them with this letter.** A prophecy is therefore a true teaching that originated from God.

Since 'love never fails' is itself a prophecy, we know Paul's reference to elapsing knowledge and prophecies cannot be inclusive. Not all knowledge and prophecies are rendered idle.

Are 'Knowledge' And 'Prophecies' Gifts?

Translations have confused this text with insertion of the word 'gifts'. (13:8; NAS) If we are to regard 'prophecies', 'languages' and 'knowledge' as 'gifts', they are universal. Everyone is capable of knowing, speaking languages and prophesying. (13:8) To prophesy, to speak language(s) and to know are universal human utilities. Personal giftedness is not the issue.

The Greek verbs for 'know' and 'prophesy' are in the present tense, indicating present-day realities. The active voice indicates that Paul, who is the speaker, is one participant of the verbs. (13:9) Even as an Apostle, he admits that he knows 'of a part'. (13:12)[94]

What Is 'Passing Away'?

Both 'vanishes away' or 'done away' in most translations, is the same word *katargethesontai* in Greek. It does not mean 'to destroy'. In my view, this is better translated, 'passing away'. In the future tense, 'passing away' implies a process that takes time. In the passive voice, 'passing away' of prophecies and knowledge is inevitable. (13:8, 10)

Paul contrasts love with prophecies and knowledge. (13:8) Love cannot fail, that is, it cannot descend to a lower position. It cannot fall. It is in

---

[94] The verbs 'know' and 'prophesy' are both present tense and active mood. 'Part' is in the genitive, meaning that it is in possession of something.

this sense that love is unique. In time, prophecies and knowledge descend from a higher to a lower status; they pass away. Love does not.

WHAT IS 'A PART'?

The Greek word *meros* is translated as 'district', 'region', 'portion', 'share', 'piece' and 'part', depending on context. In this passage, it is mostly translated 'part'. (13:9)

Is There A Difference Between *'Ek'* And *'Eis'*?

The Greek for 'in' (*ek*) is translated various ways. (13:9,10,12) But 'in' is not the meaning of the Greek, *ek*. Instead, '*ek*' should be translated 'from' or 'from-out of'. In the Greek, *eis* means 'in'.

For example, Jesus went into (*eis*) the region or part of Caesarea. (Matt. 16:13) Had Matthew used the preposition *ek* instead, we would have understood that Jesus went out of the region (part).

With the preposition '*ek*', and the context of the previous verse, the genitive noun, 'part', indicates its possession of knowledge and prophecy. 'For, knowledge from a part, we know; and prophecy from a part, we prophesy.' This knowledge and these prophecies are described by Paul as 'from a part' because they are passing away. (13:8,9)

THE 'PERFECT' TO COME

The Greek word *teleios* is most often translated as 'perfect', 'mature' or 'complete'. 'Perfect' is a neuter adjective. The verb 'comes' or 'does come' is in the aorist tense and subjunctive mood, indicating a process that does not specify the amount of time for the 'perfect' to finally arrive. (13:10) **The 'perfect' is arriving and will arrive.**

What then does 'whenever the complete does come', refer to? Given the context, 'perfect' must be the opposite of elapsing prophecies and knowledge. While some knowledge and prophecies have already passed away, this process has not yet ended. Therefore, we know from a passing part and we prophesy from a passing part. This knowledge and these prophecies continue to pass until the end. (13:8,10)

Completion Of Scripture?

Much of conservative scholarship holds that the 'perfect' to come is the completion of scripture.[95] Based on a supposed 'gift of prophecy' that was operational for "approximately the first 70 years of church history", it

---

[95] Larry D. Pettegrew, *The New Covenant Ministry of the Holy Spirit*, 2001, P. 181-182

is assumed that God was engaged in revelation through unappointed prophets.[96] By assuming 'knowledge' and 'prophecies' to be supernatural revelatory gifts of the Holy Spirit, they deduce that when Scripture is completed, these 'gifts' will no longer be needed. But, as stated earlier, Paul does not say that 'knowledge and prophecies' were revelatory Corinthian 'gifts'. The confusion begins with the assumption that 'gifts' had passed away, rather than actual knowledge and prophecies.

If the 'perfect' to come refers to the completion of Scripture, then the writing of Scripture must also be the cause of the passing of knowledge and prophesy. (13:8,10) But, the writing of the NT did not cause OT knowledge and prophecy to pass away, it added to and explained OT knowledge and prophecy. OT scripture did not expire, when the NT was written. The supposition that 'perfect' refers to the completion of Scripture, therefore, does not fit the context of passing knowledge and prophecies. (13:8)

The Lord's Return?

Others suggest that 'perfect' is a reference to Christ's return. As indicated above, the verb 'comes' or 'does come' is in the aorist tense and subjunctive mood. This is an ongoing process that does not specify the amount of time for the 'complete' to arrive. It's in the active voice, meaning that the perfecting is a current process! Christ, on the other hand, comes in the 'twinkling of an eye' after a prolonged journey to earth. (15:52) When the 'complete' comes, is therefore <u>not</u> a <u>specific</u> reference to the return of Christ.

SUMMARY

Both the arriving and the arrival of perfection requires that prophecies and knowledge pass away. But how is this possible? Were there defects in the knowledge and prophecies? No. They had to elapse because they were 'from a part', separate from the whole. Though they were means to perfection, they were not part of the whole.[97] Knowledge we presently 'know', and prophecies we now 'prophesy', belong to 'a part', not the whole. (13:8,9) The Apostle explains further with a childhood and a mirror analogy.

---

[96] Robert L. Thomas, *Understanding Spiritual Gifts,* 1978, p.61, 80-82

[97] *Thayer's Greek Lexicon, ek:*"of the measure or standard: so that each is part of the whole." V-3.

PAUL'S CHILDHOOD ANALOGY

He states that when he was a child he thought, understood and spoke like a child. As stages of childhood pass, so also does juvenile speech, thoughts and reasoning. With the aorist tense 'is come', Paul implies that he also is experiencing the coming of perfection, but not yet ultimate perfection. (13:10) With the third person plural, 'we', Paul includes himself as one who is also still a child. (13:12)

CHILDREN'S KNOWLEDGE IS AGE-APPROPRIATE

All children behave according to their age in speech and reasoning. They are not expected to think and reason like an adult. Inability to understand adult reality is normal for all children. As the child grows, his garbled pronunciation wanes. Then, they become aware that they are growing and begin to anticipate the reality of becoming a man or woman. Paul explains that childhood 'knowledge and prophecies' would fade away when they became adults. Since portions of knowledge and prophecies necessary for childhood development no longer applies for adulthood, they elapse as the child grows. The 'perfect' is coming. In time, their incomplete perceptions of knowledge and prophecies elapse. (13:11)

CHILDREN ARE EXPECTED TO GROW

Paul teaches that the growing experience causes the 'putting aside childhood ways', the fading of childhood knowledge. In the life of the children of God, this is accomplished as they grow in grace and in the knowledge of their Lord. (2 Pet. 1:2,3; 3:18) Paul prays for the church "to know the love of Christ which passes knowledge; that you may be filled with all the fullness of God." (Eph.3:19) Milk is good, but we need to grow to 'eat the meat' of His Word. (3:2)

CHILDHOOD MEANS ARE USEFUL

Child-play is useful for the mental and spiritual growth of children. They begin to learn adult principles with toys and adult mime. As children grow into the next phase, what was important to them then is naturally set aside. This simulates the believer's journey to adulthood. Though, we, as children, are yet unable to understand, reason and speak as an adult does, our 'knowledge' and 'prophecy' is not useless. The usefulness of some prophecies and knowledge fades as we transition from infancy to adolescence. Knowledge and prophecies do not fade, because they are no longer true. They pass away because their usefulness expires.

CHILDHOOD IS NOT 'COMPLETE'

However, since all believers are still spiritual children, 'perfection' has not arrived. We have not yet become adults. Even the Apostle Paul, who we would consider mature and accomplished humbly anticipates a day when he will know in full. Not rooted in past achievements, Paul pressed forward to the upward call of God in Christ, knowing that he had not yet been perfected. (1 Cor. 13:12b; Phil. 3:12-14) He was still growing. Childhood knowledge and prophecies 'diminish' until we finally become adults. In this way the 'perfect' is arriving and will arrive.

SUMMARY

Paul does not belittle childhood experience, neither does he imply that prophecies and knowledge of childhood are defective. They are, however, the <u>means</u> by which a child grows mentally and spiritually. Some of the knowledge and prophecies he has acquired will become dated, and therefore pass away, yet they are effective to train children for adulthood. As children approach adulthood, their childhood perceptions give way to the mature understanding of an adult. Childhood development progresses until we reach adulthood, when the 'perfect' finally has arrived.

PAUL'S MIRROR ANALOGY

As has been stated, where this has been translated 'in part', it is literally 'from a part'. First, Paul illustrated 'a part' with childhood. This time, 'from a part', implies a source for external guidance through a mirror. It represents 'a part' from which we discern knowledge and prophecy. The mirror symbolizes another essential means to attain spiritual adulthood. (13:12)

Archaeology provides some additional context for Paul's 'mirror'.

> "Bronze was also commonly used for mirrors, and many of these artifacts have been unearthed in ancient Corinth. These mirrors were typically small, round, held with a handle, and had molding or engraving designs around the rim or on the reverse side. Because metal was difficult to form as a wide, flat, and thin surface, in addition to properties causing inaccurate color rendering and the constant need for polishing, in the Roman period, these mirrors produced distorted, dark, and unclear images."[98]

---

[98] Dr. Titus Kennedy, *Drive Thru History*, https://drivethruhistory.com/corinth/

Paul compares our inability to fully perceive knowledge and prophecy with a mirror. *Esoptron* is translated as 'glass' in the KJV in 1 Cor. 13:12 and Jas. 1:23. Most commentaries interpret 'glass' as 'mirror',

> "... in a mirror; the reflection *seeming* to the eye to be behind the mirror, so that we see it *through* the mirror. Ancient mirrors were made of polished brass or other metals. The contrast is between the inadequate knowledge of an object gained by seeing it reflected in a dim mirror (such as ancient mirrors were), compared with the perfect idea we have of it by seeing it directly." [99]

This background shows that *esoptron* was not made from glass. Paul was referring to a metal mirror that needed to be polished. (13:12)

The Mirror Of Knowledge

While polishing this mirror, children gain added discernment of some of the shadowy features reflected in this mirror. Again, 'from a part' indicates another source for knowledge and prophecy. From this mirror, Paul knows. (13:9, 12)

With the use of the first-person plural "we", Paul also includes himself among those who knows and prophesies from a clouded reflection of this mirror. He identifies with the assembly when he states that 'now we see' through a mirror, indicating that he too was one who did not have complete knowledge. (13:9,12) Even he was not yet able to discern all the details from this clouded mirror.

The Mirror Of Childhood

After learning to appreciate the fact that the face in the mirror is their own, children soon discover that the details of the reflection were obscure. Still one of God's growing children who had not yet reached manhood, Paul, too, was unable to discern everything in the 'mirror'.

Every child of God, to various degrees, is unable to comprehend the knowledge and prophecies his metaphoric mirror reflects. Though he soon learns that as the mirror is polished, the refection becomes clearer, he still will not be able to discern all that the mirror reflects. Yet, this mirror prepares His children for the adulthood that awaits them, when the 'complete' or 'perfect' does come.

---

[99] *Jamieson, Fausset and Brown Commentary on the Whole Bible*, 1 Cor. 13:12, page 1217

The Mirror of Present Reality

Speaking from the same vantage point of every believer, Paul admitted that he, too, only had a 'face to image' perception of reality. His 'face to face' encounter was yet future. Anticipating his future 'adulthood', he asserts, 'I shall know'. By this, he expresses his own faith for the full future disclosure of all knowledge pertinent to spiritual manhood. (1 Cor. 13:12)

Though this 'mirror' is insufficient to reveal many details of our heavenly debut and eternal state, it is more than adequate to show what is needed now, for true worship and godliness. The Scriptures are essential for now, but what about our future?

The Mirror Is Unnecessary For Our Future Reality

Acknowledging that he also knows 'from a part', Paul asserts, however, that a future awaits him, when he will see the reflected image without a mirror. He will see everything 'face to face', not face to mirror. (13:12; 1 Jn. 3:2) There is coming a day when inspired descriptions of the glory of Christ will be set aside because we will see Him face to face.

> "Behold, now we are the sons of God and it doth not yet appear what we shall be: but we know that, when he shall appear, we shall be like him; for we shall see him as he is." (1 Jn. 3:2; KJV)

No longer will we need the mirror of Scripture for knowledge and prophecies. In heaven, inspired descriptions of Christ and our glorification will become vivid visual reality. Believers will personally experience the 'images' of truth they saw in the mirror. Believers are assured that a day would come when they would experience the clarity of the image with 'face to face' reality. (1 Cor. 13:12)

Summary

Through a process of spiritual growth, knowledge and prophecies are naturally set aside. Despite its dim reflections, with careful handling, God's revelatory mirror reflects more than enough truth for the believer's maturation. But, when the 'complete' arrives, this mirror of knowledge will then be rendered idle. Then 'face to face', we will be experiencing things that we could barely perceive in the 'mirror of prophecy'. Though now the 'perfect' had not yet arrived, Paul declared, 'now I know from a part, but then I shall know even as I am known'. (13:12) Like everyone, adulthood could not be experienced in childhood. Until then, the guidance from the mirror is our only resource.

EXAMPLES OF 'PASSING'

Scripture provides us with examples of prophecies and knowledge that have passed. In due time childhood perceptions are set aside. From a brief review of biblical data, it is evident that some knowledge and prophecies were temporal by design. Again, it is important to emphasize that knowledge and prophecies did not elapse because they were defective. Prophecies elapsed because they were fulfilled or no longer needed.

SOME PROPHECIES EXPIRE

Peter informs us that the Scripture is prophecy, given to us through men were moved to write by the Holy Spirit. (2 Pe. 1:20,21) What are some examples of expired prophecies?

SACRIFICES:

The large Jewish component of this church knew that God had legislated animal sacrifices. The prophetic lessons of the gospel taught in physical and ceremonial administrations of the tabernacle had expired. When the predictive element of sacerdotal service was fulfilled, this prophecy of God's revealed will, was no longer needed. Though commanded by God through Moses, this prophecy became useless and vanished away when Christ came. (Heb. 8:13-9:1)

GOD PRESCRIBED CIRCUMCISION

At the Council of Jerusalem, it was determined that circumcision was one prescriptive prophecy that elapsed. (Ac. 15:24)

PENTECOST:

Joel's prophecy of the pouring out of God's Spirit, was fulfilled in Jerusalem by the "sons and daughters" of Israel. (Joel 2:28; Ac. 2) After this, His disciples were not instructed to wait in Jerusalem for more 'little Pentecosts' and outpourings to come. Joel's prophecy had been fulfilled.

THE LORD'S RETURN:

Jesus told us not to be troubled because He would return to receive His people unto Himself. (Jn. 14:1-3) However, after He comes, the predictive element of this prophecy will be of no further use. (1 Cor. 15:51,52) The prophecy to wait for His return will be rendered idle.

THE CALL TO BE SAVED

The scriptural prophecies to repent and believe on Christ will also be rendered idle when He returns.

SUMMARY:

Paul does not teach that the "gift" of prophesying will stop. He says that in time some prescriptive and predictive prophecies no longer apply. All prophecy cannot fail, because the statement that 'love never fails' is itself a Scriptural prophecy. (13:8; 2 Pe.1:19-21)

SOME KNOWLEDGE EXPIRES.

Like prophecies, the Greek indicates that knowledge will also 'vanish away', or expire. Some knowledge becomes redundant and elapses with time - some does not.

KNOWLEDGE OF PEOPLE ON EARTH PASSES AWAY

Solomon states that knowledge of the living is forgotten when they die. (Eccl. 8:10; 9:5) Even the memory of famous people fades in time.

KNOWLEDGE OF TROUBLES PASSES AWAY

Isaiah prophesies that former troubles will be forgotten. (Isa. 65:16) Knowledge of most of our childhood hardships are forgotten.

KNOWLEDGE THAT INFORMS THE CONSCIENCE ELAPSES

In chapter 8, Paul addressed their lack of knowledge regarding food that had been offered to an idol, (1 Cor. 8:2, 7)

> "And if anyone thinks that he knows anything, he knows nothing yet as he ought to know." (8:2)

Some younger converts were still avoiding food offered to idols. However, as believers grow, the conscience is informed to know that eating meat offered to idols has no bearing on one's relation to God.

PERSONAL KNOWLEDGE OF SIN PASSES AWAY

John assures us that the world is passing away with all its lusts. (1 Jn.2:17) Isaiah shows how our gracious God causes His repentant people to forget the shame of their youth. (Isa. 54:4,5)

KNOWLEDGE OF CHRIST DOES NOT PASS AWAY.

All knowledge cannot pass away, because in Christ are hidden all the treasures of wisdom and knowledge. (Col. 2:3) In heaven, the prints in His hands and feet will be eternal reminders of His redeeming grace.

KNOWLEDGE OF TRUTH DOES NOT PASS AWAY

Vital knowledge of God consists of truth, grace and peace. Knowledge of His spiritual benefits cannot pass away. (2 Pe. 1:2; 1 Tim. 2:4)

REVIEW

Obviously, Paul did not teach that all prophecies and knowledge would elapse, when the 'perfect' arrived. Neither did he teach that knowledge and prophecies was restricted to a few 'gifted' believers. (13:8) Gifts do not fade away; prophesies and knowledge do.

THE SOURCE OF KNOWLEDGE AND PROPHECIES

With *ek* meaning 'from', Paul taught that there was a twofold source of knowledge and prophecies. 'We know from a part and we prophesy from a part.' We know and prophesy 'from a part' that is our experience of childhood. (13:11) And, we know and prophesy 'from a part' a 'mirror' that reflects God's guidance and our future reality. (13:9, 12) This 'mirror' represents Scripture. 'From a part' of childhood growth and external guidance, believers mature up to adulthood, when the perfect arrives.

ELAPSING KNOWLEDGE AND PROPHECIES

With the childhood analogy especially, Paul explains the necessity for knowledge and prophecies to pass away. As children outgrow their elementary speech, thoughts and reasoning, believers also experience the elapsing of knowledge and prophecy. Until adulthood, the children of God, go through successive phases of growth and guidance. Knowledge and prophecies that are no longer relevant for the growth stage we are in, pass away or expire. Thinking like children is appropriate for children, but not for adults. As children destined for adulthood, knowledge and prophecies continue to elapse.

A Contemporary Illustration

A concrete high-rise is built with forming, shoring and a crane. The tower crane hoists and pours the concrete for each level. After it cures, the forming is removed. When the final bucket is poured, and all building materials delivered, the tower crane is dismantled. After the building is finished, there is no further need for the forming and the crane.

As essential as the concrete forms were, they continued to be removed until the construction was finally complete. And, as essential as the crane was to pour the concrete, its usefulness also became redundant when the building was done.

Like some knowledge and prophecies, the forms and the crane are 'from a part' that is passing away until the project is completed. The 'complete' is coming and will come.

The Perfect Is Coming

This current perfecting process for every believer is accomplished by means of knowledge and prophecies. We are being perfected as we grow in knowledge and instruction. (2 Pe. 3:18)

When The Perfect Does Come

When the 'perfect' finally does come, we will all be adults, no longer subject to the limitations of childhood and hard to understand guidance. Both childhood and reflected reality are incomplete. They will expire. We will no longer need written words to communicate to us the glory of Christ; we will see Him.

Paul anticipates a day when all believers will be united in doctrine and knowledge of the Son towards a perfect man. (Eph. 4:13) The purpose for knowledge and prophecies now, is future maturity or perfection in Christ Jesus. (Col. 1:28)

Indeed, Paul teaches believers to be mature. (1 Cor. 2:6) But, as one who still knows from a portion of his spiritual 'childhood' and prophesies from a portion of his mirror of spiritual guidance, he also had not yet been made complete. (1 Cor. 13:12; Phil. 3:12) The 'complete' to come is the day that we appear in heaven, whether by death **or** the Lord's return.

But, there is knowledge and prophecy that does not elapse. They are three essential gifts.

15. THE CHARACTER GIFTS

Paul declared that should one be in possession of prophecy and the knowledge to understand mysteries, this would amount to nothing without love. (13:2) If love were dependent on knowledge and prophecies, it could not abide. And, languages change. Even useful knowledge and prophecies elapse. (13:8) Yet, love is always an unfailing present reality in the life of every child of God.

Paul now highlights three character qualities that do not elapse or change. Growth and guidance necessary for every believer, cannot impact these intrinsic qualities. They are love, faith and hope. (13:13)

Abilities in languages, discernment, prophesy, knowledge, faith to overcome difficulties, abilities in administration, teaching, generosity, helps and so on, have no power over sin. None of these gifts alone were credible evidence of their faith in Christ. Despite abilities, people are still impatient, unkind, envious, ostentatious, arrogant, rude, self-seeking, easily provoked, evil thinkers, rejoices in sin and deception. Much, much more than ability gifts are required to be a somebody. (1 Cor. 13:2)

> 'Now, however, abide faith, hope, love, these three specific things, but the greatest of these is love. Earnestly pursue the love, and earnestly desire the spirituals [guidance], now rather, that you may prophesy.' (1 Cor.13:13-14:1; Based on Interlinear, biblehub.com)

> "Now abide faith, hope, love, these three; but the greatest of these is love. Pursue love, and desire spiritual *gifts*, but especially that you may prophesy." (1Cor.13:13-14:1, NKJV)

CHARACTER GIFTS ABIDE

Among true believers, love was and is always present, even as some prophecies and knowledge became obsolete and as languages cease. Despite changing guidance for growth, there is one attribute that does not change. Through all the phases of growth and guidance, in every stage of the believer's development, love is never demoted to a lower status. (13:8)

Some knowledge and prophecy becomes irrelevant with time. Languages change and become extinct. Therefore, status and recognition gained from the possession of 'all knowledge' is only temporal. He is still nothing, without love. One is not distinguished by the kind or quantity of knowledge and prophecy he possesses.

Paul highlights the three gifts that do.

FAITH

The necessity of faith is implied with the phrase 'bears all things'. In verse 2, Paul alludes to someone who might have the faith, the personal confidence, to move mountain-sized obstacles. In verse 7, he is one, like Paul, who 'bears all things', such as burdens, deprivations, trouble, hardships and toil.[100] (1 Cor. 9:12)

Secondly, Paul says that love believes all things, that is, all things "that are to be believed, all that God says in his word, and all His promises...".[101] These are the 'spirituals', Paul exhorts believers to desire. (1 Cor. 12:1; 14:1) Acceptable faith requires that all things, all 'spirituals' are believed.

HOPE

The believer also has an abiding hope. (1 Cor. 13:7,13) He 'hopes all things' doesn't mean that he can hope to have all his dreams fulfilled. However, God has given believers many things to hope for. We know that all things work out together for good to the one who loves God. (Rom. 8:28) Every believer has this hope as an anchor for his soul. (Heb. 6:19) We eagerly await Christ's return because we love Him. (1 Cor. 1:4-8) If our hope is in a Messiah that is not raised from the dead, then we have hoped in Christ for this life only, and we are to be most pitied for believing a lie. (1 Cor. 15:18,19) However, because Christ did indeed rise from the dead, our hope is certain.

LOVE

Love does not fail.[102] Unlike aspects of prophecy and knowledge, all the features of love never 'drop away.' Love always looks the same, unaffected by changing circumstances.

Paul also stated that love is greater than faith and hope. Love is greatest because it was by His love that we have come to know and love God. (1 Jn.4:16) Love is the greatest, because it shows our faith to be real.

---

[100] *Meyer's New Testament Commentary*, 1 Cor. 13:7

[101] John Gill, *Gill's Exposition*, commentary on 1 Cor. 13:7.

[102] Fail:- "drop away, to be driven out of one's course; fig. to lose or become inefficient." (Strong's Concordance, 1601)

(Jn.13:35) Love is the greatest because it is the only reason why God sent His Son to pay an unimaginable price for our sin. (1 Jn.4:19) Love is also the greatest because God by His Spirit causes believers to truly love others when there is no reason to.

It is possible for someone to give all his possessions to the poor and still not have love. Philanthropists may be impatient, unkind, and arrogant. But humanitarianism is not love. Love does not rejoice in one's own childish deceptions. Love rejoices with the truth. Love believes God's revealed word. Love is the greatest because it is the believer's visible expression of our faith and hope in God.

SUMMARY

Faith, hope and love, abide. While some knowledge, language and elapse or change with time, these character gifts do not. Paul writes that love is greater than faith and hope, but he does not say that faith and hope were not essential or optional.

Faith, hope and love are abiding essential qualities of our relationship with God and one another. Despite changing circumstances, faith, hope and love remain constant. Though at first, like children, these gifts are barely evident, they are intrinsic, growing possessions of every believer. Apart from these character gifts, people will stand before God empty-handed. We must have all three; they are not options.

CHARACTER GIFTS ARE DESIRED

Paul instructed the church to pursue love and desire 'spirituals' earnestly. (1 Cor. 14:1) Most translations have Paul exhorting the church to desire 'spiritual gifts', especially, to prophesy. But, why would Paul now be instructing the Corinthians to keep on competing for an ability to prophesy, when he had illustrated with the body analogy, how unloving this is? They already were pursuing the best gifts according to their own ambitions; so, to deduce that Paul is instructing them to desire the best ability gifts, especially a prominent gift like prophecy, is to promote the same conflicts they already had. Since the Holy Spirit has given abilities to all, there is no need to search for ability gifts, which they already had.

Instead, Paul is exhorting the Corinthians to zealously pursue love and desire earnestly spiritual teachings more, in order to prophesy.[103] Paul

---

103 "*Mallon*" means 'more, to a greater degree, rather.' *Thayer's Greek Lexicon*. It is translated 'especially' in NKJV, NASB and ESV in 1 Cor. 14:1.

exhorted them to chase the abiding, permanent character gift of love. His desire for the churches was that their love would abound more and more. (Phil. 1:9; 1 Thess.3:12)

Already gifted by the Holy Spirit with various abilities, Paul exhorted the church to pursue love and earnestly desire 'spirituals', that is teachings and guidance from the written word. Paul implied that they had not desired the Scriptures (spirituals), in order to prophesy. It was a matter of 'desire', not giftedness. (14:1) The Corinthians needed to apply themselves to learn the Scriptures.

THE EXCELLENT WAY

Regardless of ability, faith, hope and love are essential for every believer. Anyone having love, will also have faith and hope. They come in a package. Only those in the body of Christ have these character gifts. (1 Cor. 13:4,5; 14:1) They are gifts of character.

The Character Gifts Are Evidenced By Love

Paul says that it is not a matter of having some love or more love; it is a matter of having love or not having love. (1 Cor. 13:2) It is one 'abounding love'. (Phil. 1:9)

The Character Gifts Remain

These character gifts remain. Unlike ability gifts, these do not expire with time, or become outdated. They are a perennial reality.

The Character Gifts Are Essential For Profit

Again, these character gifts are essential for rewards. Despite varying abilities, these three character gifts are constants in this divine equation, without which the product will always be zero. Seeking a profit by multiplying our abilities with zero faith or zero hope or zero love, still yields zero profit. But with these "greater gifts", spiritual profit is certain to be made. (1 Cor. 12:31) Paul had given them reason to doubt their conversion. Apparently, some had even denied the knowledge of the resurrection. (1 Cor. 15:2)

People must love God to be known by Him. (1 Cor. 8:3) They must be saved. He warned them about the rebellion and idolatry of loveless Israel in the wilderness. (1 Cor. 10:1-12) Some also did not really have the knowledge of God. (1 Cor. 15:34) Not assuming that everyone he wrote to was a believer, Paul stated that if any man does not love the Lord, let him be accursed. (1 Cor. 16:22) Love is the key evidence of true faith. (1Jn.3:14,15) 'Without love I am nothing.'

The Character Gifts Are Essential For Salvation

Still like rude, attention demanding children with clanging cymbals and noisy gongs, some professing believers in Corinth apparently had not yet acquired three essential character gifts. (1 Cor. 13:1,11,12) How could they have missed the prophecies about love? Love is not defined by how much one gives to the poor. Even the noble work of generosity can be done without love! It will be sobering for most church people to wake up in eternity to find that their works of 'charity' and donations to 'charities' were loveless, then to hear the Judge say, 'you are nothing.'

Love Is The Greatest Character Gift

Being in possession prophecy and knowledge is possible without having a love for God or man. But without love, these ability gifts amount to 'nothing'. There is no middle ground between being a somebody and a nobody; it's one or the other. If I am truly a 'somebody' in God's economy, I am in possession of His love, which guarantees me a profit.

The Character Gifts Are Not Universal; They Are Transcendent

The ability gifts are universal; these three character gifts are not. Faith, hope and love are the essential character credentials of every member of the body of Christ. These character gifts are systemic in each member of the body of Christ. They are transcendent. Every believer is in possession of these character attributes, thus assured that he will profit from the abilities the Holy Spirit gave him.

This is the excellent, the surpassing way. Ability gifts fade but faith, hope and love abide. (1 Cor. 12:31)

16. PROPHESYING WITH LANGUAGE

Crispus, the previous leader of the synagogue, had been converted along with his household. (1 Cor. 1:14; Ac. 18:8) Despite what appears to be a sizeable Jewish representation in the assembly, they seemed to be ignorant of the OT Scriptures. Paul admonished the church for not disciplining immorality, saying that such behavior is not even found among the Gentiles. (1 Cor. 5:1) By repeatedly asking them, 'do you not know...?' he implies that he had an expectation that they had been taught the Law and the Prophets. Paul references the people of the wilderness as "our fathers", indicating a large Jewish presence in the church. (1 Cor. 10:1) More was expected of them because, as Jews, they ought to have been well versed in the Law and Prophets. (1 Cor. 14:21) Unfamiliar with the Word, they had failed to communicate the Scriptures. Their prophecy was minimal. They failed to excel in prophecy. Lack of knowledge and propriety evidenced their lack of interest to excel in prophecy. But they were eager to talk in a language that others might not understand.

What Does Paul Want Them To Prophesy?

Paul defines what he means by the verb 'prophesy'. As per 'spirituals', Paul had expected the church to be informed. (12:1) He wants them to be able to prophesy these 'spirituals'. Scripture is prophecy. (2 Pe. 1:20,21) As informed believers, they were to be equipped to 'tell forth', that is, prophesy the spirituals of Scripture, not personal prognostications or opinions. (14:1) It was to be based on the Scriptures they were given, propositional.

Prophesying Was Not Ecstatic

Paul stressed that believers not offend the sensitive consciences of new converts from pagan idolatry, by eating meat that had been offered to idols. Had Jewish converts participated in pagan gibberish and 'ecstatic utterance' of the Gentiles, Paul would have censured them immediately. 'Tongues' was and is a pagan practice that Paul would not have allowed.

Translators have failed to translate *glosse* (tongue) as 'language'. In King James 1611 English, 'tongue' would be understood to be a 'language'; today, we use the word 'language'.

TRANSLATION MUST BE UNDERSTANDABLE

Translations engage in logical dissonance. For example, Bible versions typically write something like, 'for he who speaks in a tongue, does not speak to men but to God...' (14:2a) This sounds like someone speaking in 'a language' speaks only to God, whether someone is present or not. However, it is obvious that one who speaks in a language does indeed speak to men and God. How would one even come to know a language without speaking to men?

But, there was a language problem. Note especially the comma after (language) in the first line in each of the following literal translations:

> 'For the one speaking in a tongue (language)**,** not to men speaks, but to God; for no one hears; in the Spirit (spirit) however, he utters mysteries'.[104] ('language', brackets added)

Another interlinear has a similar translation,

> "For he that speaks with a tongue (language)**,** not to men speaks, but to God: for no one hears; but in spirit he speaks mysteries."[105] (brackets added)

Given that punctuation is not inspired, it needs to be assessed. Had the comma been placed after 'men' in both of the above translations, instead of after 'tongue' (language), the meaning would be different. It would then read, **'for the one speaking in a language not to men, speaks but to God**...' (14:2a) Then it becomes clear that a language 'not to men', was a learned language not understood by the hearers. In this case, only God would understand the language.

LANGUAGE MUST NOT BE A BARRIER TO COMMUNICATION

New converts brought with them minority languages unfamiliar to the majority. If this multilingual mix was left unmanaged, corporate communication would be limited and the believers' opportunities for prophesying His word would be compromised. (14:2)

The text implies two cases:

- When a person speaks a language he knows, to men, he is not speaking mysteries, because his hearers understand him.

---

[104] http://biblehub.com/interlinear/1_corinthians/14.htm
Interlinear Greek of 1 Cor. 14:2

[105] *Interlinear Greek-English New Testament*, George Ricker Berry, p. 459. Also, note that "there is no authority anywhere for the punctuation." Introduction, p. ii.

- Or, when a person speaks a language he knows, not to men, he is speaking mysteries, because his hearers do not understand him.

In the first case, the language is known to both speaker and hearer; in the second case, the language is known only to the speaker and in both cases the language is known to God. In the first case, the speaker is not speaking mysteries because his hearers understand his language; in the second case, the speaker is speaking mysteries because the hearers do not understand his language.

Some who had been chosen to be part of the service on any given Sabbath, had spoken in a minority language not understood by most. Unbelievers would know that all of them understood the vernacular, yet some spoke their native language in the service without interpretation! Unbelievers would think they were insane. (14:23)

The Gospel Was Prophesied At Pentecost

Believing that the Holy Spirit supernaturally enabled the Galileans to speak languages they had not learned, it is commonly taught, even among Cessationists, that He also conferred this supposed ability upon believers in Corinth.[106] As discussed earlier, the Galileans prophesied in their own learned languages, which the hearers understood. In Corinth, some did not prophesy because they were speaking their own learned language, which the hearers did not understand. But at Pentecost, believers were glorifying God and prophesying in languages understood by the hearers.

Mysteries Are Knowable.

Charismatics think that 'mysteries' supports the idea of 'private prayer language', where people utter meaningless syllables that only God understands. Such claims that God hears ecstatic speakers because he understands ecstatic speech is like saying that one can get up in a group and bark like a dog and God will understand what he says. (as per the "Toronto Blessing", which is really a curse.) Whether the language was understood or not, they were learned languages, not ecstatic utterances.

Not only did Paul want to speak languages appropriately, he wanted them to speak knowledgeably. (14:1) Only when knowledge is articulated in a language everyone understands is it possible for mysteries to be diffused. Since, to prophesy requires communication of truth in the language of the listeners, 'ecstatic utterance' can be categorically ruled out.

---

[106] Robert L. Thomas, *Understanding Spiritual Gifts*, P. 36

Jesus spoke real human language his hearers could understand. He spoke in 'mysteries', but it was not in gibberish or ecstatic utterance. (Matt. 13:10,11,15) Multiple times, Paul asked the Corinthians, 'Do you not know?' Truth available from the Scriptures and Apostles, remained an unnecessary mystery to them.

Despite their linguistic smorgasbord, the Corinthian assembly had a limited appetite for spiritual sustenance. Apparently, they had very limited knowledge to communicate. This was the bigger problem.

PROPHESYING PROVIDES SCRIPTURAL GUIDANCE

Not only must the language be understood, it must communicate the truth. As indicated earlier, regardless of their language, they couldn't prophesy because they had not earnestly desired spiritual teachings.

> "...and he who is prophesying to men doth speak edification, and exhortation, and comfort; he who is speaking in an (unknown) tongue (language)", himself doth edify, and he who is prophesying, an assembly doth edify; and I wish you all to speak with tongues (languages), and more that ye may prophesy, for greater is he who is prophesying than he who is speaking with tongues (languages), except one may interpret, that the assembly may receive edification." (14:3-5, YLT, 'language(s)' added)

Having already repeatedly queried them on their ignorance, Paul revisits this matter as it relates to prophecy. (12:1; 14:1) The languages of some could not be understood and others, though understood, were not prophesying spiritual food. He wishes they were all multilingual so they could all understand one another, but that too would be of no avail if they remained ignorant. Elementary at best, knowledge necessary to prophesy in any language, was deficient. (14:4,5)

Paul contrasted one who spoke with a language that was <u>not</u> understood ('does not speak to men'), with one who spoke in a language that was understood ('does speak to men') (14:2,3) Anyone who prophesies must speak knowledgeably in an existing understood language.

'What Shall I Profit?'

Not only were most of them not able to understand the various languages spoken, they were uninformed. Paul explains that even if he came speaking all the languages unapprised, he would not profit them.

> "And now brethren, if I come unto you speaking tongues (languages), what shall I profit you, except I shall speak to you either in revelation, or in knowledge, or in prophesying, or in teaching?" (14:6, YLT; brackets added)

Yet, cessationists suppose that "the tongues utterance produced understandable revelation, knowledge, prophesying, and doctrine." [107] According to this theory, in order for tongues to edify the church, someone with the 'gift of interpretation' needed to translate the 'tongue'.

> ""The interpretation of tongues" was an ability to translate into one's native tongue from a language that had not been learned by natural means."[108]

There is nothing in the text that suggests that anyone had a supernatural ability to translate a language he had not learned or reveal something not in Scripture.

Paul did not want them to remain ignorant. (12:1; 14:1) Whichever one of the many languages Paul knew and spoke, his intent was to profit his hearers by communicating the truth. Unless they were informed by apostolic revelation, wise counsel, prophecies of Scripture and doctrine, people would remain ignorant. Had the Corinthians truly been receiving supernatural revelations from God, Paul would not have had to admonish them the way he did, or even write this letter. [109]

'How Shall It Be Known?' (14:7,9)

Paul likens different spoken languages to the sound of a flute or harp. If one 'spoke' the 'harp' or 'flute', the words must be distinct to understand the meaning. Due to heavy accents, communicating in the Greek vernacular, proved to be a challenge for many.

So, Paul exhorted them to speak clearly. Unless 'you' bring thought into harmony with appropriate sounds and syllables of the language used, 'you' would be speaking into the air. 'There are, it may be, many sources of sounds in the world and none of them are mute.' Everybody can make a noise. And, any language, not spoken clearly or not understood, is just noise. Because of this, some remained foreign to one another. There was a communication problem.

---

[107] Robert L. Thomas, *Understanding Spiriutal Gifts*, 1999, P. 92

[108] Ibid. p. 37

[109] The Corinthians were not gifted to receive direct revelations from God. Revelations from God would not be subject to analysis as Paul advised regarding the 'prophets' in the church. (14:29, 37)

'Who Will Prepare For Battle?' (14:8,9)

The trumpet may have sounded but because the note was uncertain, no one prepared for battle. Rather than letting speech be as mere sound in the air, Paul exhorts them seek to excel to edify the whole assembly with words that can be understood. It is impossible to prepare to fight sin in the flesh or battle the evil one, when the language can't be understood.

FAILURE OF ZEALOUS SPIRITS. (14:12)

Again, the insertion of the word 'gifts', hinders a right understanding of this verse. Similar to the errant translation to "desire spiritual *gifts*", Paul's statement is now distorted to be an affirmation of their zealousness for gifts. (14:1, 12) Why would Paul exhort them to 'desire spiritual gifts', then later affirm them for being zealous of 'spiritual gifts'? The translation makes Paul contradict himself.

"Spirits" is in the genitive. The translation should read,

> "So also ye, since emulous ye are of spirits, for the building up of the assembly, seek that ye may abound."[110] (14:12)

Paul actually says that they are zealous of "spirits", not 'spiritual *gifts*'. Though 'willing of spirits', to participate in ministry, some Corinthians had failed to seek to edify the church. Their zealousness counted for nothing.

SUMMARY

Unable to prophesy from scripture, they spoke much, but said little. Secondly, some were unable to communicate because they lacked familiarity with the common language. Thirdly, zealousness was misplaced. Paul exhorts them to channel their zealous spirits to the building up of the assembly.

Prophesying is to communicate spiritual knowledge from His written Word in a known learned language.

---

[110] *Interlinear Greek-English New Testament*, p. 461

17. FRUITFUL COMMUNICATION

Paul likened the Corinthian problem to the speaking of foreign languages in their assembly. But when foreigners speak to each another, they speak in real human languages, not 'ecstatic utterances', and they understand one another very well. Paul's exhortation arises from the inability of people to understand other indigenous languages in their meetings. They may as well have had a foreigner speak to them. (14:11) Paul provides the church his solution.

THE NECESSITY OF INTERPRETATION

Given the multiple languages represented in Corinth, it was necessary for Paul to provide some guidelines to accommodate them. Rather, than forbid the use of languages, he advises that they be interpreted.

THE TWO-FOLD MEANING OF 'INTERPRET'.

Paul uses the word '*hermeneia*' meaning 'interpret.' (12:10; 14:26; Thayer's) Another word also translated, *diermeneuo*, 'interpret', means to 'unfold the meaning of what is said, explain, expound.' (Thayer's) This word is used in 12:30; 14:5, 13, 27.

Whether translating the meaning of one language into another, or expounding a text from one language to another, the Greek for 'interpretation' requires the conscious, logical, propositional exercise by the mind of one who knows both languages. By definition, both Greek words, *hermeneia* and *diermeneuo,* require human intellectual expertise. In either case, interpretation precludes spontaneous revelation.

THE ACTUAL PROBLEMS

Some who attempted to speak Greek were ineffective, like bugles played with incorrect notes. Listeners did not understand the 'message of the music.' So, also language, if it is not 'played' with the right 'notes' cannot be understood. (14:8,9) They were unable to speak the vernacularly well enough to be clearly understood.

And others, unable to speak '**the** language' everyone could understand, spoke 'a language', which most or all the rest could not understand. Consequently, the listeners were not edified. (14:11,12)

PUBLIC PRAYER (14:13)

Should someone be permitted to pray in church in his own language? (14:13) Paul concludes that 'even' when they speak a minority language, they also have the potential to communicate if their prayer is translated.

Erroneous Cessationist Contravention

It is somewhat puzzling that even cessationists hold to the notion that the Corinthians were given this supposed supernatural gift to speak 'with tongues'. Note the following commentary on 14:13,

> "It was possible for a person to speak with tongues publicly and still benefit the church if he did so solely for the sake of the interpretation that would result. A guided zeal for using the gift demanded that its use be with interpretation as the objective. Stated negatively, the tongues speaker could not with propriety embark upon a tongues prayer unless he was assured in advance that an interpretation would follow." He begins the next paragraph, "<u>That the prayer of verse 13 is a tongues prayer and not a prayer intelligible to the listeners is a necessary conclusion.</u>" Then down the page a bit more he adds, "It is far more harmonious, ...therefore, to understand "pray that he may interpret" in verse 13 in the sense of "pray with the tongue in order to generate an interpretation."" [111] (emphasis added)

Why would the Holy Spirit give a non-human 'tongue' that is humanly not translatable? If this prayed 'language' is non-translatable, it cannot be interpreted, as per the Greek definitions.

Paul did not instruct the one who prayed to 'generate an interpretation'; he instructed him to "interpret". Interpret is an exercise of one's intellect, in this case man, by which the meaning of one language is transposed into another. He was not to expect a 'heavenly' interpretation to fall into his head.

The notion that Paul expected the Corinthians to believe a personal 'interpretation' of someone's own supposed 'prayer language' is contrary to everything Paul taught regarding discernment. He wanted them to be familiar with the Scriptures to avoid being deceived. Unlike real languages, this supposed 'prayer language' is unique to the person and therefore cannot be verified. Gibberish is not checkable.

---

[111] Robert L. Thomas, *Understanding Spiritual Gifts*, P.95-96

The Scriptures Were Interpreted

Is there any scriptural precedent where one who speaks in 'a language not to men', then prays **for** a supernatural ability to interpret? When the Jews returned to Israel, the OT Scriptures were explained to them and translated as necessary without prayer for a translation ability. No one told them to pray **for** a special "gift". (Neh. 8:1-8) Why was it not necessary to pray publicly for a gift of interpretation before Christ, but it was after Pentecost? No such prayer was offered when people spoke languages at Pentecost. Neither did Ezra and his assistants pray for this 'ability'. It is not plausible that Paul here advised one who spoke in a 'tongue' to pray for the ability to 'interpret' his 'tongue' into a language he didn't even know, then expected everyone to believe that whatever he blurted out, was God's revealed Word. (14:13) No precedent exists where one who spoke in 'a language', prayed for the ability to interpret it, then interpreted it.

To 'Interpret' Is Impossible Without Knowledge

As discussed above, the Greek meaning of the words translated, 'interpret', do not mean 'reveal'. The one who interprets must be able to demonstrate that he knows both the source and target languages. If he does not know them, he can't interpret. What does Paul say?

'Interpret' Implies A Known Human Language

Though eager, some had failed to prophesy (reveal the Scriptures), because they spoke languages that were not understood and others spoke the common language unclearly. (14:6-12) So, Paul mitigates this misplaced zealousness with advice to those who were not speaking 'the' language in public prayer. Following is a literal translation of the Greek for verse 13,

> 'Therefore, [112] him speaking a language, let him pray – to the end that he ought to interpret.' (14:13)

It stands to reason that anyone speaking 'a language', was not speaking 'the language', in a public prayer. Not wanting to limit believers' participation in the service, Paul said, 'Let him pray.' Despite the language barrier, believers were to be involved in the service. Multiple languages were not forbidden. (14:39) But there was a caveat.

---

[112] The Greek *dioper* translated as 'therefore' or 'wherefore' in 14:13 is a conjunction meaning "Thru-Which-Even" (scripture4all.org) The only two other places this conjunction is used is 8:13 and 10:14. Even normally accepted foods should be deferred if it has been offered to idols.

The subjunctive mood of the verb 'interpret', indicates that an action should happen that was not happening. Some had been praying publicly in 'a' language foreign to most of them, without translating it.

The verb 'pray' is in the middle/passive voice. In the middle voice, the one who prays both initiates the prayer and participates in the prayer. In this case, he thinks and speaks his prayer. Contrary to popular belief, this context does not imply that one who prays in 'a tongue' is passively receiving a 'prayer language' from God. Paul's clear command is that he must interpret, not receive an 'interpretation'. Both context and grammar precludes the passive voice, where the speaker is being acted upon by an outward influence.

He only granted permission to one speaking "a language" to pray publicly, if he himself could translate (*diermeneuo*) his words into the vernacular. Though he may not know the Greek nearly as well as his first language and might have to search for words to convey his meaning, he must be sufficiently bilingual to translate his prayer from his preferred language. Everyone must understand the language of the prayer so that listeners may respond with an 'amen'. (14:13,16)

FUNCTIONS OF THE SPIRIT AND UNDERSTANDING

Perhaps one Scripture portion most twisted to teach that mystical behavior is justified, are verses 12 to 17 of 1 Corinthians 14. Two major terms of these verses is the spirit and the understanding.

WHAT DOES 'SPIRIT' MEAN?

This battered portion of scripture is misused to affirm irrational and mystical behavior where the mind is neutralized or disconnected from the spirit. Often translated as 'mind', erroneous inferences emerge. Some claim that the spirit can pray in a 'prayer language' with a mind that is disengaged. First, what is the spirit? (14:12-17)

Paul explains what the spirit is. "For what man knows the things of a man except the spirit of man which is in him?" (2:11; NKJV) In this context, 'spirit' is the source and repository of knowledge. Man knows things about himself that others do not. Right or wrong, his spirit contains information, convictions, opinions, preferences, abilities and data that no other person knows. (14:14, 15) Of course, the Bible has impacted and continues to correct error in the spirit of the believer. But it must be emphasized that to 'pray with my spirit', one must retrieve knowledge of personal information, emotions and desires from his spirit in him. Thus, the believer prays by means of his spirit.

WHAT DOES PAUL MEAN BY 'UNDERSTANDING'?

'Understanding', however is different. One cannot pray without the 'spirit', but is it possible to pray without understanding? (14:14,15) The 'mind' or 'understanding' is the 'intellective faculty' by which man is able to perceive or judge. (Thayer's)

How Does Paul Use 'Understanding' Elsewhere?

Additional Pauline references of the word 'understanding' or 'mind', serve to help us determine its meaning.

- The mind or understanding can be reprobate. (Rom. 1:28)
- Paul quotes from the OT, 'Who has known the mind of the Lord?' The ways and judgments of His mind cannot be discovered. (Rom. 11:34) The mind is a custodian of knowledge.
- Believers' minds are to be renewed, in order to prove the perfect will of God, to not think of himself more highly than he ought to think. (Rom. 12:2,3) Knowledge of the mind must be updated.
- Each one is to be assured in his own mind, not the judgment of others. (Rom. 14:5, 10) Each person is to think his own thoughts.
- Differences with one another are endorsed by being of the same mind, the mind of Christ. (1 Cor. 1:9, 10, 12)
- The Lord does not need instruction, but man does. Having the mind of Christ, believers are enabled to evaluate thoughts and behavior correctly. (1 Cor. 2:16)
- Believers are not to mimic the unsaved because their minds are vain. (Eph. 4:17) Thoughts of the mind generate behavior.
- The Christian is not to be beguiled by the arrogant, legalistic influences of the 'fleshly mind'. (Col. 2:18)
- Fleshly impulses are described as the 'law of sin' that war against the 'law of my mind' in the Christian. With the mind we serve the law of God. (Rom. 7:23-25) Since conversion, the law of the mind has changed. Where once he loved the things that God hated and hated the things that God loved, he now delights in the law of God after the inward man. (Rom. 7:14-25) The believer, therefore, has the capacity to judge himself rightly, according to the law of God.

Generally, Paul's use of (*nous*) 'mind' in these passages indicates personal character, revealed when the understanding or mind judges or evaluates an issue with his own knowledge.

Praying With The Understanding Also

Since the 'spirit' is the personal reservoir of knowledge, 'understanding' or 'mind', evaluates the knowledge articulated. Paul states that if I pray in a language, "my understanding" is unfruitful. Praying with "my understanding" (mind), and praying with "the understanding" are different. One is fruitful; the other is not. Therefore, one 'mind' has judged correctly; the other has not.

Since one who prays in 'a language' is unfruitful, it follows that one who prays with 'the understanding' made a correct evaluation, by not speaking 'a language'. What then is this language?

Paul specifically stated that 'a language' is one that is **not** interpreted. (14:13) Therefore, '**the** understanding' must be the evaluation that '**a** language' must be translated into '**the** language'. If one does <u>not</u> also pray with '**the** understanding', his choice will be incorrect and blessing others with knowledge of the spirit is forfeited, because they do not understand what is said. Edification is then compromised. (14:15-17)

There are two evaluations based on two 'understandings'.

Since one who prays with 'his (**my**) understanding', is praying in '**a** language', one who prays with '**the** understanding', is not praying in '**a** language.' Therefore, the one who prays with '**the** understanding' must be praying in **the** language, understood by everyone. (14:13-16)

Fruitful Prayer Is Made With 'The Understanding'

Willing and even eager 'spirits' must prayer and sing in **the** common language, not '**a**' language. (14:12-14) In this context, one's understanding errs, if it fails to communicate in language that everyone knows. Given that Paul's letters were written to the churches in Greek, it is implied that Greek would have been the vernacular.

When public prayer in 'a language' is left uninterpreted, my spirit prays, but 'my understanding' has erred in judgment, which rendered it unfruitful or barren. (14:13,14) If public prayer is to benefit the hearer, it must be understood, so that he can say 'Amen' to the prayer. (14:16)

Rather than just praying with the spirit and 'my understanding', Paul concludes that one should pray with the spirit and with **the** understanding. (14:14,15)

Purpose

The meaning of *idiotes* is not 'ungifted' as some translations have. (14:16,24) It means unlearned or uninformed or uninstructed. Everyone in the "room" remains 'uninstructed' up until he is instructed or informed. The only means by which that occurs is through language the listeners understand.

SUMMARY

In Paul's context, 'the spirit' of a man is productive in prayer regardless of the language employed. But his 'understanding' has erred in judgment if listeners do not understand the prayer. 'The understanding', in this context, is the evaluation that correctly concludes that communication to everyone is essential, in order to be fruitful.

Since 'a language' is understood among foreigners, yet not understood by listeners in this assembly, 'the understanding' is the evaluation that the vernacular is the practical means of communication to everyone.

A REVIEW OF VERSES 6 TO 17

The following questions and answers is a review of the preceding explanations of verses 6 to 17.

- Who are the barbarians? (14:11) Paul is referring to those who do not speak Greek. (Rom. 1:14)
- What language was common? The common language were not the languages of the barbarians, so it must have been Greek.
- What language did Paul use? Writing in Greek, Paul exhorted that his letters be read to the churches. (Eph.3:4; Col. 4:16; 1 Thess. 5:27) He made no specific instructions to translate the Greek.
- Who are the people that speak 'a language'? Paul is referring to 'foreigners' who speak a known language other than Greek.
- Do barbarians speak gibberish? No. When 'barbarians' speak to one another, they can understand one another.
- What is meant by 'a language'? 'A language' therefore refers to one of the minority languages. Context shows that 'a language' means a real spoken language, but understood only by a few, if any. (14:2)
- How does Paul characterize unknown languages of the barbarians? He characterizes them as unintelligible sounds, voices, and tones. But, these sounds are not without meaning because they are actually part of a human spoken language, other than Greek. (14:10,11)

- How does Paul illustrate the problem of speaking 'a language' not to men? (14:2,9,11) The Greek also, becomes like a foreign language when it is spoken so poorly that it is not understood by Greeks.
- Is an 'unfruitful' language good? 'Unfruitful' means barren and in no way could this be considered a compliment. Paul is critical. Charismatics falsely teach that the prayer is 'unfruitful' because the one praying doesn't understand what he is saying. Did Jesus then somehow miss this when He taught His disciples to pray with real words they could understand? Jesus was not a charismatic!
- When was the mind 'fruitful' in prayer? The mind or understanding was not fruitful in prayer when others understood the prayer. (14:17)
- When then was the mind unfruitful in prayer? The understanding was unfruitful in prayer when the listeners could not comprehend the prayer. (14:16)
- What is the personal evidence of prayer? Paul's words are explicit, 'my spirit prays.' The one who prays gives thanks from the spirit. No spirit prays without knowing what is said. (14:14, 16, 17)
- How was the understanding involved? The understanding was responsible for initiating the prayer.
- Why was the mind of the one who prayed unfruitful? The mind of the one who prayed determined to speak in 'a language' not known by the others, and for that reason the mind was unfruitful. (14:14)
- Does 'unfruitful' imply an inability of the mind to understand what was prayed? No! (14:16,17)
- Does 'unfruitful' imply that the mind did not know what the spirit was communicating? No. (14:4,16)
- What, then, is 'a language'? 'A language' is one that is not understood by the majority and needed to be interpreted. (14:13, 16)
- What is the function of the spirit? The believer's spirit functions as a repository of knowledge. (2:11)
- Does the spirit of a man know what he knows? Yes. (2:11)
- How does one bless with a prayer? One may bless with a prayer by the spirit and **his** ("my") understanding, and not be understood by the hearers, or one may bless with a prayer by the spirit and "the" understanding "also" and be understood by the hearers. (14:14,15,16)
- What is the function of 'understanding'? Like a judge, the 'understanding' presides over what is said.

- What should we expect from understanding? The understanding is expected to be fruitful. (14:16,17)
- Is it possible to pray without understanding? No. (14:15) One prays with either his (my) understanding or 'the' understanding.
- Which 'understanding' did Paul disapprove of? He disapproved of 'my understanding'. (14:14)
- Why was 'my understanding' unfruitful? 'My understanding' was unfruitful because the hearers did not understand the language spoken and was left uninterpreted. (14:16,17)
- Why did Paul not write instead, 'For if I pray in a language, my spirit prays, but my 'language' is unfruitful'? (14:14) The context indicates that 'language' is not unfruitful because language is necessary, even when praying alone. It is the mind, however, that determines whether he will edify others besides just himself.
- When does a public prayer bless with the spirit only? A prayer blesses with the spirit only when someone does not understand what is prayed. (14:16, 17)
- How is it known when 'the understanding' is fruitful? The understanding is known to be fruitful when listeners respond with an 'Amen'. (14:16,17)
- Can prayers be made without personal comprehension? No. 'My spirit prays' means that real thoughts of the spirit are consciously expressed by means of a real human language. To pray and sing with the understanding "also", then, means that not only will the speaker understand, but also the listeners. (14:15-17)
- What does a fruitful understanding accomplish? The fruitful understanding informs and edifies the listener. (14:17)
- Who are the "uninformed"? These are the listeners who do not understand the ethnic languages spoken. (14:11,17)
- What is the relationship of the spirit and the understanding? They are both the means [113] by which knowledge is communicated. The knowledge of our spirit functions as the source of our prayers and songs. The understanding is manages the delivery of the knowledge of the spirit. (2:11,12)

---

[113] Benjamin W. Brodie, *1 Corinthians*, page 593 Both 'spirit' and 'understanding' are dative of means or instrument.
http://www.versebyverse.com/sitebuildercontent/sitebuilderfiles/1cor.pdf

- Is ecstatic speech implied? There are two known human languages implied: the un-interpreted translatable language, and the common language, which everyone knew. (14:13-15)
- Is there such a thing as a 'private prayer language?' Emphatically no! If one prays in 'a language' in this context, it is a public exercise. Secondly, the speaker understands the language he is speaking. It is not a supernatural event. (14:13,16,17)

CONCLUDING SUMMARY

The spirit is the repository of knowledge. The understanding manages the delivery of the knowledge of the spirit.

Since 'a *glossa*' is an actual language spoken by foreigners, 'ecstatic utterance' is ruled out. Secondly, there is no supernatural component to this context, where anyone spoke in an unlearned language, as the cessationist presumes. At Pentecost, everyone heard Peter preach in one language; at Corinth everyone would have understood the Greek.

To pray with "my" own understanding in this context, then, is to pray with a real human foreign learned language that only God understands. (14:2) To pray with "the" understanding is to pray in the common language, which both the congregation and, of course, God understand.

Since saying a prayer with 'his' understanding alone in 'a language' is unproductive, it is necessary to pray with 'the' understanding. (14:13-15) Therefore, Paul permits one who speaks a minority language to pray and sing publicly, if He can mentally interpret his language into the common language. Speaking 'a language' does not 'bless with the spirit'.

'Prayer Language' Interpretation Is Incredulous

It is important to emphasize the fact that supernatural 'prayer language' could not possibly be part of Paul's context. Charismatic, continuationists and some cessationists are expecting their students to believe that people could turn their 'prayer' gift on at will to speak in 'tongues'. Then, to suggest that this is a 'gift' of the Holy Spirit, who would supernaturally interject a prayer that the speaker himself could not understand, is preposterous. There is no record of God-glorifying testimonies accompanying the supernatural 'gifts' they are alleged to have had. Yet, we are asked to believe that people in Corinth were speaking unlearned languages, or 'prayer' languages? Claims that they were voluntarily speaking unlearned languages, does not meet any standard of reason, not to mention biblical exegesis. There is absolutely no mystical transmission of knowledge. There were no charismatics, continuationists or cessationists in Corinth.

The Church Was Ignoring The Vernacular

Paul was not advising a charismatic class of spiritual elites on how to use their 'gift'. 'A language' was spoken that could not be understood. This begs the question. Was there a language everyone could understand? Yes. As in any multilingual society, even today, most people can understand English, but cannot speak it very well. In Corinth, they all understood Greek.

Writing to them in the Greek, it follows that they understood Greek. He had not given instructions that his letters be translated into other languages, when publicly read. The majority in the assembly understood Greek and that was 'the' language into which other languages would be translated. In situations where "a language" (not the vernacular) might be spoken without an interpretation, they were to keep silent. (14:27,28)

From Paul's words, 'he who speaks in a language not to men', it is implied that some could 'speak in a language unto men.' This means that there was one language the majority understood, a common language, which made it possible to 'speak unto men.' Despite the linguistic complexity of this congregation, as with many even today, most could understand the common language well enough.

Wanting to participate in the service, volunteers spoke in 'a language' not understood by those present. Or, they attempted to speak the Greek vernacular, but couldn't speak it well enough to be understood.

PAUL'S LANGUAGE UNDERSTANDING

It is believed that Paul himself supernaturally spoke in unlearned languages or communicated with God mystically with ecstatic utterances. But the scripture shows that he was not ever a charismatic.

Paul was a Jew, born in the city of Tarsus, where he became familiar with the philosophy and the poetry of the Greeks. This early exposure to the Greek language enabled him to preach from Mars Hill in Athens. His parents moved to Jerusalem when he was still very young where they provided him an education under the respected rabbi Gamaliel. Trained as a rabbi he was required to know Hebrew. He was a 'Hebrew of Hebrews' who excelled above his peers.

PAUL'S LANGUAGE RESUME

Paul could understand and speak Hebrew. (Ac. 21:37; 26:14; 40-22:2) Paul could speak Greek. (Ac. 21:37) Paul admitted that he was not good at speaking, yet he was not deficient in knowledge. (1 Cor.2:1-5; 2 Cor. 10:10; 11:6) Paul was fluent in both Koine and classical Greek.[114] Israel was under the domination of the Romans at that time, so Paul would also have known at least some Latin. Many were converted when Paul was confined in Rome. Paul knew Greek, Hebrew, Aramaic and Latin.

But could Paul speak more? Verse 18 is usually translated, 'I thank my God that I speak in tongues more than you all.' With placement of "more" after 'tongues' it is erroneously inferred that Paul spoke 'heavenly tongues' more than all of them. Rather, this should be translated, 'I thank my God I speak with more languages than you all.' Scholars have deduced that Paul spoke learned languages,

> "*with more tongues than ye all.* I am able to speak more foreign languages than all of you. How many languages Paul could speak, he has nowhere told us. It is reasonable, however, to presume that he was able to speak the language of any people to whom God in his providence, and by His Spirit, called him to preach. He had been commissioned to preach to the *Gentiles*, and it was probable that he was able to speak the languages of all the nations among whom he ever travelled. There is no account of his being under a necessity of employing an interpreter wherever he preached."[115]

Where ever Paul went, he knew the languages spoken and could speak them.

PAUL'S UNDERSTANDING

Paul adds, "yet in the church I would rather speak five words through *(dia)* my understanding, that I may teach others also, than ten thousand words in a language." (14:19 YLT) Paraphrased,

> 'Yet in the assembly, I desire five words to speak through my understanding to instruct others also, rather than 10,000 words to speak in 'a language' through my understanding that does not instruct others.' (14:19)

---

[114] Quency E. Wallace, *The Early Life and Background of Paul the Apostle*,
See the following link. http://www.biblicaltheology.com/Research/WallaceQ01.html

[115] *Barne's Notes on the New Testament*, 1 Cor. 14:18

From this verse, it is inferred that Paul spoke with 'understanding' publicly, but privately he broke into a mindless 'prayer language'. However, claiming to speak more languages than all of them, it is untenable that these many 'languages' were acquired through mystical ecstasies. No reason in Paul's exhortation has yet emerged, where the Corinthians would understand 'languages' as supernatural. They would have agreed that Paul indeed could speak more human languages than any of them.

Therefore, having the option to speak a language that would teach others, Paul states that he would exercise that option with "my understanding". If everyone present understood Aramaic and no one understood Greek, Paul would have spoken Aramaic instead of 10,000 words in Greek.

Paul could speak five words with his understanding for the purpose of teaching others. Or, he could speak ten thousand words with his understanding in a language his hearers did not comprehend and leave them untaught. Naturally, his choice was the former.

Despite his ability to speak many words in other languages he had learned, his mind determined a different option based on purpose. He would speak fewer words in the language his hearers understood for the purpose of instructing them. With a hyperbolic contrast of 'five and 10,000 words', Paul depicts the chasm between one who communicates and one who does not; between one who instructs others and one who does not. The appropriate language and knowledge are both vital.

It must be emphasized that there is nothing in the text that remotely suggests that Paul was in the habit of speaking unlearned languages. Neither is there any context to suppose that Paul would promote or engage in the pagan practice of speaking impulsive or 'ecstatic utterances'.

PAUL'S OPTIONS

Paul had two options: he could speak 10,000 words in a language most of his hearers did not understand or five words they all understood. Both options require speaking; both options require listeners; both options require knowledge; both options require linguistic abilities; both options require understanding; both options require teaching. But, only one option teaches "others also"!

18. THE SIGN OF LANGUAGES

Charismatic 'tongues' has gripped many believers because of a failure to grapple with Paul's statement that 'languages cease' and that 'languages are for a sign'. Speaking with languages is certainly a 'gift'. But in the Jewish context it is also a sign. Through their captivities, Israel had learned to speak languages other than Hebrew.

Despite the immaturity of many in the church, the evidence does not suggest that they were trying to show off their linguistic interpretation skill. It only suggests that they were eager but unqualified. Rather, Paul exhorted that languages be interpreted.

HEAVENLY LANGUAGES

Paul's reference to speaking in the languages of men and angels does not imply that many of them were fluently multilingual. With this hyperbole and the ones following, he explains that even if they were in possession of greater multilingual skills they would still be nothing without love. (13:1) The common notion that this church competed in multilingualism doesn't fit the context. It appeared to be the opposite where people were speaking a minority language and didn't care whether they taught 'others also.'

Secondly, 'languages of men and of 'angels', does not imply that men were speaking 'heavenly' languages.

LANGUAGES CEASE

Languages cease.[116] Paul does not say language (singular) shall cease, for if he had, we would immediately understand that communication by any and all languages would come to an end. He is talking about languages, not gifts or abilities. Throughout the centuries man has always had the ability to speak in his own learned languages. Inserting 'gift' in 13:8 introduces a noun that does not belong there and changes the meaning.

"They will cease" is in the future middle voice. In the middle voice the subject acts upon itself. An interlinear translates this as 'tongues, they shall

[116] Vine's: ('cease' means 'to stop' , 'a willing cessations')

be ceasing.'[117] Paul was stating a fact that in time languages become extinct. Over time the very languages the Corinthians were speaking would fade from usage. He says that languages (plural) shall cease of themselves.[118] And that is exactly what happened and continues to happen. Most of the ones spoken in Paul's day have become extinct, and those remaining would not be recognized today.

To teach, as cessationists do, that Paul is referring to the ceasing of the 'gift of languages', which they believe is to speak unlearned languages, creates huge textual problems. As discussed earlier, there is no statement that people spoke unlearned languages even at Pentecost. Secondly, it is inferred that people speaking unlearned languages in Corinth was initiated by their own will. Thirdly at Pentecost, the Holy Spirit prompted believers to glorify God with the truth in their <u>own</u> languages. Fourthly, unlike Pentecost, listeners could not understand the speaker. Fifthly, people today still have the gift to speak multiple languages, which means that the gift, has, in fact, **not** ceased.

The allegation that this language gift was supernatural, given for the completion of scripture, is also not credible because the Corinthians, due to their own ignorance, were not even prophesying knowledge available to them from the scripture they already had. If they had been prophesying revealed truth by the Spirit, why did Paul even have to write his letter? Secondly, God appointed certain men who were moved by the Holy Spirit to write scripture. There were no openings for this job.

The Corinthians didn't suddenly become multilingual after their conversion. Management of speaking and interpreting foreign languages facilitated fellowship and evangelism in the services. After their conversion, the Corinthians were still gifted to speak multiple languages.

He exhorts them to be mature. Then with a quote from an OT prophecy, Paul shows how multiple languages was a sign to unbelieving Jews.

THE TWO-FOLD PROPHECY

Under the direct control of the Spirit at Pentecost, learned languages were employed to boldly glorify God! Conversely, at Corinth there is no record of anything said that glorified God! Paul says,

---

[117] scripture4all.org, 1Cor. 13:8

[118] Note languages that have become extinct: http://linguistlist.org/forms/langs/get-extinct.cfm

> "In the law it hath been written, that, 'With other tongues (languages) and with other lips I will speak to this people, and not even so will they hear Me, saith the Lord;' so that the tongues (languages) are for a sign, not to the believing, but to the unbelieving; and the prophesy *is* not for the unbelieving, but for the believing," (1Cor. 14:21-22; YLT, brackets added)

God would speak to His people in two ways: with 'other' languages and with 'other' lips.

GOD SPOKE WITH 'OTHER' LANGUAGES

Paul's quotation from Isaiah to explain the 'sign' of languages, is erroneously linked to Pentecost. (14:21)

The Languages 'Sign'

God had even spoken audibly to His people in Hebrew at Sinai. For centuries after, He spoke through the Prophets, who recorded God's words in Hebrew. Having ignored God's many warnings to repent of their sin, He arranged for Israel to be taken captive, where apparently most lost the ability to speak Hebrew. They were judged with the imposition of foreign languages, as prophesied by Moses. (De. 28:49)

Under the leadership of Ezra, a scribe and priest, God would provide the synagogue to facilitate the teaching of His Word, but no longer with the singular use of Hebrew. Ezra had the Law read in Hebrew, then had it interpreted and explained. (Neh. 8:8) Translation and explanation of the Hebrew into Gentile languages became necessary. Consequently, a major shift developed in worship. Gentile languages became an essential component of Jewish assemblies.

God had spoken to His people through the Prophets in the Hebrew language they knew. Later, He also spoke to the Jews in Greek through Paul the apostle, who could easily have written his epistles in Hebrew. As a sign of judgment for belligerent rejection of Him, God would speak to them in 'other languages'. (14:21) Ironically, God did exactly that, by speaking to them in the synagogues through oral translations of the Hebrew into Aramaic. This was a sign to the unbelieving Jews.

They could also have known God's call to maturity from the Scriptures (14:20) He expected the Jews among them to know that they began to speak multiple languages when they were taken into captivity by the Babylonians and the Assyrians. No longer speaking Hebrew as their first language, Gentile languages was evidence of God's prophesied censure.

The Jewish unbeliever was left with a 'sign' of their idolatrous ways - languages. (14:21,22) Multiple languages in Israel bore witness of God's past judgment; it was not a sign of God's blessing.[119] Paul alludes to the reason for the origin and advance of multiple alien languages in Israel. It was a sign to unbelievers, but the Jews did not see the sign.

Is Joel's Prophecy Relevant?

Keeping in mind that the Law and the Prophets were mostly written in Hebrew, and that sacred services were still conducted in Hebrew, it is particularly noteworthy that the Galileans broke out with joyful proclamation of the wonderful works of God in languages other than Hebrew at Pentecost. Despite God's languages censure, He would bless this special Pentecost by the outpouring of the Holy Spirit to Jewish believing sons and daughters, who then prophesied in 'other' languages, not Hebrew. God spoke through multilingual Jewish Galileans believers.

GOD ALSO SPOKE WITH 'OTHER LIPS'

But Isaiah prophesied that with 'other lips', God would also speak to this people. (14:21) Not only would He speak to His people through believing Jews, such as the Prophets, He would also speak to Jews through converted Gentiles. After God had judged Nebuchadnezzar, he came to his senses. He blessed the King of heaven. (Da. 4:33-37) We can be certain that he would have spoken his own language. Through non-Jewish lips such as these, God spoke to His people.

He used the 'lips' of a Gentile and his household to preach the gospel with languages other than Hebrew to Jews in Israel and fellow Gentiles! (14:21) Cornelius' and his Gentile household heard the gospel, believed, was baptized with the Spirit, and spoke in languages and prophesied. Here was an uncircumcised foreigner prophesying the truth back to the Jews right in Israel, together with other converted Gentiles. (Ac. 10:23-24, 45-46) God spoke the gospel to Jews through Jews with 'other languages'.

Paul's quote from Isaiah should really have jolted this majority Jewish church into reality. Even as they were being taught the Scriptures in their Gentile languages, God also spoke to them with 'other lips' of the participating uncircumcised Gentiles among them.

---

[119] Predicting Assyrian captivity, Isaiah's 'language' is singular. (Isa. 28:11) Paul's plural 'languages' in14:21, is Isaiah's inspired summary of the "law", comprising of the 'law and the prophets', which also include the Babylonian captivity and the possibly Rome. (De. 28:49; Jer. 5:15)

SUMMARY

The Jews were oblivious to the fact that Aramaic, Latin, Greek and languages other than Hebrew employed in worship was a sign. (14:22) God had been arranging events to fulfill prophecy such that through these 'other' languages and the people of these languages, He would continue to speak.

Joel prophesied that Jewish believers would prophesy to Jews. Isaiah prophesied that Gentiles would prophesy to Jews.

THE IMPORTANCE OF THE SIGN

It is wrongly inferred that languages is a 'sign gift.' (14:21, 22)

Despite Paul's teaching, continuationists believe that God gives His people a gift to pray in a non-human language. This is known as speaking in 'tongues' or mystical glossolalia. It is inconceivable that believers would receive a 'gift' to make meaningless sounds, that mimic the practice of pagans and cults.[120] Paul did not say that the '**gift** of tongues are for a sign'. He said that '**languages**' are a sign.

And, despite Paul's teaching, cessationists teach that God gave His people the gift of speaking unlearned languages. This too, for reasons already pointed out, did not happen. Again, Paul says that languages are for a sign; he **does not** say that the '**gift** of languages are a sign.' (14:22)

God gifted Assyrians, Babylonians, Romans, Greeks, Americans, Canadians, Europeans, indeed the whole world with the ability to speak languages. Whether one can speak one or five, it is a gift. However, this gift of languages is not a sign. But, the sign is 'languages' – plural.

'LANGUAGES' IS A WARNING SIGN

In the first phase of this prophecy, Hebrew faded from common use as they adopted the languages of their captors. This involuntary infusion of other languages into Jewish society was a sign to unbelieving Israel. The very people through whom the gospel was first prophesied and proclaimed, continued to reject it. They failed to ask themselves, 'why have we lost the ability, as a nation, to speak in the language of the Law?' And, 'why as God's people, are we speaking in the languages of Gentiles to carry on Jewish business?' If they had searched the Law, they would have discovered that this was the prophesied consequence of their own unbelief

---

[120] *Speaking in Tongues and The Mormon Church* https://beggarsbread.org/2012/09/23/speaking-in-tongues-and-the-mormon-church/

and rebellion! Paul reminds believers and professing believers that multilingualism was a sign of judgment to Jewish unbelievers. As a fulfillment of prophecy by Moses, Isaiah and Jeremiah, Israel was still being chastised for their unbelief. (1Cor. 14:21,22)

Isaiah prophesied that Israel would not hear. (Isa. 6:9,10; 30:9; 66:4) Sadly, Israel's refusal to hear God is a repeated theme in scripture. (Psa. 135:16,17; Jer.11:10; 13:10,11; Zech. 7:11-13) Phony claims of being the ones who honored the Law, Israel continued down the path of unbelief, which later moved them to kill Jesus.

Did Israel read the 'sign'?

'Languages' Is A History Lesson For Corinth

Having alluded to Jewish history, Paul drew a comparison between professing believers in Corinth and Israel. (14:21,22) Professing believers apparently had forgotten that before his captivity, Israel was also religious. They were as unaware of their immaturity, as was Israel. God had spoken through god-fearing Jewish prophets like Moses, Isaiah and Jeremiah. Might these professing believers ignore Apollos, Peter and Paul like the deaf professing law keepers of captive Israel? (10:1-11; 14:20,21; Jer. 7:1-8)

Were The Corinthians Speaking Assyrian?

Languages not spoken clearly or not understood was a reminder from Isaiah, that God would speak to Israel through a language that sounded to them like 'stammering lips', a language at the time of the prophecy was foreign to them. (Isa. 28:11) Paul's point is that if people are not understanding one another, they might as well be listening to the Assyrian of Isaiah's prophecy.

Languages Was A Sign Of God's Censure

Imposed languages for unbelieving monolingual Jews were a sign of judgment, not a blessing or a gift. Despite the censure, God's prophet, Ezra, interpreted and explained the scriptures to the people in Aramaic. The Corinthians, however, in their aimless eager desire to be heard, minimized the necessity of interpreting spiritual teachings. The Jews among them were unaware of God's languages censure.

The Sign Of 'Other Languages'

Unlike Pentecost, where languages were clearly understood, the Corinthian church failed to communicate the 'wonderful works of God'. Paul was showing them that the 'other' languages they had been speaking were a sign of God's displeasure with His people. From their captivity to their return under Nehemiah and Ezra, God had imposed foreign languages as a sign to unbelieving Jews. Paul reminded the Corinthian believers that Israel was judged by the imposition of **other** languages, through which most would lose Hebrew as their first language. Truth prophesied in languages, other than Hebrew, at Pentecost was not a good sign for belligerent Jewish unbelievers. Yet, God in His mercy continued to speak the gospel to Jews even in their adopted Gentile Aramaic and later Greek and Latin. With the prophesying in Gentile languages and Peter's Hebrew sermon, many Jews and proselytes would finally come to understand and believe the gospel, though most still remained in unbelief.

Why would Corinthian believers permit multiple languages in assembly, especially without interpretation, when historically, languages were a sign of rebellion? Mostly Jewish, the Corinthian church should have observed that God's prophecies were orally translated from the Hebrew into Aramaic. For unbelieving Israel, 'other' languages were a 'sign' of judgment, not a gift! (14:21,22)

WHEN THE SIGN OF LANGUAGES IS NO LONGER NEEDED.

Yet, through Gentiles' languages, His Word was clearly understood even when it was translated from Hebrew. (14:21,22) Despite centuries of prophesying to His people, through Jewish translators from the Hebrew into their acquired languages, they continued to disobey. God gave them these languages as a sign to point them back to the reason for it. Multiple languages were an easily observable indicator to the Jews of their national, historical belligerence. With the climactic demonstration of the prophesying of Cornelius and his household, God spoke through Gentiles to Jews in languages other than Hebrew in Israel. With the sign of multiple languages God censured the Jews for their unbelief, yet they would not only hear the gospel of salvation but would also hear it in the languages of their Gentile captors. But most did not read the sign.

SUMMARY:

Speaking a language not understood by the listeners made the Corinthians non-communicative just like the pagans of Assyria and Babylon were to the Jews when first taken captive. Immature use of languages in the assembly raised questions concerning their faith. So, Paul exhorts the church that languages are a sign to both unbelieving Jews and Gentiles among them, as it was to unbelieving Israel. (14:20-22)

The Corinthians didn't have the supposed 'sign gift' of languages any more than the Assyrians and Babylonians and Greeks. In fact, the Corinthian supposed 'sign gift' sounded more like the 'sign gift' of Babel. God had judged Israel's pride and rebellion with languages as He had judged man's pride at Babel with languages. Again, multiple languages was a sign of censure by God. It was not a gift.

The Hebrew Vernacular.

Up to the point that Israel had been taken captive, they had one common language - Hebrew. Required to speak in "other languages" in captivity, they lost the ability to communicate in the Hebrew vernacular they all knew. Yet, God graciously provided for His prophecies to be discovered in Aramaic, the common language of most Jews in Israel, and Greek, the common language in Corinth. (14:2,3,23,24)

God Was/Is Still Gracious

Though languages were an additional hurdle to understand His Word, God graciously continued to speak to His people. God proved Himself true to His Word by revealing His truth, as the Hebrew Scriptures were taught in the languages of the Diaspora. And, in the NT, it was primarily written in Aramaic and Greek.

How gracious God has been to all mankind, not only to the nation of Israel! He has not yet stopped speaking! He continues to call out His chosen people from among Jews and Gentiles in languages other than Hebrew.

'Sign Gift' Is A Misnomer

The notion of 'sign gift' is a misnomer. From our study to this point, there is no evidence to suggest that any language was spoken supernaturally. All languages spoken, were learned. Languages are not for a 'sign gift'; languages are for a sign. (14:22)

19. THE CHURCH BULLETIN

Both biblical and extra-biblical context serves to provide a better understanding of synagogue and church services in Corinth. Scholars agree that church services were initially modeled after the synagogue services, which originated during Israel's captivities.[121] Migrants returning to the Promised Land, recognized the leadership of Ezra, the priest and scribe. He led the people in organized worship by offering prayer and praise to God, reading the Law in Hebrew, translating and then explaining it to the people (Neh. 8:1-8; 1Cor. 14:21) Centuries later, the Jews were still experiencing "other languages" in their synagogue services. Long gone were the days when the civic and religious affairs of Israel were conducted in Hebrew alone. (14:21)

Yet, Hebrew remained the religious language of Judaism, still learned and spoken by devout Jews even after centuries of speaking 'other' languages. With the continuation of the synagogue system, biblical evidence shows that Jews were able to read the Hebrew Scriptures.

THE APOSTOLIC BIBLE

The utility and availability of Hebrew "Scripture" in the days of Christ and Paul enhances our understanding of how languages were used.

BIBLICAL EVIDENCE PRECLUDES TRANSLATIONS

Many think that Christ and the Apostles used a Greek translation.[122] Yet, 250 years after this translation, known as the Septuagint, was allegedly written, Jesus said that 'not one jot or tittle' would pass until all these were fulfilled. (Mt. 5:17,18)[123] Christ was referring to Scripture then in existence, not a supposed older Greek translation. Greek does not have 'jots' and 'tittles', so clearly Christ and his listeners must have had access to Hebrew manuscripts. Therefore, the Hebrew Scriptures could not have been inferior to any earlier Hebrew manuscripts from which the

---

[121] Merrill F. Unger, *Unger's Bible Dictionary*, Moody Press, Chicago, 1976 C, p. 1053

[122] Please see Septuagint in NOTES.

[123] Jesus spoke Hebrew with the woman at the well in Samaria. "The Samaritans preserved and spoke Hebrew, not Aramaic." – *An Introduction to Ancient and Modern Hebrew* c. 2010, by Al Garza, ThD., PhD. p. 17.

Septuagint was supposedly translated. Unaffected by time, even these small Hebrew Scripture letters with its 'jots and tittles' would not pass away. Jesus' own words indicate that His generation had the 'authorized' version of the Hebrew manuscripts and were using them, not a Greek translation. The 'newer' manuscripts were as good as the 'older'.

Scripture Is Not A Translation

A Greek or any translation of the Law and the Prophets is not 'Scripture' because it is initiated by the will of man, therefore cannot be inspired. Scripture is not a product of man's will. (2 Pe. 1:20,21; 2 Tim. 3:15,16) Timothy was taught from 'holy scripture'. The gospel promised beforehand was through the prophets in the Holy Scriptures. (Rom.1:2) Jesus read from "Scripture", the scroll. After having read the Scripture in Hebrew, He then sat down and explained it to them. (Lk. 4:18-21) There is a difference between copies transcribed from the autograph and a translation. The Holy Spirit moved men to write Holy Scripture not 'holy' translations.

Though multiple languages were spoken in Christ's day, the Hebrew Scripture remained central to Jewish religious life. The same Hebrew in the Law and Prophets, read each Sabbath in the synagogues, remained part of Christian bibliography in their gatherings. The Berean Jews searched the Scriptures not Targums or translations. (Ac.17:10,11)

None of the many references to 'Scripture' in the NT suggest or imply that the OT Scripture of their day was deficient. It is very important to emphasize that the Septuagint was not inspired; it was only a translation.[124] Their copy of the OT was as good as the one from which the Septuagint was allegedly translated.

'Have You Not Read?'

When Jesus addressed the scribes, Pharisees and Sadducees, He asked them if they had not read the 'Law', the 'Psalms' and 'Scripture.' (Mt.12:3,5; 19:4; 21:16,42; 22:31; Mk. 2:25; 12:10, 26) He would not have been asking these educated men of the Law and Prophets if they had read these things in a Greek translation. The Ethiopian was reading from

[124] Considerable controversy swirls around the authenticity and origin of the Septuagint, much of it driven by King James Onlyism. The Bible does NOT inform us that the prophecy came as holy men of God were moved to translate the original into the KJV. (2 Pe. 1:20,21) KJVO are guilty of the same charge they level against LXX, that of treating a translation as inspired by the Holy Spirit. More discussion on the Septuagint is found in the NOTES.

Scripture not a translation. (Ac. 8:28-32) Moses is read in the synagogues every Sabbath. (Ac. 15:21) Paul laments that even when Moses is read to the present day, a veil lies over their heart. (2 Cor. 3:13, 14) 'To the present day', implies that Moses was read from the time of Ezra, before the Septuagint is even supposed to have been written.

"It Is Written"

When Jesus declared 'it is written', He must have referred to existing exact copies written in Hebrew. Again, it is inconceivable that Jesus would be appealing to educated religious scribes of the day with quotations or citations from a very flawed Greek translation. He would have either quoted directly from the Hebrew or targummed His quotation orally into Aramaic. Undoubtedly, He referenced existing Hebrew Scripture, not a Greek translation. "It is written," means that He knew what the Hebrew autograph actually stated.

Writing to mostly Jewish Corinthian believers, Paul references the Scriptures with the words, 'it is written.' (1:19,31; 2:9; 3:19; 9:9; 10:7; 14:21; 15:45) By stating that Christ arose according to the Scriptures, Paul appealed to inspired authority of the prophets, not a biased translation. (15:3,4) Paul knew what the original said.

Argument From Silence

Had there been even one translation, it is certain there would have been recorded debate about its validity. English translators were martyred for their translation efforts. We can be sure that the scribes and Pharisees, who fussed about minor issues of the Sabbath, would certainly have something to say about an existing translation of Scripture!

Other Evidence Preclude Written Translations

Over time, diminishing familiarity with the Hebrew, however, necessitated the public reading of the Torah and the Prophets to be accompanied with a translation or paraphrase by the meturgeman (translator) This process was strictly governed. One paragraph from the Law would be read in Hebrew, then translated, three paragraphs from the Prophets, then translated. To avoid the perception that the meturgeman might be reading directly from the Law, copying and reading these targums (translations) was not permitted. It was not until the mid-second century A.D. that these Aramaic translations (targums) were written down.[125]

Therefore, the supposition that the Jews in Alexandria were using a Greek translation of the OT authorized by Jewish leadership in Jerusalem for synagogues in Alexandria before Christ, directly conflicts with Jewish practice. Strict rules governed the public communication of God's word from the Hebrew into Aramaic.

SUMMARY

The 'text' of both the synagogue and church was the sacred Scriptures. Since written translations of Scripture were not read in first century, synagogues or churches, it was necessary that it be orally translated after it was read.

SYNAGOGUE SERVICES

Because Scriptures were Hebrew, a "running translation into Aramaic", the common language of Israel, was required.[126] Though Ezra standardized an Aramaic script, the language remained Hebrew, like English and German have mostly the same alphabet, yet are completely different languages. Undoubtedly, from Ezra to Jesus' time, the Law and the Prophets used in the synagogue was written in the Hebrew. [127]

Scholars differ regarding the extent and familiarity of Latin, Greek Aramaic and Hebrew in Israel. Latin and Greek words and names were assimilated into Aramaic indicating a mixing of populations, but Aramaic remained the dominant language, with Greek as the minority. Though not prevalent for civic affairs, Hebrew certainly remained the language of rabbinical schools and the official language of Judaism. But, the ancient practice of orally translating Hebrew into Aramaic, was still required tradition for synagogues.[128]

Translation was left to qualified, designated 'meturgemen', (translators) who had also set up a guild. Some of these translators became Christians and it is believed that Paul references these in 1 Corinthians.

---

[125] Josh McDowell, *The New Evidence that Demands a Verdict*, Thomas Nelson Publishers, c.1999, p. 86,87

[126] Rev. William Fairweather, D.D., *The Background of The Epistles*, Published by T & T Clark, Edinburgh, 1935, P. 85

[127] John J. Parsons, *Did Jesus Speak Hebrew*, http://www.hebrew4christians.com/Articles/Jesus_Hebrew/jesus_hebrew.html

[128] Rev. William Fairweather, D.D., *The Background of The Epistles*, Published by T & T Clark, Edinburgh, 1935, P. 85, 110.

(14:28,29) [129] Copies of the Hebrew scriptures were confined to the synagogue, where the Jews came to hear them read, then translated into Aramaic, a process begun in the days of Ezra.

Elements Of The Synagogue Service

Ten men from those present at the meeting were appointed by the ruler of the synagogue each Sabbath to conduct the service. The messenger of the congregation read the prayers. There were seven readers of the Law. One read the prophets. When the Hebrew text was not understood by the congregation, a meturgeman was required. The preacher was also selected from the congregation. Over time these duties were assigned to one person. But in the time of Jesus and the Apostles, this change had not yet occurred. [130] [131]

The chief parts of the service were the recitation of the Shema, prayers, the reading of the Torah and the prophets, the blessing of the priest. After the blessing the sermon any adult Jew delivered the sermon. The service closed with a blessing.[132] (The Shema is an invitation for Israel to hear, quoted from De. 6:4-9; 11:13-21; Nu. 15:37-41.) The Scripture read in Hebrew, was orally translated into Aramaic, the common language of the Jews inherited from their Babylonian captivity.

THE CORINTHIAN WORSHIP SERVICE

From Paul's exhortation to the Corinthians we get a glimpse into the worship service and its similarity to the synagogue service.

Elements Of The Corinthian Service

The Corinthian church service consisted of time allotted for prayer. (14:13-16) At the rebuilding of the temple they sang praise from Scripture to God responsively. (Ezra 3:11; Psa. 136) This may be the singing with 'spirit' and 'mind' Paul referred to. Up to three were permitted to speak in their own language with an interpreter. (14:27,28) Two or three prophets (preachers who taught scripture) spoke as others analyzed the accuracy of what each one said, based on the Law and the Prophets. (Neh.

---

[129] E.H.Plumtre, Cassell, Petter & Galpin, *The Bible Educator*, London, Paris & NY, P.215

[130] *The Biblical World*, P.144, https://archive.org/stream/jstor-3140264/3140264#page/n1/mode/2up

[131] *Synagogue, Scripture and the Sermon*, Online: https://www.biblicaltraining.org/library/synagogue

[132] Merrill F. Unger, *Unger's Bible Dictionary*, Moody Press, Chicago, 1976 Cp. 1054

6:7; Zech. 1:4) (14:32; 15:3,4) Also, Paul's letter would be read to the congregation as the inspired word of God. (14:37; Col.4:16; 1Thess.5:27)

One other vital element of the service was the reading of scripture. Jesus read from the book of Isaiah, when He identified Himself as the fulfillment of prophecy. (Lk. 4:17) Jesus read from the Hebrew.

Paul inspires Greek rendition of OT Scripture with a translation of his own into the Greek. (1 Cor. 1:30-31; 2:9; 3:19; 9:9) He begins his quotation with the words, "it is written." With his knowledge of Hebrew, Paul authoritatively translated his quotation from the Hebrew manuscript into Greek. That they were not to think beyond that which 'is written' implies that they had access to the Hebrew writing. (4:6) The record of the wilderness idolatry of Israel is, "as it is written" and were "written for our admonition." (9:7,11)

Corinthian Church Bulletin:

The following is a suggested summary of the parts of the Corinthian service:

- Call to worship – perhaps the Shema (with translation?)
- Reading the Hebrew manuscript- standing. (ie. Ezra, Jesus,)
- Meturgeman translation into vernacular implied.
- Prayers
- Praise – responsive singing from the Psalms
- Maximum three discourses in minority languages.
- Three discourses translated into the vernacular (if necessary).
- Preachers/prophets: max. 3 each followed with critical analysis.
- Reading of Paul's letter.
- Closing blessing.

The number of persons required is eleven without interpreters, similar to the synagogue service.

Regulations For The Church Service

Whenever Paul preached in the synagogue, there was never any hint that the order or content of service was an issue.

How To Accommodate More Languages:

In addition to Hebrew, Aramaic and Latin there were also dialects that needed to be interpreted.[133] Doric, Aeolic, Arcadic, Attic and Iconic were dialects spoken in various parts of the Roman Empire. Paul instructed the

---

[133] *Collins English Dictionary*, Third Edition, 1991

Corinthians to permit 'other languages' but only when there was an interpreter present, since these languages might not be understood.

Everyone could not speak the various languages. (12:30) Paul even wishes that everyone could speak in languages, implying that many spoke only one, though they all understood Greek. (14:5) Secondly, only two or at the most three were permitted to speak, each in turn. Thirdly, if there was no interpreter, speaking 'a language' was not permitted. (14:27,28)

How Time Would Limit Translation In A Service.

But was one minority language translated into every other minority language? If at one service the specified maximum of three were allowed to speak in their native language ('a language'), each accompanied with qualified a translator for Greek, we would have a total of four languages. Allowing each of these three speakers ten minutes how much longer would the service be if it were expected that each sermon also be translated into the minority languages? To translate into just three minority languages would add one and a half hours to the service.

To wait for interpretations into numerous languages would only have exacerbated the inattention and disorder Paul wanted to avoid. Only one interpreter (singular) for any of these minority languages was required. If Paul had intended that each language be translated into the other two or three minority languages, then he would have required more than one interpreter. Paul does not say, 'if there are not interpreters. . .' 'Interpreter', being single, implies that each minority language be translated into one language, the vernacular which everyone understood. (14:27,28) Permission granted to speak other languages, therefore, was based on the condition that they would be translated into the Greek.

Guidelines For The Lord's Table

Paul needed to address the selfish behavior of some at the Lord's Supper.

Allowance For Reading Apostolic Letters

Among the converts in Corinth was the ruler of the synagogue, Crispus, who along with the others had a strong Jewish influence, which impacted the liturgy of the NT church.[134] The reading of the Law and the Prophets was one. (Ac.13:27) But there was one new addition to the

---

[134] *The Synagogue and Nazareth* – Synagogue Worship and Arrangements
http://www.ccel.org/ccel/edersheim/lifetimes.viii.x.html

content of service. Written in Koine Greek, Paul instructed the church to read his letters publicly as scripture. (Col.4:16; 1 Thes.5:27) This is especially significant because even written Targums had not yet been authorized to be read in the synagogues. Jewish believers would need to recognize that Paul's letters were to be read as the Word of God in the churches.

CONCLUSION

Since there is clear biblical evidence that Hebrew manuscripts were used in the synagogues, that Christ and the Apostles referenced Scripture, not written translations, no other conclusion can be drawn except that the Hebrew Scriptures were being orally read, quoted and translated in the churches. (2 Pe. 1:19-21) NT Greek quotations of the OT that appear similar to or the same as the LXX only show the reality that translators can independently arrive at the same interpretation.

Translation is necessary, but it is not Scripture, by definition. Translation is the necessary lens by which those who do not know Greek and Hebrew can look into the Scripture. Great care must be taken that these lens are not smudged with the translator's errant bias.

Paul's references to the Scriptures in his letter imply the necessity of interpretation in the services! Scripture is prophecy, the 'sure word of prophecy' to which translations have no claim. The language that was not "other" still needed to be interpreted for the purpose of knowing prophecy. (12:30; 13:2; 14:21)

Speaking languages in Corinth was already a reality and not a supernatural event. Though multiple languages were spoken, there was always a common language which most understood. The use of multiple languages in services was not unique to churches. But ecstatic speech and gibberish was completely foreign to both the cultures of Jewish/Christian worship. In short, there is no mystical context to languages and communication in the churches.

20. FAITH FOR A MIRACLE

Numbered with the twelve Apostles, Paul would have concurred with their teachings. The Apostle James, believed to have written the letter by that name, wrote to the Jews who were scattered abroad before 49 AD. Paul's first letter to the Corinthians was written about 55 AD. Having already been sent out to Jews in Gentile cities, it is certain that Paul was familiar with the book of James.

Since Paul would not have been opposed to any of James' teachings, it is curious that he never mentioned oil as a means of healing. Neither did Paul exhort believers to pray their way out of trouble into prosperity. Yet, it is believed that this is what James taught. (Jas. 5:13-15) However, upon a contextual, grammatical review of this passage, James' teaching may not be the answer most of us want, though it is certainly the answer all of us need.

FAITH IN SUFFERING

What did James teach on praying by faith for miracles?

JAMES' AUDIENCE

James writes to his Jewish brothers who are scattered throughout many countries. However, as in Paul's letters, James also does not assume his entire readership to be believers. Every genuine confession of faith is backed up by works. Faith unaccompanied by works is dead. After all, even the devil believes. (Jas. 2:17-19) He reprimands the wealthy for not paying their laborers according to their work and for fraudulently withholding payment agreed to. Caring only for earthly treasure, some were living for personal pleasures, even murdering the just. (5:1-6)

SUFFERING IN PATIENCE

James also writes to believers. At the beginning of his letter, he reminds them that hardships are used by God to produce patience and endurance. He encouraged believers to 'be patient until the coming of the Lord.' As the farmer must wait for the early and latter rains, so also must the Christian wait for his final relief from afflictions. He exhorts believers to establish their hearts, not their bodies. They were not to grumble against one another. The real Judge, standing at the door, can hear everything you say. (5:7-8)

Examples Of Suffering

James then holds up the prophets who spoke in the name of the Lord as examples of suffering and patience. Truly these are blessed, because they endured. He cites Job as an example of perseverance. Whether hardships are due to afflictions brought about by the loss of health, wealth or family, or by persecution, the solution is the same. He wanted them to strengthen their hearts, endure with patience and not grumble. (5:9-11)

Works Is Not Accomplished By An Oath

James says to let your 'yes' be 'yes' and your 'no' be 'no'. (5:12) It appears that some among them thought that if they said 'yes' or 'no' without an oath, they could change their minds. However, by his own example, Peter lied with an oath. (Matt. 26:69-75) It is just as easy to lie with an oath as it is to tell the truth. James exhorts them to dispense with the Jewish practice of swearing and oath.

How Should Believers Live?

James instructs the suffering to pray. However, despite the suffering of some, if anyone is cheerful, they should sing psalms. (5:13)

Overwhelming Fatigue

He asked them if any one among them was 'sick'. (asthenei, which means ill or weak; 5:14) Paul uses this same word when writing to Timothy to refer to hardships and afflictions, not illness. (2 Tim. 2:9; 4:5) The other word translated as 'sick' is '*kamnonta*' and is used in only one other place in the NT. (5:15) This word also means 'weary' and is translated 'weary' in Hebrews 12:3. Overwhelmed with hardships some had become weak. James was concerned that they strengthen their hearts. (5:8) Persecution, in some places, had left some physically, mentally and spiritually exhausted, so he advised them to call upon the elders.

The Older Men's Hospitality

When these older believers arrived at the home of the afflicted, they were to anoint them with oil and pray for them.

Anointing of Oil

Some suggest that the anointing of oil was for the purpose of medicine. But the Apostle would not know what medicine to apply in every case. For Timothy Paul specifically prescribed a little wine for his stomach's sake.

The Samaritan applied both oil and wine for open wounds. (Lk. 10:33,34) So, it doesn't make sense that James' intent was medicinal. Oil was also used for consecration and coronation, which clearly was not the intent here either. Since the context seems to preclude both a ceremonial and medicinal application, what then did the oils represent?

The word for 'anoint' used here is <u>not</u> '*chrio*', which is ceremonial, signifying consecration. (Ac. 10:38) The word for anoint used is *aleipho*, which was more than just a dab. Oil was a staple cosmetic in Israel. Jesus censured the Pharisees for their hypocritical attempts at looking 'spiritual' by appearing in public without oil. (Matt. 6:16,17)

Luke's narrative about Christ's visit with Simon discloses what the expected etiquette was. (Lk. 7:45,46) Mary had brought oil with her and anointed Jesus with a pound of ointment, yet, as a guest of Simon's, Jesus was not even afforded the usual greeting of a kiss and anointing of oil.

Daily routines would include the application of oil to the skin when visiting others. (Ruth 3:3) It was an expression of joy. (Psa. 23:5) The righteous ones are anointed with the oil of joy. (Psa. 45:7; Heb.1:9) However, unpleasant circumstances caused some to abstain from using oil. Refraining from the use of oil indicated grief. Mourners would not use oil. (2 Sam. 14:2; Da. 10:3)

Familiar with his culture, James anticipated the neglect of the daily application of oil because of weariness, exhaustion and grief. So he instructs the older believers to anoint with oil, a symbol of gladness. (Isa. 61:3) Of course, the oil could not give joy, but as a symbols of joy, conveyed to the troubled recipient that this was the expected outcome. Oil does not represent the Holy Spirit.

The Afflicted One Is Called Upon To Pray

These older men of the church were called to pray about the matter ('over' does not mean hover) 'having anointed' him in the name of the Lord. There is no laying on of hands.

Note that it says that the 'prayer of faith will save the weary.' (Jas. 5:15) The singular 'prayer' means that at some point it is expected that the person who needed the help would personally call upon God as is specifically stated in James 5:13.

Pray In Faith

By faith it is meant that their circumstances, were recognized to be under the sovereign control of God and might not change. By faith, it is also implied that He alone could forgive sins and restore one's heart immediately. So the personal prayer of faith for forgiveness of his sins will raise him up, that is restore to him the gladness he once knew. If he had sinned by denying Christ or grumbling, they would be forgiven him and in this way preserved. (saved)

Many had been so overwhelmed with the trials of the day that they were no longer cheerful. (1:2, 3) James instruction to pray indicates that the purpose of their prayer was to gain contentment and cheerfulness, not healing of a physical sickness. (5:13) Healthy people also complain. Thayer's lexicon explains that He 'will cause him to recover.'

PRAY FOR STRENGTH

The answer to the prayers of the elders may not be immediate, but these prayers were enjoined to encourage the subject that the Lord will bring about His deliverance in due time. (5:14) This was not an exercise in signs and wonders of healing gifts. To raise them up does not imply that the persecution or affliction would go away. But James' concern was that their hearts be strengthened, not their bodies. (5:8) His concern was that their weariness would be replaced with an ability to 'count it all joy when they would fall into various trials.' (1:2) Despite their continuing affliction, the Lord would raise him up in the affliction not out of the affliction.

What is the meaning of the word 'healed' in verse 16? Various scripture use this word to describe spiritual restoration. (Matt. 13:15; Jn. 12:40; Ac. 28:27) The confession of sins does not heal the body but it will invariably heal the heart. It will strengthen the heart.

"The effective, fervent prayer of a righteous man avails much." is not correctly translated (Jas. 5:16b) Rather, 'the prevailing petitions of one just man are working'. The sense is that our persistent petitions to God may not appear to have an impact, but they do. Trials do linger, but God has designed them to provide us impetus to continually petition Him for persevering strength and joy even as trials persist.

PRAYERS OF ELIJAH

Elijah, a prophet who also suffered affliction, is set forth as an example of prayer in afflictions. He was in the place of prayer that is, "before the Lord" even as he was speaking with Ahab. Note that Elijah stated, "before whom I stand", not 'before whom I stood'. (1 Kg. 17:1) This prophet actually announced to King Ahab while standing before the Lord, his prayer for drought! Ahab, of course, only saw Elijah and did not discern Elijah standing before the Lord. This is the background to James' reference to this Prophet. (5:16-18)

The word *proseuche* is defined as 'prayer' or a 'place of prayer'. It does not mean fervent. (Jas. 5:17) Elijah was not repeatedly begging God to send drought. Though he also saw himself as a sinner, he had a righteous standing before God, therefore, knew exactly what to ask for. He was standing in the presence of the Lord.

Elijah's prayer of faith was not to have a good time. Nothing in his communication when he first 'prayed' for rain to stop gave him a clue as to how God would provide for him. God revealed His provisions for Elijah as time went on. His faith was such that he could pray for a negative petition though it would also impact his own life. Being a man of like passions as the believers James was writing to, Elijah would not have enjoyed the prospect of having to find food to eat. Though this trial was not a consequence of God's displeasure with Elijah, he would also experience it. He accepted it without complaint.

Elijah prayed in trials and for trials without grumbling. The airborne food caterers God had prepared for him was all he needed, but for some to whom James was writing, this would be reason for grumbling. Who would want to eat food delivered by ravens? Elijah's prayer for the rain to stop contained no petition for food. He did not know when God would end the drought, but he was faithful to Him during that time. God orchestrated the beginning of trials through the prayer of Elijah and He also conducted the end of the trial of drought by the prayer of His Prophet. James uses this OT example to show that God 'raises up' His people up, without removing trials. A true faith does not remove the trial.

King Ahab had done more than any of the other kings before him to provoke the Lord with the worship of Baal. (1 Kg. 16:32,33) Near the end of the drought, Elijah initiated a contest with the prophets of Baal. Having won the contest, he commanded them to be killed. Again, God told Elijah to go to Ahab to tell him that He would send rain on the face of the earth, before Elijah had prayed. (1 Kg. 18:1) James tells us that Elijah prayed that it might not rain, but the second time he prayed, it does not say that he had prayed for the rain to start. It says only that he prayed again and the sky poured rain. James was referring to Elijah's prayer that fire would consume the wood and offering. He didn't have to pray for the rain because that had already been told to him earlier. But Elijah did pray that the people assembled at an intentionally drenched altar would know that He is Lord. (1 Kg. 18:37,38)

But when Jezebel found out about the elimination of her prophets, she vowed to find Elijah and kill him by the same time the next day. The rains had come but the hardship remained. Now fleeing for his life, the burdened prophet was so discouraged that he prayed for the Lord to take his life. But God did not leave him; He came to him and restored him, though He didn't remove Jezebel. Even this highly regarded Jewish prophet was not above the normal human emotions of sorrow and fear. He also prayed!

PRAYER OF FAITH

From James' instruction and the example of Elijah, he presents key features of the prayers of faith.

- Prayers of faith are to one Person only – the God of the Bible.
- Prayers of faith begin with confession of sin. Being a righteous man, Elijah knew himself to be a sinner and acknowledged it before God.
- Prayers of faith exclude fleshly appetites.
- Prayers of faith submit to the sovereignty of God.
- Prayers of faith are not demanding.
- Prayers of faith do not grumble.
- Prayers of faith expect to be delivered from despair.
- Prayers of faith expect God to strengthen the heart.
- Prayers of faith expect God to bring victory over sin.
- Prayers of faith are in accord with His will.
- Prayers of faith are based on His word, not personal opinion.
- Prayers of faith expect that God will give joy in due time.

The prayer of a righteous man in a right standing before God is operative in all circumstances of life. But the words and context of James have nothing to do with an expectation of health and wealth. If it were, there would be no need for patience or for hearts to be strengthened. (5:8) The believer's prayer of faith is a reality despite remaining physical illness and other calamities. Answered prayer is not measured by physical healings or financial gains.

CLOSING OBSERVATIONS

Indeed, there are anomalies where God coincides the prayers of the needs of believers with His eternal plan. (Rom.8:28) God does direct the prayers of His people as a means of accomplishing His will. Prayer is one of the means by which the believer participates in the Sovereign plans and works of God. If God is truly Sovereign, the prayers of His people in prosperity and distress are also under His control.

Should we not expect to receive a supernatural miracle? But when one is cheered in the midst of severe trial, how could that not be a supernatural miracle? By comparison, to be made cheerful by supplying all physical needs and removing persecution, is not a supernatural miracle.

THE MIRACLE CREDIBILITY GAP

Confronted with stunning claims of healings, speaking unlearned languages, visions and other supposed phenomena, many people including believers, are inclined to believe them without question. How should the believer evaluate these claims?

MIRACLE TESTIMONIES ARE UNIVERSAL

Even conservative Reformed believers testify that believers have been healed of various maladies after laying on of hands, prayer and anointing of oil. There are no shortages of testimonies healing rituals. In addition to professing evangelicals, Catholics, Mormons and other cults all claim healings.[135] 'Evangelicals' do not have a monopoly on supposed 'healings'.

DISCERNMENT

Neither do 'evangelicals', so-called, have a monopoly on credibility. Their stories are not any more believable than the stories of non-evangelicals. From advertisements for merchandise to politics to religion, man is constantly bombarded with calls to 'believe' something. What 'better' way is there to gain adherents to any movement than the prospect of health and wealth? Having adopted similar tactics, Simon Magnus type 'evangelicals' have also become professional financiers and healers.

CREDIBLE TESTIMONIES

A biblically credible testimony includes a confession of sin, a repenting of sin, and an abiding faith in Christ alone for salvation from his sin. Additional claims to having experienced a supernatural miracle of physical or financial recovery proves nothing. Credible testimonies do not brag of

---

[135] Archangel Raphael, *Holy Healing Ministry*. http://www.straphaeloil.com/testimonies/

great exploits for God but rather express how God has enabled them to accept their hardships in life.

WHAT ARE WE REQUIRED TO BELIEVE?

There is no biblical requirement to believe testimonies of 'healing' and wealth or dreams and visions. Everyone is commanded to believe on the Lord Jesus Christ for salvation. (Ac.16:31) We are to believe the Scriptures, which record the miracles of the Prophets and Apostles as well as Christ. (Jn. 5:46-47)

James does give us one thing that we can believe about one another. James advice is to confess our sins one to another. That is what we confess. These testimonies we can believe.

WHAT WAS JESUS' ADVICE CONCERNING THE SUPERNATURAL?

When Jesus healed a leper, He instructed Him to show himself only to the priest so that he would no longer need to be quarantined. (Matt. 8:4) This man disobeyed, distracting the crowds from the message to the healing. (Mk. 1:44,45) Jesus raised Talitha and commanded that no one else was to be told about it. (Mk. 5:42,43) Jesus commanded the deaf man He had healed not to tell anyone. (Mk. 7:36) Jesus raised Jairus' daughter from the dead but instructed that this not be told. (Matt. 9:26; Lk. 8:56)

It is clear that even when Jesus performed real supernatural healings, He did not want people to talk about it because they would seek Him out for the wrong reason. They wanted His miracles but not His message of repentance. Why should we think that these guidelines no longer apply? Books written on 'miracle' experiences are in violation of Jesus' own words.

ANSWERS TO PRAYER

But God does answer prayer! Unusual events <u>do occur</u> as an answer to prayer and unusual events <u>do not occur</u> also in answer to prayer. In situations where it appears that an extraordinary medical remedy occurred in answer to prayer, it is best to give thanks for God's provision. Thank God together with the circle of friends who walked through the valley with you. But be certain of this, that our prayers do not give permission to God for Him to get involved in our lives as some extreme charismatics teach. God is Sovereign and He will not permit any answer to prayer contrary to His will! In other words, people will continue to suffer bodily infirmities, despite prayers of faith.

Where are those who have been 'healed' of stage four cancer, whose main desire is to talk about God's substitutionary death on the cross, forgiveness of sins, and expectations of His coming, how God is bringing people to Himself and growing His people even in the most severe trials? Even when our prayers for health improvement are answered, with the services of a medical doctor, our praise and thanks ultimately should go to God, because He arranged that too.

Graciously, God does answer the prayers of His people in ways that cannot be explained. God continues to be involved in the concerns of His people by occasionally providing physical needs in unusual ways. Remissions of disease and other internal remedies have indeed occurred after prayer, but these cannot be assigned the category of supernatural miracle. We are inclined to see the mountain top experience as 'miraculous', forgetting that God's invisible delivering hand of grace had also been 'miraculously' sustaining us in the valley.

Share stories of how God has answered prayers for the salvation of friends and relatives, of struggles in the battle against sin, of how much God has shown his love to us in the day to day affairs of life. Testify of how God has saved us from sin, how He has brought us to repentance. These are the healings about which we should boast. The miracles we are required to believe are recorded for us the Bible. But the supernatural occurrence that thrills our souls and surpasses every event on earth ever, is Christ rising from the dead!

SUMMARY

Certainly, every believer has held views, later found to be errant. Many who attend charismatic churches, do not endorse aspects of charismatic teaching and many have left. If you have been attached to this movement, I pray that you would be reminded that God's Word alone governs right thinking and delivers anyone from the emotional upheavals that bad teaching engenders. Christ did real miracles, yet, in the end everyone left Him! Miracles do not make disciples.

This is also an appeal to otherwise doctrinally sound continuationists who in some measure believe, as do the charismatics that supernatural 'gifts' continue to this day. They are complicit with the charismatic enterprise as a whole and are part of the problem. Though less extreme they have contributed to the credibility of the charismatic heresy.

What Is An Example Of Answered Prayer?

Thankfully there are countless genuine testimonies of true believers who in the midst of extraordinary hardship have demonstrated a 'supernatural' faith in God. The subjects of the following example have prayed for strength and endurance in times of extreme difficulty.

MIRACULOUS STORY THAT CAN BE VERIFIED AND NOT BORING!

Only God knows the countless examples of how the ability gifts of the Holy Spirit have been exercised by many believers to profit for all eternity, for God's glory. The Holy Spirit has worked and developed His ability gifts in the lives of two prominent believers, Ken Tada and his wife Joni Eareckson Tada. Gifted in various ways, Joni used her gift of 'miracles' (strength) to deal with the plight of unbearable physical handicaps and life threatening sickness, not to mention incessant pain. Her husband Ken, has served her with his gift of helps. Despite periodic discouragement, he also demonstrates his love for God and Joni, by consistently attending to her demanding needs, both physical and emotional. Together they have encouraged countless in the gospel with yet another ability gift: prophecy. They would be the first to admit that others have served them also with varied abilities. But few of us are called to go through such extended, unending periods of exhausting trial, so I marvel at how God has sustained them. It is beyond astonishing that the strength (miracle) of God is made most evident in the midst of such crushing weakness! It is so very gratifying to hear their testimonies because they always give loving glory to God! They love Christ! And God's profit principle at work in their lives is obvious.

I suggest the reader listen to 'Joni and Ken' on line – An Untold Love Story and other sites like it.

21. 'ECSTATIC UTTERANCE' DECEPTIONS

Following is a summary and review of a few Bible words from which Pentecostalism and even cessationists draws false inferences.

WRONGLY INFERRED FROM 'SIGNS AND WONDERS'

The Bible does not imply that 'signs and wonders' are gifts of miracles. (P. 118-120) Signs and wonders is something God does independent from a personal ability. Gifts were/are distributed by the Holy Spirit to everyone and is not supernatural. However, signs and wonders are supernatural and were primarily performed by the Apostles to lend credibility to the Gospel message. (Ac. 2:43 ;5:12) There are no signs and wonders performed today.

WRONGLY INFERRED FROM THE WORD 'KIND'

Paul states that some have been given 'kinds' of languages. (14:10) Kind *(genos)* must refer by definition and context to real spoken human language. Paul has in mind a language already existing from another country or race. Jesus uses *genos* to describe different sorts of fish caught in one net. (Matt.13:47) But they were all fish. The 'kinds' of languages to which Paul refers were all human languages and recognized as such. Ecstatic utterance is not a "kind" of anything close to being a language.

WRONGLY INFERRED FROM THE WORD 'TONGUE' [136]

It is supposed by some non-charismatic conservative commentators that because 'tongue' is singular that Paul was addressing the drift of ecstatic utterances from pagan worship into the church. (14:2,4, 13, 14) This is not tenable for a couple of reasons. First, 'glossa' means physical organ of the human body, or language, plural or otherwise, not gibberish. Second, if this had been going on in the public gathering of the church, Paul would have dealt with it like Moses did the idolatry of Israel in the wilderness. (10:6-11) Imperatives against mimicking idolatrous worship

---

[136] Charismatics derive some of their support for their ecstatic utterances from 'unknown tongue' in KJV. It should be emphasized that 'unknown' is italicized in every case, indicating that the word does not appear in the original. (14:2,4,13,14,19,27) Let's be clear that if we are to understand from the context a language as 'unknown', it is because the language was certainly understood by the speaker, but not by the listener.

are not mentioned at all. Rather, he instructs the church how the use of actual language(s) should function within the church.

It is proposed by Cessationists that the singular for 'tongue' in 14:2 is used because that's the only way gibberish can be expressed. This reasoning isn't plausible because it eliminates the usage of the singular form to refer to one normal language. Paul wishes that all could speak in languages. If someone then spoke in 'a language', it was real, not gibberish. (14:5,26,39)

Wrongly Inferred From The Word 'Spirit'. (14:2)

Paul's use of the word 'spirit' is never depicted as an unconscious or mystical function. Paul presents the spirit of man as having the capacity to know, just as the Holy Spirit knows the thoughts of God. (1 Cor. 2:11,12) Being the repository of knowledge, man's spirit may be informed by the Holy Spirit, who knows and communicates the thoughts of God with the words of God, revealed in the Scriptures. When man hears the Scriptures read, preached or when man reads the written word of God, his spirit is educated with the words of an existing human language.

The Holy Spirit bears witness to man's spirit of man that he is a child of God. Based on the knowledge that he has been saved and sanctified, the spirit of man testifies of his personal faith in Christ and walk with the Lord, according to the Scriptures. (Rom.8:16) When the Samaritan woman learned who Jesus was and who she was, her spirit was informed to be able to worship Him in spirit and in truth. (Jn. 4:24)

From the spirit, we communicate with God as we give thanks in our prayers. And, from the spirit, man is also able to bless one another with the truth. (14:16,17) It is impossible for God to be honored with irrational garble. The Bible does not provide any support for the notion that God communicates to the spirit of man with gibberish or even an unlearned language that needs interpretation. Having the mind of Christ, believers do not attribute hypnotic behavior, meaningless gibberish, erratic utterances or babble to a word from the Holy Spirit, to man's spirit.

Wrongly Inferred From The Word 'Baptism'

Jesus instructed His disciples to wait in Jerusalem where they would be 'baptized' with the Holy Spirit. As stated in earlier chapters, Peter's quote from the Prophet Joel at Pentecost, indicates that baptism means the 'pouring out' of something in possession of the Holy Spirit. As the events of Pentecost unfolded it is obvious that the Spirit gave His disciples an immanent, unified understanding of OT knowledge that Jesus was indeed the prophesied Messiah. The Spirit baptized them with information!

The power the disciples received at Pentecost was evidenced by their boldness to break with the tradition, by interrupting the service, by speaking in the languages they were most familiar with, and by witnessing to the reality of the most important historical events in human history – the death and resurrection of Christ. (Ac. 1:8) They got the 'power' according to God's sovereign plan. They did not ask for it.

Has this 'power' been replicated since? When was the last time a group of more than a hundred believers sitting in a large Roman Catholic service hearing the Scriptures in Latin, suddenly started joyfully speaking in their own languages about the glories of Christ's great salvation by faith alone, not by works? Or, when was the last time a hundred true believers instantaneously interrupted a large international 'Christian' ecumenical conference by just getting up out of their seats to rejoice with one another in how God in mercy had sent Jesus to die for their sins to save them from eternal torment?

Wrongly Inferred From The Word 'Filling'

Without evidence continuationists infer that the 'filling' of the Holy Spirit caused people to speak in languages they had not learned.[137] To be filled with the Holy Spirit is to be filled with His knowledge. Paul exhorted the Ephesians to keep on being filled by[138] the Holy Spirit, not to be drunk with wine. (Eph. 5:18) Wine inhibits the Holy Spirit's work of informing the believer's spirit. At Pentecost, believer' delighted in being informed by the Holy Spirit about the person and work of the Christ.

Wrongly Inferred From The Word 'Revelation'.

Paul explains that he who thinks himself to be a prophet or spiritual is not to be recognized, unless they do two things. They must speak the commandments of the Lord and they must agree with Paul's writing. (1 Cor.14:36-38; 2 Thes.3:14) This precludes charismatic assertions that 'the Lord told me,' or any claim to have received a 'special word of knowledge or wisdom'. Paul specifically declared that anyone could not initiate new

---

[137] Wayne Grudem, *Baptism and Filling with the Holy Spirit*, P. 19 http://storage.cloversites.com/valleybrookcommunitychurch/documents/Baptism%20in%20and%20Filling%20with%20the%20Holy%20Spirit%20(Grudem).pdf

[138] 'With' should be translated 'by'. (Eph. 5:18) Already indwelt by the Holy Spirit, every believer has all of the Holy Spirit he needs. However, he needs to be informed by the Holy Spirit.

revelations or new prophecies. These 'prophets' did not have the so-called 'revelatory' gift. Other scripture clearly indicates that Paul received revelation directly from the Lord. (2 Cor. 12:1,7; Ga.1:12; 2:2; Eph.3:3) However, the only way the Corinthian believers could claim a 'revelation' was by disclosing truth already given in the Scripture, or apostolic teaching. (14:37) As discussed earlier, primary revelation came directly from the Lord <u>to</u> the Apostles and Prophets; secondary revelation came from the Lord through the writings of the Apostles and Prophets.

No one since the Apostles can claim they have heard from the Lord.

WRONGLY INFERRED FROM THE WORD 'MYSTERY'

Mystery simply means secret. 'Mystery' is information that can be made known a through language that is understood. Once known, it is no longer a mystery. So, one who speaks information in a language not understood by the hearers speaks only to God. Note that the word is 'speaks', not mumble, not babble, not bark, not laugh, not gibberish.

Paul writes, "For what man knows the things of a man, except the spirit of man which is in him? No one knows the things of God except the Spirit of God." (2:11) God had not revealed His thoughts in gibberish. He has articulated them with a known language, so that they are understood. Paul wants the church to consider him as a steward of the mysteries of God. (4:1) Did Paul write 'gibberish'? Yet, the charismatic teaches that God speaks His mysteries in gibberish to people.

WRONGLY INFERRED FROM THE WORD 'UNFRUITFUL'.

Paul's use of the word 'spirit' and 'mind' (understanding) is distorted to teach that when praying to God with 'tongues', the spirit energizes the prayer, but because he doesn't understand anything his mind is unfruitful. [139] (14:12-17) This completely ignores the context.

The one who prays in a language certainly understands what he is praying but his mind remains unfruitful because his hearers do not understand. Personal comprehension of the prayer when he 'blesses with the spirit' is still reality. The presence of mind, coherent thought, ability to perceive, judge and determine has not been compromised in any way. (14:13-17) Unlike the Pentecostalism's ecstatic utterances and gibberish, the unfruitful prayer can be interpreted. When the knowledge of one's

---

[139] *Vine's Expository Dictionary* defines mind (nous) generally as "the seat of reflective consciousness, comprising of the faculties of perception and understanding, and those of feeling, judging and determining."

spirit is communicated with one language into 'the understanding' of the hearers also, they are informed the mind is no longer unfruitful. (14:11,13, 15, 16)

Charismatics and continuationists distort this to be a 'prayer language' where the mind is believed to be disengaged. But the 'mind', in Paul's context is capable of rational thought and communication. 'Fruitfulness' of the mind is gauged by the ability of people to understand. (14:28) Paul's own words sum up what it means to pray. Silent or oral, prayer is real conscious thought expressed to God. "But if there is no interpreter, let him keep silent in the church, and let him speak to himself and to God." (14:28, NKJV)

'A language' is translatable; gibberish is not. (14:13)

Wrongly Inferred From The Word 'Edify'.

It is contended that Paul had nothing against self-edification. (14:3) Some had yet to learn to curb childish, fleshly impulses to speak, caring little that they were understood. (14:20) Some had become preoccupied with their own abilities, having become puffed up and rude. (13:4,5; 14:12-14, 20) Studying scripture and praying in words of a learned language are biblical means of 'self-edification'. Gibberish is not.

Summary:

It is alarming how various distortions have even rendered conservative believers spellbound, afraid to speak up to oppose self-centered doctrines lest they be charged for causing division in the body. Quite the opposite, unity among believers is only achieved, when we agree on the meaning of Bible words. Though bold and joyful at Pentecost or rude and disorderly at Corinth, there is no hint that anyone was mesmerized with a 'prayer language', by gibberish or even by speaking an unlearned language. As immature as the Corinthians were, no one was performing ecstatic utterance routines. Paul exhorted them to be mature and walk like adults.

All languages spoken were humanly understandable. Where a language might not be understood in church, it was to be translated into the vernacular. Ecstatic utterances are not fruitful.

22. CHARISMATIC CARNALITY

Drawn to a variety of health and prosperity miracle claims, many people have made charlatans wealthy, while they remain sick. To add to the deceit, these preachers mesmerize their Christianized audience with a flash focus on Christ, making their story time healing testimony tactics accepted without question. This charismatic side-show detracts from the supernatural power that it took for Christ to retrieve one sinful, wicked soul from the gates of hell. Regrettably, Continuationists have assisted the Charismatic calamity, as some of the following aspects will show.

Charismatics Are Selective About The Miracle's Difficulty

They are highly selective in their choice of how difficult their 'miracle' will be. If their miracles were genuine, they would go to where the people are sick rather than draw the sick to their crusades.

Charismatics Are Selective Of The Kind Of Miracle It Will Be.

Charismatics claim various signs and wonders for themselves as gifts, yet, avoid the judgment of sin as in the death of Ananias and Sapphira for lying to the Holy Spirit. (Ac. 5:1-11) They boast about healings and miracles but have no interest in signs and wonders that might show what God's attitude toward the sin of deceit is.

Charismatic Behavior Is Not Limited To Christianity.

Various cults and religions claim to have the ability to speak in 'tongues' and heal. That these are practices done in the name of Christ is nothing more than a Satanic ploy to distract and deceive.

Cults Like Mormons And Catholics Also Claim Healings.

A boy is said to have been healed after nuns pray for him.
http://www.nydailynews.com/news/national/vatican-confirms-colorado-boy-healed-thanks-miracle-article-1.1318597

Charismatics Emphasize The Spectacular.

Simon was amazed at the miracles of the apostles. Wanting that same 'magic' power, he was willing to pay for it. Are we like the 'Simons' who are easily impressed with the visibly 'supernatural' caring little or nothing for the gospel message? (Ac. 8:9-24) Multitudes saw Jesus feed 5000 plus with five loaves and two fish. They 'believed' until they heard His doctrine. Man loves the miracles if he doesn't have to know the truth about himself and God.

Charismatics Feign The Spectacular

It has been repeatedly shown that the charismatic 'healings' and 'tongues' are not real. Some have even used various electronic transmission devices to secretly learn a person's history in order to gain credibility for a 'word of prophecy' in 'healing' meetings.

Charismatics Devalue The Unspectacular.

Another distracting aspect of stories of people who have 'heard' the gospel in spectacular ways is that it diminishes the less 'spectacular' experiences of 'ordinary' people who have come to a true faith in Christ without these stunning events. After all, who wants to hear a 'boring' testimony?

Charismatics Disobey Scripture.

Christ instructs His disciples not to believe others who come with signs and wonders. (Matt. 24:23-26)

Charismatics Add To Scripture.

Invariably, they testify that the 'Lord told me'. The Lord told them nothing that is not available for all to read in the Scriptures. This is easily countered by replying with the words, 'God also told me something' – 'I can show you in the Bible what He told me!' God bore witness by the apostles through the working of signs and wonders and various miracles. (These were not gifts of the Holy Spirit.) (Ac. 2:3,4, 43; 2 Cor. 12:12) God told the Apostles and Prophets what to say and write.

Charismatics Claim A Higher Level Of Christian Experience.

At Pentecost, no person performed a miracle and no one spoke in unlearned languages. All believers spoke about Jesus and exalted Him! The truth about Christ was prophesied; people understood the gospel and many were saved. None among the 3000 saved, claimed a 'healing' experience or spoke in unlearned languages, yet charismatics erroneously make their mystic experiences the standard for the filling of the Spirit.

Charismatic Performances Cannot Be Verified.

Healings in the Bible were verifiable. Everyone knew who the blind man and the lame man were. People knew that Lazarus was dead. Even the skeptical, hostile Pharisees acknowledged that Jesus' healing was real, yet, complained that He was doing it on the Sabbath. Credible documented evidence of the supernatural had been given to us by appointed Apostles and Prophets, which charismatics cannot produce.

THE CHARISMATIC MIRACLE MESSAGE IS DEPRESSING.

Many are persecuted for their faith in our Lord without any relief, suffering poverty, and even torture and finally death. Now, how does telling these suffering saints about how people have been allegedly delivered from sickness, calamity and hardship through miracles, help? While hearing of others who were prayed for and supposedly 'healed', other victims hang onto a false hope. This only adds to the misery.

THE CHARISMATIC MIRACLE MESSAGE IS NOT CREDIBLE.

Must the sick accept the many testimonies of those who claim to have been healed of some cancer or other malady without question? Jesus Himself warned of many wolves dressed in sheep's clothing. Unfortunately, Christians hear some Bible words and without any due diligence accept what they hear. Let's be like the Bereans.

CHARISMATIC 'FAITH' AND PRACTICE INSULTS THE HOLY SPIRIT

The very words that the Holy Spirit wrote down for our salvation and sanctification are twisted into rights to a happy life on this earth, thus making the Holy Spirit a liar. Furthermore, ungodly behavior attributed to the Holy Spirit really assigns the work of the flesh to the Spirit.

CHARISMATIC CLAIMS TO PROPHECY ARE PERSONAL OPINIONS.

They have extracted the word 'prophecy' from its biblical context and redefined it. Similar to their view of 'word of knowledge', to them this gift permits them to predict or sense another's need. They have applied the word subjectively when in the scripture it is used objectively. There is no record where even the Apostles went around sensing people's needs, then prayed for them. 'Agabus' is erroneously considered a support for continuationist thinking. Please see Agabus in Notes.

Charismatics invoke the Lord's name, 'The Lord told me'. Non-charismatics join them with words like 'the Lord prompted me.' Though such claims of divine authorization or a divine experience are subjective, they are rarely challenged.

What did the Apostle James say? Believers were not told to say, 'The Lord told me to go to that city and stay a year.' He did not advise them to say that the Lord prompted me to go into business. He states plainly that we ought to say 'the Lord willing we will go there or do this or that.' (Jas. 4:13-16) For believers then to claim that the Lord told them to do something is arrogance according to James.

Charismatics Divert The Focus Away From God's Word.

Citing Agabus, the 'prophet', even continuationists along with charismatics teach that believers can prophesy with less than 100% accuracy. The Corinthian prophets' 'revelation that is made' is not by the Holy Spirit; it is by the preacher, therefore not authoritative. (1 Cor. 14:29, 30, 37) Paul exhorts the Corinthian 'prophets' that they could not declare that what they said was the Word of God apart from what was Scriptural. It was on that basis they evaluated each other.

Charismatic Propaganda

Much has been written alleging supernatural miracles, dreams and visions. *The Case For Miracles*, by Lee Strobel, is one of many authors who rehearses testimonies by many who believe that they've experienced a miracle of healing or had a vision for God's guidance.

Bible Miracles Are Supernatural

Lee Strobel's 'miracle' stories are not believable for the following reasons,

- It is impossible to verify these healing stories.
- Benevolent 'miracles' happen to heretics like Mormons, Mystics Charismatics and Roman Catholics, just to name a few.
- No distinction is made between prayers of unbelievers and prayers of believers. Catholics pray to Mary and other 'saints'.
- Strobel equates the miracles of Jesus with charismatic healings of today.
- Scripture is rarely applied and when it is referenced, it is out of context and misinterpreted.
- The 'miracle' stories are contradictory.

Some of the physical recoveries, touted as 'miracles' were medical anomalies, misdiagnosis or misrepresented.

The miracles that Christ and the Apostles performed were supernatural. When Jesus commanded both the wind and the sea to 'be still', natural law was suspended. Even a recovery from what is believed to be a terminal illness, is not a supernatural miracle when compared to miracles in the Bible. In God's providence, He continues to work His ways by natural means, sometimes using medics.

Visions And Dreams

Strobel rehearses accounts of people who claimed to have visions of Jesus. A professing converted Muslim, Nabeel, said that he had dreamt a parable from scripture that he had not previously read. (p. 140-141) But, what was not stated is Islamic tradition describes heaven as having eight doors. The dreams of everyone including Muslims, are affected by what they have already been taught.

Strobel alleges, without proof, that thousands of Muslims are being saved through dreams and visions. He doesn't tackle the issue of why many 'converted' Muslims revert. Muslims believe in Isa of the Koran, not the Jesus of the Bible. Yet, they claim to have seen Christ in a vision.

Besides the influences of our own philosophies, religion and environment, the devil himself may also participate in these visions. As an angel of light, Satan deceives professing Christians with an image people would think is Jesus. One central feature of these 'Jesus visions is that he makes people feel good about themselves. (p. 148-149)

Having analyzed Strobel's examples, I find it impossible to believe them. His record of 'miraculous' events and visions are no more supernatural than the illusion of a magician.

SUMMARY

Peter informs us that we love Christ, whom we have not seen. (1 Pet. 1:7,8) This implies that no one knows what Jesus looks like. Supernatural guidance through visions cannot verified. If they cannot be verified, they should not be believed. The only supernatural dreams and visions which we are required to believe, are found in the Bible. Dreams and visions were among the signs of the apostles. Since then, no one has been chosen to reveal new information. (2 Cor. 12:12) We now have the written word of God; His revelatory work is done. We have everything we need to know from the Scriptures concerning the occurrences of visions, dreams and the supernatural.

Apostolic teachings included no directives on how future saints could carry on the 'art' of signs and wonders. They wrote about who Christ is, what He has done, who man is and what he has done and the righteousness God requires for eternal life. The Prophets and Apostles showed people how to get right with God. Why not be amazed at the miracle of miracles: the new birth, whereby we have now been made to love the things that God loves, and hate the things that God hates? The real miracle is the supernatural working of the Spirit of God who makes man aware of how vile his sins, then raises him to spiritual life, thus enabling him to repent! The real miracle is about God's grace, not physical wellbeing or a divine communication. We need to remember that God also communicated to Balaam directly! Was he not also a deceiver? (1 Pe. 2)

Though God has the power to save His people out of a corrupt theological system, as He did Martin Luther, those who embrace and support deviant doctrines obscure and even deny the gospel of Christ. And, similarly, even within overt Pentecostalism, there are those whom God has brought to repent of their sin and trust Christ alone to provide them His righteousness. Having had a few charismatic friends and acquaintances over the years, I am quite certain that some knew the Lord, but, others – not so much.

However, the fact that there is such a sizeable portion of Christianity that has embraced the Pentecostalism heresy, is evidence of deception. Pentecostalism is just an illusion of biblical reality, a litany of charismatic deceptions.

(Please see Visions and Miracles in Notes, page 237)

23. EPILOGUE

All true believers acknowledge that the scriptures are God-breathed, therefore, without error as given in the original autograph. Men were inspired by the Holy Spirit to speak and write truth from God. (2 Pet. 1:20,21) Still, this conviction does not guarantee that all our doctrines will comply with Holy writ. Many doctrines are not unanimous among true believers, yet each side claims that their position is biblical. Since both sides cannot be right, the reader is asked to be critical of any teaching, including the teachings in this book. To this point it must be obvious that these viewpoints contrast sharply with most 'evangelical' teaching today. It is for the reader to discern these important matters of doctrine by searching the scriptures like the Bereans did.

THE CHURCH IN CORINTH

In Corinth they divided according to leadership preference. (1:10-12) Permissive attitudes regarding immorality in the church jeopardized their testimony. By eating meat offered to idols, believers did not care that they might offend newer converts. Still content with the wisdom of the world, professing believers remained ignorant. They took one another to court, and horded food at the Lord's Table. They failed to discipline professing believers, for their selfishness, at the Lord's Table. They competed for prominence and failed to yield to the Apostles and Prophets. (1 Cor. 14:37)

Some Corinthians were speaking languages most did not know and others couldn't speak the vernacular clearly. Because of prevailing biblical ignorance and their quest for recognition, their prophesying was deficient. Where in Corinth were the charismatics, who supernaturally healed people of their physical weaknesses? How could these carnally minded Corinthians, some not even saved, perform miracles?

There were no signs and wonders taking place in Corinth. Not once did Paul enjoin these immature believers for their preoccupation with physical healings. Not once did Paul give the slightest intimation that supernatural events of any kind were happening in the Corinthian church.

THE CHURCH IN JERUSALEM

The church in Jerusalem, however, was of one mind. There were no divisions based on leadership preferences. (Ac. 1:14; 2;46; 4:24; 5:12) Instead of hording food, they contributed food. Instead of taking one another to court, church leadership judged. Unlike Corinth they devoted themselves to prayer and the Word. (Ac. 1:14; 2:42) When problems arose, they submitted to the authority of the Apostles. (Ac. 15)

There were no language issues before, during or after Pentecost. They prophesied speaking their "own" learned languages. Unlike Corinth, they spoke as the Holy Spirit impressed them with truth pertaining to Christ and His Word. (Ac.2:4,33) And, unlike Corinth they glorified God, not themselves. In Jerusalem there was evidence of gospel joy.

Signs and Wonders

However, the supernatural was indeed evident in the signs and wonders performed by the apostles. (Ac.2:43; 4:30; 5:12; 14:3) Displays of power, such as the supernatural healing of the lame man, are never referred to as gifts (charisma) in Acts. If this were so, then Peter also had the "gift" to kill dishonest people like Ananias and Sapphira. It is noteworthy that in Paul's second letter to the Corinthians, he aligned his ministry with the most eminent of apostles not by ability "gifts", but by signs, wonders and mighty deeds.

> "Truly the signs of an apostle were accomplished among you with all perseverance, in signs and wonders and mighty deeds." (2 Cor. 12:12, NKJV)

Note the reference to the term 'signs of an apostle.' Paul could not confer upon any in Corinth or anywhere else, power to perform signs, wonders and mighty deeds. Even Paul could not choose other Apostles. He told them that these signs and wonders had been done among them – past tense. The Corinthians did not possess this power, because they were not Apostles. Therefore, signs and wonders must be distinguished from ability gifts; ability gifts are never supernatural.

THE CHURCH TODAY

The Corinthian condition is not unlike most of the church today. Yet, they did retain an appreciation for orthodox ministers, Peter, Paul and Apollos. They received Paul's admonitions and made some changes, as his second letter reveals. Despite continuing issues, even they had not yet coddled charismatic teachers.

Today false teachers elicit unbiblical cravings for the supernatural. But Charismatics aren't alone in exploiting the professing Christian's carnal cravings. More recently, Charismatic cousins called Emergents have regurgitated old asceticism and mysticism with 'spiritual disciplines' or 'spiritual formation', 'contemplative prayer', 'the silence', 'solitude', disguised this as biblical, then fed it to an unsuspecting church. They, like Charismatics, whose 'praying in the spirit', visions and dreams, ecstatic speakers and 'speaking in tongues', promote this same mystical malady. Like the Pharisees, Emergents and Charismatics have promoted a spiritual elitism based on religious disciplines, by distorting and adding to scripture. Masquerading as holiness experts, they manipulate the unlearned to pursue self-esteem.

Faith healers, deliverance ministries and prosperity preachers appeal to the aspirations of the needy and when their 'miracle' fails to happen they are accused of not having faith. The entire Pentecostalism movement is a accomplished by twisting scripture.

Conservative Inclusivism

Charismatics are perfectly content if most of true evangelicals don't teach their doctrines as long as they are regarded evangelical. They deceive by making the more conservative believers look intolerant, unloving, making themselves look spiritual and others unspiritual. Like all heresy, it mutates into subtle strains and spreads like a plague until it sickens and destroys fellowships. These teachings are a satanic ruse under the guise of biblical Christianity. It should be noted that the devil has some evangelical views. (Jas. 2:19)

Though there seems to be a spiritual famine within the professing church, yet God does have His elect, even today. The gates of hell will not prevail against it. God's people still exist!

CONCLUDING OBSERVATIONS

When important matters of scripture such as this are misunderstood and distorted, God honoring ministry is greatly diminished and even eliminated altogether. Following are some key observations,

- that doing 'greater works' does not mean supernatural works.
- that the Galileans could speak as many languages or more than the inhabitants of Jerusalem and Judea.
- that the 'other' languages they spoke were their own as the text says, therefore spoke learned languages at Pentecost.

- that Hebrew was the one language no one learned from birth.
- that God gave abilities, persons and character as gifts.
- that the ability gifts of Corinth were not supernatural.
- that the character gifts abide and are transcendent.
- that the character gifts are in sole possession of believers.
- that supernatural miracles were not happening in Corinth.
- that signs are to be distinguished from gifts.
- that 'signs and wonders' were temporary external manifestations.
- that everyone is born with gifts by the Spirit.
- that all supernatural sign miracles after Christ, occurred through the apostles and those directly associated with them.
- that the common language of Corinth was Greek.
- that the Corinthians varied in their abilities to speak the languages well, but they could understand the vernacular.
- that the Corinthians gave little evidence of the proper use of any ability gift.
- that languages (plural) was a sign, not a 'sign gift' at Pentecost.
- that 'sign gift' is a misnomer.
- that the Holy Spirit always works in accordance with the word, not by arbitrary proclamations of 'thus says the Lord'.
- that person gifts were appointed as messengers of God's word to His people and the world.
- that the Corinthians did not recognize the authority of the person gifts.
- that character gifts are necessary to profit from our ability gifts.
- that believers are not exhorted to search for abilities, but rather to follow after love and spiritual teachings.
- that ability gifts can only function for God's glory in the body of Christ by the baptism of the Holy Spirit.
- that only the true believer can profit from his ability gifts.
- that 'languages cease' means that they become extinct, but the gift of languages does not cease. People continue to be multilingual.
- that the Corinthians were boasting in knowledge not in the Lord. (1:31)
- that abilities are not given to make us happy.
- that abilities do not confirm conversion.
- that both believers and unbelievers misuse ability gifts.

- that the presence of God-given faith, hope and love confirm conversion.
- that James was not advocating anointing with oil as a means to heal the physically ill.

SUMMARY

If believers are not of one mind in vital biblical doctrines affecting the salvation of sinners and the sanctification of believers, professions of unity ring hollow. Can it truly be said that the charismatic and continuationist movements contribute to the health of God's people?

Corinth Did Not Resemble Pentecost!

If, as the charismatics and some continuationists claim, the Corinthian 'tongues' experience is a direct extension of Pentecost, then it would be reasonable to expect that the condition and behavior of the church in Corinth bear resemblance to the manifestation of the Holy Spirit as at Pentecost. It doesn't! Had their language speaking been understood their listeners would have testified that they were glorifying God as they did at Pentecost. Unlike Pentecost, in Corinth they ignored the revealed word of God. Yet Charismatics would have us believe that the Holy Spirit was causing these doctrinally unsound Corinthians to speak 'ecstatic utterances'. Continuationists insist that the Holy Spirit was causing doctrinally ignorant Corinthians to speak truth in languages they had not learned or pray in 'ecstacy'. Millions of professing Christians have been deceived to think that 'ecstatic utterances', is evidence of saving faith.

People With Abilities Are Cast Out!

And, unfortunately others derive their assurance of faith from the use of real abilities. But abilities are not ever an evidence of the new birth. Everyone who believes that Jesus is Lord has this knowledge by the Holy Spirit. But simply being able to say "Jesus is Lord", does not a Christian make, for many in the last day will say, "Lord, Lord" and He will say, 'depart from Me'. Unless profit is made from the abilities received, man will be sentenced to the same fate as the slave who buried his talent. Thankfully, the believer's baptism by the Holy Spirit into the body of Christ, secures for us the love necessary to make our abilities profitable.

Ability Gifts Are To Be Used For God's Glory

Giftedness is presumed to make people happy. Paul had abilities he used for the glory of God, but abilities did not make him joyful. We are called upon to do unpleasant things with the abilities we have been given. But some boastful and rude Corinthians tried to satisfy themselves with their abilities.

WHAT IS HERESY?

Charismatics believe that Jesus died and arose from the dead and even draw some to Christ. But their teachings of 'tongues', health, wealth and prosperity directly inhibit the sanctification of the believer and promote an unbiblical view of the Holy Spirit. Balaam also believed in God. He even obeyed God. But he didn't want to. Craving the wealth Balak could provide, he didn't care whether he led God's people to sin. He promoted an unbiblical view of God.

Charismatic prophetic claims of new truth along with deviant behavior are no different than monastic, Roman Catholic, and other cultic prognostications. A dismissive or a permissive attitude in this matter is to condone heresy even if one does not claim to 'speak in tongues.' The Holy Spirit has clearly communicated to man words that are easily understood, His written word. Yet 'professing believers' claim to be speaking in tongues, gibberish that no one can understand, in the name of the Holy Spirit, no less. How insulting is that?!

This has even become a reality in non-charismatic denominations. Consequently, churches once evangelical no longer are.

A FINAL CHALLENGE

As stated in the last chapter, I have no hesitation in acknowledging that people have come to genuine faith in Christ in a charismatic environment. It is also true that no denomination has a flawless understanding of all biblical doctrine. God's power alone regenerates the human heart, regardless of doctrinal distractions and even heresies. Indeed, Martin Luther and others saw the Light, amidst cultic conditions. Pentecostalism is only one of many that has dishonored the Holy Spirit and stunted the growth of believers.

Of course, not all differences have moral and eternal implications. Different opinions on the mode of baptism or different views on certain aspects of eschatology, do not impinge the believer's relationship with God. But the doctrine that man can be saved by baptism, prepares people for hell. The false doctrine that one can 'believe on the Lord Jesus Christ' as Savior without having Him as Lord provides a false sense of security to many professing believers. (Ac.16:31) The charismatic doctrine is also heresy because its adherents believe man can lose his salvation, that gifts like 'speaking in tongues' are evidence of salvation and a 'spiritual' Christian. Really, this movement appends the gospel with man's words and works. These and other teachings are examples of how they, like the Pharisees, have added rules for the believer's salvation and sanctification. More seriously, this fleshly work is attributed to the Holy Spirit.

Right doctrine is not based on a right result. Moses got exactly the right results despite ignoring God's word to speak to the rock. God's people's thirst was quenched, but he was denied entry into the Promised Land. Neither is right doctrine determined by what we think it should be. Despite Abram's sinful union with Hagar, he had produced a legal heir. Since God had made it clear that his wife Sarah, would bear a son who would be heir, Ishmael was not acceptable. Yet, Abram laughed and still prayed that Ishmael would be his heir! (Gen. 17) The end doesn't justify the means. Moses' experience of getting exactly the right results by hitting the rock when he should have spoken to it, or Abraham's experience of getting a legal heir and then praying for this heir contrary to the Promise, illustrates how even believers obscure God's Word with personal emotion and opinion. Experience does not determine right doctrine!

Though there are notable differences within Pentecostalism, whether extreme or mild, its dogma compromises the believer's spiritual health. Claims that God still speaks personally, deflects the focus away from God's Word. The charismatic movement along with the continuationist, is not an inconsequential violation of God's Word. Many other books have been written, which detail the aberrant and ungodly, unbiblical behavior these doctrines engender.

Claims of hearing from God, speaking unlearned languages, prayer language, tongues, ecstatic utterance, of angelic visitors, supernatural healings, faith healing, the anointing, etc., are charismatic contrivances. Only the truth of God's word can heal these deceptions.

Created in the image of God, man has been afforded the great and wonderful privilege to be assisted by the Holy Spirit to speak in prayer to his Father with his own learned language. First, with sincere, sorrowful and contrite confession of sin, heartfelt appreciation for the Person and work of Christ, with confession of Him as Lord, then intercession for the sanctification of others, we actually honor God! As believers we have this unending advantage of engaging our Lord, as not only our Savior and

King, but also our faithful Friend, who knows our every need and cares for us as only God can. That is amazing!

The Cure For Pentecostalism

The only reality the charismatic movement can legitimately claim is that its origin is of the flesh and in some cases of the devil. Unfortunately, the Continuationists are complicit. Since neither in Acts or First Corinthians were believers supernaturally speaking in 'tongues' or languages, it is therefore concluded that charismatic dogmas are human fleshly fabrications imported into scripture. Reading Scripture out of context, changing the meanings of words and adding words that should not be in the text, have contributed to an erroneous God-dishonoring narrative. Only the pure Word of God can dispel these spiritually dangerous and even deadly deceptions.

Though some Corinthians in the assembly were very immature and some were not saved, even they would have associated the behavior of today's Charismatic with pagan worship. The Corinthians would have understood that Jesus taught His disciples to pray with real words in a real learned language, not a 'prayer tongue'.

The Holy Spirit did not begin the cult of Pentecostalism. He is not, and never was the least part of Pentecostalism. Having shown how the charismatic and continuationist heresies conflict with scripture, I recommend that the word of God, not experience, as the cure for Pentecostalism.

24. NOTES

'GIFTS' IN HEBREWS

Following is a passage of scripture needing some discussion because the Greek word '*merismos*' is translated as 'gifts', instead of 'distributions', in most translations chapter 2, verse 4 of the book of Hebrews.

The following is a paraphrase of Heb. 2:1-4,

> 'For this reason it is more abundantly necessary to take heed to the things we have heard, lest we drift away. [2] For, if the word having been spoken by messengers was unchangeable, namely, every transgression and disobedience received a just recompense, [3] how shall we escape, having neglected so great salvation? Which having received a preeminence, to be spoken, through the Lord, by those having heard, it was confirmed to us. [4] God also, bearing witness with them of this by signs and wonders, and various acts of power and distributions of the Holy Spirit, according to His will.'

The context is essential to understand what the author of Hebrews was referring to with '*merismos*', translated 'gift'.

The Message And The Messengers

In times past, God spoke by the Prophets to the Jewish fathers. (1:1; 2:2) Writing to Jewish readers, Hebrews is concerned that they take earnest heed to what they have heard. The Law, having been spoken through the Prophet-messengers, was steadfast. Under the law, sin received just punishment, showing the need for salvation. Before only a prophecy, but now fulfilled in history, Christ's salvation was magnified, yet it appeared that it was being neglected. They, too, would not just escape recompense for sin. (Heb. 1:14; 2:1-3) ('Angels' should always be translated 'messengers'. The 'messengers' or angels are the Prophets iof 1:1.)

The Gospel 'Preeminence' And 'Confirmation'

Now fulfilled in Christ, His salvation, that is His death and resurrection, necessary for man's deliverance from sin has now received the preeminence. It was spoken through the Lord. The Lord gave the

Apostles the words that the Father had given Him, hence, 'spoken through the Lord.' (Jn. 17:8) It was confirmed to "us" Jews, those who were the recipients of the Law and deserved the penalty for disobeying it. (2:3)

How Did They Bear Witness?

God bore witness of the Law through the Prophets with signs, wonders. Similarly, God also bore witness through the Apostles with signs, wonders, miracles and distributions of the Spirit. As God had made Himself known through prophecy before Christ, He would also prophesy about Himself at the time of His first Advent.

Signs And Wonders And Miracles

'Signs and wonders' are often coupled together in the NT. 'Miracles' essentially means power. With outward 'signs and wonders and miracles', God authenticated the message of the Prophets and Apostles in unusual ways. The calamities Moses pronounced upon Pharoah, the fire lighting Elijah's water-drenched sacrifice, Elisha raising the Shunammite's son to life, Paul striking the sorcerer Elymas with blindness, Paul's resistance to the deadly bite of a viper and Peter predicting the death of Ananias and Sapphira for lying are just a few examples of how God bore witness through His messengers with signs and wonders and miracles.

Signs, wonders and miracles were external visible manifestations of God's power to authenticate the message of the Prophets and Apostles.

Distributions (Gift) of the Spirit?

Many commentators suggest that these 'distributions' are gifts as per 1 Cor. chapters 12 and 14. But the real meaning of 'distributions' is foiled when *charisma* and *mersimos* are assumed to be synonyms, the context is ignored and the chief role of the Holy Spirit is diminished. Hebrews implicates Jews for their disobedience and rebellion, because they ignored the message of the Prophets, who God had sent to them. (Heb. 2:1,2)

Throughout scripture, Prophets and Apostles claim that the Spirit spoke to them. David testified that the <u>Holy Spirit</u> spoke by him. (2 Sa. 23:2) The <u>Spirit of God</u> came upon Zechariah to warn the people that they had broken the commandments. (2 Chr. 24:20) The <u>Spirit</u> of the Lord spoke to Ezekiel. (Ez. 11:5) The Lord specifically assured His disciples that after He departed, He would dispatch the <u>Holy Spirit</u> to help them remember what they had been taught. (Jn. 14:26; 16:13) By Peter's ministry, through the Holy Spirit, many at this Pentecost heard the Gospel, were convicted by it and repented of their sin. (Ac. 2:33,38) Peter declared that the message that the Holy Spirit had given him. (Ac. 2:33; 2 Pe. 1:21,22) With signs, wonders and miracles, God certified Prophets and Apostles, that their words were the 'distributions' of the Spirit. (2 Cor. 12:12) God, by His Spirit, repeatedly and graciously revealed how man could escape the penalty of sin. The Holy Spirit 'distributed' to them the necessary knowledge by means of spoken words, for the remedy.

SUMMARY

Signs, wonders and unusual power (miracles) of the Prophets and Apostles, were external affirmations that they had been sent by God to reveal His Word, the 'distributions' of the Holy Spirit. (Ac. 2:42,43 5:12; 1 Cor. 14:37; 2 Cor. 12:12)

The Holy Spirit Distributes Gospel Knowledge.

Appointed by God, the OT Prophets were to declare the truth about sin and salvation. The priests were to communicate what the Prophets revealed. At Pentecost, the Holy Spirit 'distributed' to the Galilean believers 'utterance', which enabled them to speak about the Christ's salvation, who just died and rose 50 days prior. The pouring out of the Holy Spirit at Pentecost upon the Galileans, causing God's Jewish believers to be immanently cognizant and united in the sudden realization that Jesus was the prophesied Messiah-Savior, could certainly be regarded as 'distributions' of the Holy Spirit. (Heb. 2:1-3) Thus God bore witness by words of truth from the Holy Spirit about Christ.

The Distributions Of Salvation and Sanctification

The author of Hebrews was concerned with the spiritual well-being of professing believers. Giving heed to what is heard to the word spoken by messengers and spoken by the Father through the Lord, and confirmed by those who heard Him set the immediate context for understanding the meaning of 'distributions of the Holy Spirit'. (2:1-4) The Holy Spirit communicates words necessary to remedy for our transgressions. The Holy Spirit is primarily known for these 'distributions', or communication of what has now become Scripture.

If the author of Hebrews intended ability gifts, he would have used the plain language of *charisma*. While the outward manifestations of signs, wonders and miracles served to authenticate the Gospel Messengers, both Prophets and Apostles, the distributions of the Holy Spirit serves to dispense and understandably mediate the Gospel message they delivered to us.

AGABUS

Agabus, a 'certain prophet, had rightly prophesied that there would be a famine throughout the world. Familiar with Christ's prophesies, he knew that famines were to come and correctly predicted just one of them. (Matt.24:7; Mk.13:8; Lk.21:11) But, it is not stated whether he predicted the time and length of the drought. (Ac. 11:28) He also predicted Paul's imprisonment in Jerusalem. But, was he accurate?

PAUL WAS CALLED BY THE LORD

The Lord had commissioned Paul to bear His name to the Gentiles, kings and Israel, that he must suffer for His name's sake. (Ac. 9:15,16) In accord with his calling, he was bound in the Spirit to go to Jerusalem, though he did not know what would happen to him there. Always conscious of the ministry he had personally received from the Lord Jesus, to testify God's grace, he did not hold his life dear. (20:24) Later, after his arrest in Jerusalem, the Lord personally affirmed Paul's call, saying that he must be a witness in Rome also. (Act.23:11) Nothing would deter Paul from his divine call to minister the Gospel! (Ac. 9:16; 14:19,20; 20:22,23)

THE HOLY SPIRIT GUIDES ALL BELIEVERS

Before the credibility of Agabus' prophecy is analyzed, it is important observe the ministry of the Holy Spirit, not only in the life of Paul, but also in his friends. Could the Holy Spirit give conflicting signals?

Paul's Meeting At Miletus

At his last visit to Ephesus, Paul had resolved by the Spirit to go to Jerusalem and Rome after passing through Macedonia and Achaia. (Ac. 19:21) Upon his return trip from Asia, he met the elders of Ephesus at Miletus. There he informed them that he was constrained by the Spirit to go to Jerusalem, that the Holy Spirit testifies to him that in every city imprisonment and afflictions await him. (Ac. 20:22,23) Paul's expectation in every city was that he would be persecuted. Convinced that they would not see him again, they prayed together, bid him a tearful departure and accompanied him to the ship. (20:25; 36-38) It is important to note that none of the brethren here tried to persuade him not to go to Jerusalem!

Paul's Meeting At Tyre

When he met with some disciples at Tyre, they advised him through the Spirit that he should not go to Jerusalem. (21:4) However, it appears that after having prayed, his friends accepted Paul's plan.

Paul's Meeting At Philip's House

When he arrived at Caesarea, he stayed with Philip, the evangelist. While there, Agabus joined them from Judea. He also implies that he is informed by the Holy Spirit about what he will encounter in Jerusalem.

IS GUIDANCE THROUGH THE SPIRIT CONFLICTING?

On the one hand, Paul had been constrained by the Spirit to return to Jerusalem, and on the other hand friends, disciples and elders advised Paul by the Spirit not to go. Is the Spirit giving contradictory advice?

Paul Informed The Elders About The Spirit's Calling

Paul informed brethren from Ephesus that he was constrained by the Spirit to go to Jerusalem. Furthermore, he stated that the Holy Spirit testifies to him that bonds and afflictions awaited him in every city. (20:22, 23) Interestingly, after his exhortation and benediction, no one spoke to advise him 'by the Spirit' not to go to Jerusalem. Accepting his testimony of the Spirit's leading, they knelt and prayed with him, in sorrow, embraced him and accompanied him to the ship. (20:36-38)

The Fellowship Did Not Know His Calling

At Tyre, 'they kept telling Paul through the <u>Spirit</u> not to set foot in Jerusalem.' Based upon what they knew of the hostility to believers in Jerusalem, it would have been unloving for them to advise Paul any differently. (21:3,4) Perhaps, unaware of Paul's own testimony of the Spirit's personal leading, they attributed their advice that he not go to Jerusalem to be the leading of the Spirit. Or, perhaps, Luke is making his own inspired observation about the spiritual character of these believers. Their efforts to dissuade Paul from going to Jerusalem was evidence of the fruit of the Holy Spirit. (Ga. 5:22,23) For that reason, Luke writes that they were pleading for him not to go.

At Philip's house, Agabus expressed concern for Paul in terms of an explicit prediction. Agabus said, 'Thus says the Holy Spirit ...'. He did not have a vision, or a dream. He wasn't hearing a voice, like Paul did on the road to Damascus. He only states in the present tense that 'the Holy Spirit is saying'. The narrative does not state or imply that Agabus was correct. Paul did not personally rebuke Agabus. He accepted everyone's concern. (21:13)

What would we think about a group of believers who were happy to learn that they would not ever see Paul again? Can we even imagine a group of Christians 'encouraging' Paul by saying to him, 'Wow, we are so glad to learn that you are about to be persecuted for the Lord's sake. You'll certainly find it in Jerusalem. How can we help you get there?' Is this how the Holy Spirit moves? Of course, not.

So, the first answer to this apparent conflict is that the Holy Spirit gave them the impetus to express their loving concern, Agabus included.

The Will Of The Lord

Having heard the Apostle's steadfast conviction, that not only was he prepared to be bound, but also to die for Christ, they relented and said, 'The Lord's will be done'. (Ac. 9:15; 21:13, 14) In other word, no prophetic warning about his plight in Jerusalem, even by someone claiming Spirit authority, could deter Paul from doing the will of the Lord.

WHAT DID PAUL THINK OF AGABUS' WARNING?

Apparently, not the slightest bit shocked by the 'prophecy', Paul replied that he was ready, not only to be bound, but also to die in Jerusalem. (Ac. 21:12-13) He paid no attention to his prophecy!

WHAT WAS THE AGABUS 'PROPHECY'

When Agabus joined the fellowship at Philip's household, he took Paul's belt and bound his own feet and hands, saying,

> "Thus says the Holy Spirit, 'So shall the Jews at Jerusalem bind the man that owns this belt and deliver *him* into the hands of the Gentiles.'" (Ac. 21:11; NKJV, emphasis added)

Though this 'prophecy' itself, does not contain any advice, those present were dismayed and tried to dissuade Paul from going to Jerusalem, based on this 'prophecy'. (Ac. 21: 11, 12)

WHAT HAPPENED IN JERUSALEM?

When the Jews discovered Paul in the temple, they seized him, dragged him out of the temple, then beat him. (21:30, 32) Upon hearing the news, the captain took with him soldiers and centurions and ran down to where the Jews were beating Paul to death. (23:26) Taking him into custody, the captain commanded that he be bound with two chains. (Ac. 21:27-33)

WAS AGABUS ACCURATE?

The Agabus 'prophecy' that Paul would be bound hand and foot by the Jews did not happen. In his defense, some have argued that Agabus' depiction of Paul's arrest indicated only that the Jews were responsible for his arrest, though they themselves had not bound him.[140] For this theory to be plausible, the Jews would have arrested Paul and handed him over to the Romans. But, this also did not happen. The Jews did not bind him and neither did they deliver him over to the Romans.

The Roman cohort took him from the mob. (21:33) Again, some think that in this case, the verb, *paradidomi* translated 'deliver', could also mean to 'surrender' or to 'abandon'. This also is not what happened. When the soldiers arrived, the Jews stopped beating Paul. If, at this point, they had truly 'abandoned' him to the cohort, it would not be necessary to seize Paul.

'Delivered From Jerusalem'

When Paul arrived in Rome, he explained to the Jews there, that he had not done anything against the Jews, yet was delivered a prisoner from Jerusalem into the hands of the Romans. (Ac. 28:17) Paul was taken from Jerusalem to Antipatris, a Roman military post, then on the next day to Caesarea. (23:31-33) Here, Paul appeared before the Roman governor. Clearly, the Jews did not deliver him into the hands of the Romans.

What Is A False Prophet?

A false prophet is one who prophesies in the name of the Lord presumptuously, and consequently, the event fails to happen. (De. 18:20-22) A prophet may also predict events that come to pass and lead people to follow false gods. (De. 13:1-5) A false prophet is one who teaches rebellion against the Lord. (Jer. 28:15,16) However, even one who reluctantly speaks the word of the Lord, as Balaam did, he is also a false prophet. Like the charismatics, he was in it for the money.

Was Agabus' Warning A Prophecy?

Familiar with current religious and secular politics of Judea, Agabus understood the intense Jewish hatred for the Gospel. As a well-known minister of Christ, Paul would be an immediate target for arrest. With this in mind, Agabus predicted that the Jews would bind Paul hands and feet. (Ac. 21:11) Under OT rules for prophecy, did Agabus prophesy?

---

[140] For example, the Jews are said to "have taken and by wicked hands have crucified" Christ. Ac. 2:23. But, we understood that they didn't nail him to the cross; the Jews were responsible for it. In this case, the Jews intentionally engaged Roman jurisprudence from the outset and delivered Christ to the Gentiles for crucifixion.

Was Agabus a False Prophet?

Based upon these OT passages, could Agabus be a false prophet? First, it must be emphasized that Agabus did not claim to be a Prophet called of God, as was John the Baptist and the Prophets before him.

Despite the fact that Agabus' prediction was not accurate, he was not a false prophet. He made no attempt to usurp the authority of Paul.

Agabus was not a false prophet because he was not interested in getting wealthy.

Agabus was not a false prophet because he did not lead God's people into sin, as did Balaam.

Agabus was not a false prophet because there is no evidence that he tried to gain a following with his reputation of having predicted a famine.

Agabus was not a false prophet because his 'prophecy' was evidence that he supported the Apostle. He wanted to protect him from harm.

Agabus was not a false prophet because his 'prophecy' was an interpretation of the prevailing religious and political conditions in Jerusalem.

Summary

Agabus was not an 'inspired' Prophet of God. Prophets are subject to evaluation and correction. Does the Apostle Paul allow for prophet errors? Paul had prescribed how the prophets should teach in the assembly. After two or three prophets spoke in turn, they were to be seated and submit themselves to the judgment and possible correction of others. (1Cor. 14:29,30,37) Uninspired prophets are not always correct.

Given Agabus' errors, Continuationists claim that the gift of prophecy might not be accurate. What is missed is that every uninspired prophet is subject to public evaluation. Uninspired prophets can be wrong.

THE LORD'S TABLE

The majority of commentators on 1 Cor. 11:30 teach that abuse of the Lord's Table was the cause of physical weakness, sickness and ultimately death among believers. However, a few hold that Paul is using these words as metaphors of moral or spiritual issues. (Valckenaer, Morus, Krause and Eichhorn) The following shows that any other view is out of context.

METAPHOR OR LITERAL?

The bread and wine consumed at the Lord's Table depict Christ's work and the believer's spiritual nourishment. (11:24,25) The words, "This is my body" do not literally convert bread into Christ's body. (transubstantiation) Christ said that 'he who eats my flesh and drinks my blood shall live forever.' (Jn. 6:51-58) Physically eating and drinking, is a metaphor for the nourishment needed for spiritual life. If bread and wine are metaphors, then words normally associated with physical ineptitude could also describe the spiritual condition of some individuals in the church, not a physical malady.

Detractors at the Lord's Table were 'drinking damnation' to themselves. Here again, is a metaphor, highlighting a very serious spiritual predicament. Since the wine is symbolic of the blood, it should not be unreasonable to deduce that some who consume these elements would also be described with symbolic language, such as 'weak', 'sick' and 'sleep.'

INTERPRETATION DILEMMAS

The majority conflate 'weak', 'sick' and 'sleep' by mixing physical with spiritual reality. Two are taken literally, the third, symbolically.

Literal or Figurative?

The majority view claims that 'sleep' is a reference to death, yet, it purports to take the scripture literally. But this view only takes 'weak' and 'sick' literally and makes 'sleep' <u>symbolize</u> death.

Condemnation Prevention

How then does the supposed physical 'sleep' of death chasten a professing believer from being condemned with the world? (11:30-32) No chastening occurs after death.

Judging Others

It is incongruous that Paul would be drawing attention to the lack of health and life as the cause of sinful behavior. Should physical weakness, sickness and death be the metrics by which Christians could judge one another? Should physical deficiencies be the basis upon which we judge maturity? This is inherent in the charismatic heresy movement, where sickness is the basis of judging the spiritual health of a Christian.

False Assurance

Since Paul did not assume that everyone in this assembly were true believers, neither would he have assumed that everyone who had fallen 'asleep' (died), had 'fallen asleep' in Christ. 'Sleep' cannot mean physical death because it does not differentiate between the saved and the lost.

Drinking Judgment

Those who drink unworthily, drink damnation to themselves. They are not celebrating their salvation, but their damnation. (11:29) Clearly, this verse is about the spiritual condition of professing believers, yet physical 'weakness', 'sickness' and physical death are considered to be a consequence of this 'damnation'. (11:30) Only unbelievers could drink damnation that would condemn them with the world. (11:32)

Conclusion

The context does not support the notion that 'weak', 'sick' and 'asleep' describe physical circumstances.

SPIRITUALLY WEAK, SICK AND ASLEEP

However, with physical symbolism, Paul is describing a literal spiritual condition in the churches.

WEAK

Various contexts elsewhere apply 'weak' to a spiritual disorder. Christ died for the 'helpless'. (weak, Rom. 5:6) Paul uses 'weak' to contrast the mind of God with the mind of man. (1 Cor. 1:26-28) Paul describes his lack of influence and authority as 'weak'. (1Cor. 4:10) 'Weak' consciences are defiled. (1Cor. 8:7-10) His body analogy depicts the spiritual assistance the members should provide one another. (1Cor. 12:22) 'Weak' does not necessarily refer to physical incompetence.

SICK

This particular Greek word for 'sick' is used five times in the NT. In the other four instances, the context is clear that physical ailments is meant. However, there is no reason why this word cannot be applied metaphorically. The context determines the meaning.

Jesus said that those who are 'well have no need of a physician, but those who are sick.' (Matt. 9:12) This, He said in reply to a question about His association with sinners. Elsewhere this word 'sick' refers to physical illness. However, in this context, with the word 'sick', Jesus identifies Himself as the people's much needed physician to cure their spiritual sin sickness. Though a different word than the one Paul used, this shows how context determines the intended meaning.

Would Paul describe anyone physically sick, when some who participated in the sacred meal gave every evidence that they discerned the Lord's body, yet physically ill? Rather, Paul would even describe the physically healthy as 'sick', because they were spiritually sick.

SLEEP

The disciples understood the normal meaning of this particular word to mean physical sleep. (Matt. 28:13; Lk.22:45) For that reason, Jesus had to explain to them that this 'sleep' of Lazarus was actually death. (Jn. 11:12-14) He applied 'sleep' metaphorically.

However, the normal definition for 'sleep' is not death. Paul uses 'sleep' to encourage the believer not to be any more afraid of dying as physically going to sleep. To die is to go to sleep and wake up in the presence of our Lord. (1 Cor. 15:6,18,20,51) The context in these references, show that the death of the believer is as harmless as sleep.

The majority view for 'sleep' at the Lord's Table is that it is a metaphor for death, as per Lazarus. But, Paul did not mean that people were physically going to sleep, so it must have a metaphorical application. Instead, 'sleep' describes the loss of spiritual discernment. Like the Hebrews, some who had come to understand the gospel, could fall away. (Heb. 2:1,2) It was a spiritual sleep.

OBSERVATIONS AND CONCLUSIONS

Since 'sleep' does not normally mean to die, most have interpreted it symbolically, while taking 'weak' and 'sick' literally. However, the only consistent interpretation is one that treats them the same. Despite having been physically nourished and strengthened at the Lord's Table, Paul describes them as spiritually weak, sick and sedated.

The Missing Challenge

If 'weak', 'sick' and 'sleep' denote physical deterioration, evidence of this, even today, should be overwhelming, since many have eaten unworthily, yet are not sick and live just as long or longer than others who have not 'eaten unworthily'. Has the church then failed in judging the illnesses that are present in the church today as failure to eat worthily? When is the last time you were challenged at the Lord's Table that the reason many are physically weak, sick and dead in the church is because of unworthy participation of the bread and wine? If not, why? If the meaning is physical, why does the church not practice it?

Would Paul Introduce A Means To Judge One Another By Appearance?

Would Paul intend that the spiritual condition of a church be based on the physical condition of her membership? Why would Paul now introduce a climate of suspicion in the church where everyone would look at the other wondering if physical 'weakness', 'sickness' or death occurred because they participated unworthily? Physical weakness, sickness, and death are realities in the life of every believer. Are we now to examine their spiritual condition based on their loss of physical health?

'Weak', 'Sick' And 'Sleep' Are Spiritual Metaphors

If these are not physical, they must then be spiritual. Failure to worship the Lord in spirit for His work on the cross, is to incur far more serious consequences than physical. The weak thought they were strong, the sick thought they were healthy and those who had fallen asleep thought they were awake. They all shared the same failure to discern the body of Christ, thus unable to worship Him at this meal. This really is a depiction of the natural man who cannot receive the things of the Spirit of God. (2:14)

PARTAKING UNWORTHILY

What is the meaning and consequence of eating unworthily? There is a translation issue: It should be 'whoever drinks of the cup unworthily' <u>not</u> 'whoever drinks of the cup in an unworthy manner'. Can a true believer eat 'unworthily?'

NOT 'UNWORTHY MANNER'

The chief purpose of the Lord's Supper is to proclaim or show forth the Lord's death until He comes. (11:26) For this reason, Paul states that to eat the bread and drink the wine one must be careful that he is worthy. Personal effort or work that appears worthy is not sufficient, which is why 'unworthy manner' does not convey Paul's meaning. Partaking unworthily was not just a matter of what they did; it was first a matter of who they were.

Evidence of Unworthiness

However, belligerent behavior might be evidence of partaking unworthily. Certainly, when others who had plenty, shamed those who had little, the evidence might suggest that they had not be truly converted. (11:18-22) It must be emphasized that sharing food does not make one 'worthy'. Some had no food to share. The hording of food in this instance was the evidence of a more serious problem.

Some of these behaviors may certainly have been present among believers, yet, as blood bought sinners, they could not participate unworthily. True believers are not perfect and may also have not behaved properly. After all, the Lord's Table is for sinners, so there must be other characteristics of unworthiness that render a person unfit to partake.

Attitude Of Unworthiness

This problem was not rooted in behavior. From the evidence, Paul concludes that they were not interested in the Lord Himself. Like the world, they retained an attitude, which despised the church. (11:20, 22) This cannot be said of any true believer. (Jn. 13:35) Though, he too will struggle in relationships, his purpose is always to honor Christ at the Lord's Table and elsewhere. .

Source Of Unworthiness

Partaking 'unworthily' results from a state or condition of the soul. Their attitudes betrayed a condition of the heart. The necessity to discern the Lord's body is basic to the true believer, yet among them were professing believers who couldn't even do the basics! Commensurate with the state of their soul, they couldn't help but make this a time of self-promotion amidst those who were hungry. Their attitude betrayed the real condition of their hearts. Therefore, they did not really come together to celebrate the Lord's Table but assembled for another purpose. The reason for their sinful attitudes originated in the heart. (11:27-29) As a man thinks, so he is. (Prov.23:7)

Who Are The Unworthy?

An unworthy person is one who is guilty of the body and blood of the Lord. The reason for the guilt of some of these Corinthians is much deeper than just their behavior. Unable to rightly discern the Lord's body unbelievers may even participate in the elements with greater outward dignity and consideration for others than some Corinthians did. But without understanding the reason for the death of Christ and the necessity of it, spiritual death looms. Without Christ's blood on the doorposts of their heart, many were eating and drinking unworthily, therefore still subject to condemnation. Everyone who participates unworthily has no capacity to truly appreciate the offense that his sin is to God and that it could only be paid for by the substitutionary death of Christ. Simply bringing food for others could not possibly ensure that partaking of the elements would be evidence that they had discerned the Lord's body.

To discern the Lord's body is an act of the spiritual man, the regenerated man. It is not a physical activity. Failure to engage the mind to discern the Lord's body is evidence of a serious spiritual deficiency, illustrated with weakness, sickness and sleep, none of which would apply to the true believer.

Consequence Of Unworthiness

The inability and refusal to discern the Lord's body incurs the guilt of the body and blood of Christ. (11:27) This penalty has no exceptions. Everyone who drinks unworthily is still as guilty of sentencing Christ to death as were the Jews and Pilate. The only exceptions were those who did not eat unworthily. (11:29) The consequence of unworthiness is not physical weakness, sickness or death. People are weak, are sick and die and yet are not guilty of the Lord's body. However, the inevitable consequence of unworthiness is condemnation with the world.

Who Are The Worthy?

It is virtually impossible to reconcile the notion, that true believers could still be guilty of the body and blood of Christ, with scripture. Since the believer's just sentence for his guilt has been paid at the cross, he cannot be an unworthy participant. The true believer has been given the righteousness of Christ and it is on this basis that he partakes at the Lord's table. It is His righteousness that makes believers worthy. Believers are not partially saved, therefore, they are not partially worthy. We are worthy because Christ has made us worthy!

EXAMPLES OF 'UNWORTHINESS'

In this letter Paul refers to incidents of Israel's first Passover and the Last Supper, which he must have had in regards to unworthiness.

Wilderness Israel

Paul sets the backdrop by referring to Israel's unworthy participation in the Passover. Like the Gentiles, wilderness Israel had been drinking the cup of demons and the cup of the Lord. (10:18-22; De.32:17,18) Like Israel many may have gone through some ceremonial motions and even believed, but had believed in vain. (15:2; Lk. 8:13) Like Israel, professing believers in Corinth, were warned not to become sharers in demons. The penalty for their drift into unbelief was denial of entry into Canaan, the Promised Land. (Heb. 3:7-12) 'Unworthiness' denies entry into heaven.

Judas' Betrayal

Paul reminds the church that the Last Supper occurred the same night He was betrayed. (11:23) Serving as an example of one who did not 'discern the Lord's body', Judas was consigned to 'his own place'. He was unworthy to go to the Lord's place. (Ac. 1:25)

As there was a Judas among Christ's disciples, there would continue to be Judases among His people. Judas was unworthy before he consumed the bread. Judas didn't get physically sick or die physically because the bread and wine poisoned him. He was already spiritually sick and dead in his trespasses and sin.

Was Peter Unworthy?

Later that same evening when the Pharisees and the soldiers came for Jesus in the Garden, Peter severed Malchus' ear, intending to kill him. Could Peter have possibly discerned the Lord's body properly? Certainly, he did not understand the means by which Christ would save His people. His boastful claims that he would never deny the Lord utterly failed, just as Jesus predicted. Did he eat and drink unworthily?

Christ had prayed for Peter that his faith would not fail. When washing Peter's feet, Jesus prophesied that though Peter did not understand then, he would later. Peter's worthiness is seen in his continuing desire to have his part with Christ. (Jn. 13:7,8) And, if Peter ate 'unworthily', why did he not get sick?

Summary

Only an unbeliever can eat and drink unworthily. Only the unbeliever has no personal appreciation for the penalty for sin Christ paid on the cross. Unless he repents of his sin and trusts Christ to save him, these professing believers continue to eat and drink to their own judgment, not salvation. It's on this basis that we are to 'examine ourselves'. (11:28)

THE CHASTENING OF THE LORD

Paul's primary concern was that those who were participating at the Lord's Table would not be condemned with the world. (11:31,32) Unless we judge ourselves, the Lord judges us with His chastening. When we hear and accept the chastening exhortations of our loving God, we give evidence that we are His true sons. (Heb. 12:8)

Perhaps, a major reason for misunderstanding the meaning of chastening is assuming that God made people sick and caused them to die for eating unworthily. As already discussed, however, these are spiritual descriptors, not physical.

Physical Chastening Of The Lord

However, there were times when He caused physical sickness and death by means of the Prophets and Apostles to punish belligerent sin.

Apostolic Censures

A lethal censure was administered under the authority of the Apostle Peter. Caught lying, Ananias and Sapphira were judged and sentenced. Paul struck Elymas blind for attempting to lead others away from Christ. (Ac. 5:1-11; 13:9-11) Paul delivers someone to Satan for the destruction of his flesh so that he might be saved. (1 Cor. 5:5)

As with healings, these were part of the signs and wonders that verified the apostleship. There were no follow-up warnings that from then on, anyone caught lying in church would die on the spot. These censures were all person-specific. God left no room to doubt who was guilty of an offense and why. The supposition that people were physically weak, sick and dying because they had participated unworthily, is general. Based on this assumption no one would know why they were weak, sick and dead. This is not how God censured people through the Apostles.

Consequential Censures

However, God does physically discipline people through the normal course of life. Certain sins bear greater physical censures than others. Drunkenness, sexual sins are laden with inherent disciplines such as family break-ups, wife abuse and disease, etc. Paul states that deeds sown to the flesh reap corruption. (Ga. 6:8) There are sins that hasten death and some that don't. (1 Jn. 5:16,17) No one is exempt from the physical consequences of sin, believers included.

Sickness Does Not Indicate Divine Judgment

However, a physical sickness or weakness still cannot possibly be a means of judging spiritual worthiness. Asked concerning a man born blind, whether it was the result of this man's sin or his parents', Jesus replied, 'neither'. (Jn. 9:1-5) Of course, Jesus did not mean that this man was not a sinner. In this case, God had arranged this man's blindness for Christ to display His power to heal. Job's calamities were not the consequence of belligerent sin. (Job 1:1) Physical deficiencies do not indicate one's spiritual condition.

Whatever the illness of the body might have been, every believer could come to the Lord's Table, with the full confidence that he has been spiritually made whole, through Christ, regardless of his physical condition.

Spiritual Chastening Of The Lord

While God does cause a variety physical afflictions and calamities to accomplish His purpose, this is not the context here. Physical weakness and death are not the means of chastening at the Lord's Table. (11:30)

To 'Judge' Must Be Consistent

Paul instructed believers to 'judge' themselves, so that we should not be judged. (11:31) If we are to accept the notion that God caused physical calamity and death for eating and drinking unworthily, then it follows that we should also 'judge' ourselves the same way. Of course, making ourselves sick and committing suicide is not what Paul teaches! Paul's point is that we should 'judge' ourselves according to the standard that God uses. That standard is His Word, including Paul's writings.

Paul explains that God's judgments are His means of discipline. If judging ourselves is not about physical self-flagellation, then, neither does God judge us with physical chastening – in this context.

The Chastening By Means Of Exhortation

Paul warns the church that if they discerned for themselves, they would not be judged. (11:31) Paul is very specific about what this chastening is. This judgment upon the church contained words. Much like the deliberations in a court of law, the defendant is arraigned and presented with reasons for his guilt, in words. When we are 'judged', we are chastened by the Lord by His word.

Parents discipline children with words. As children, we have all experienced the discomfort of receiving criticism for bad behavior, especially in the presence of other members of the family or friends. Paul commends the churches including the church in Corinth. (1:4-6; 11:1; 1 Thess 1:1-6) But after hearing words of praise, to then hear the words publicly read, "I do not praise you", was undoubtedly felt by some as a stinging rebuke, which was really a chastening from the Lord. (11:17, 22)

Paul says literally, "But when we are judged we are chastened by the Lord that we may not be condemned with the world." (11:32 NKJV) Judge means to evaluate on the basis of what is right. When God chastens His people we are judged with words on the basis of His righteousness, so that professing believers might be saved.

It is always uncomfortable to hear criticism of one's own failures and deficiencies but this is what the Lord's judgment does through His Word. His judgments are statements of current deficiencies and impending condemnation, if corrective action is not taken.

What Are Some Specific Judgments?

Well then, if the chastening is not physical in this context what are they? As already stated, they are words, written words of Paul from the Lord. The judgments are:

- they cannot be praised. 11:17,22
- they came together for the worse. 11:17
- they came together to fight. 11:18
- they did not come together to honor Christ. 11:20
- they had no interest in the needs of others. 11:21
- they despised the church of God. 11:22
- some were participating at the Lord's Table unworthily.
- unworthy participation incurred guilt of the body of Christ.
- they drink damnation to themselves.
- they did not discern the Lord's body.
- some are still condemned with the world. 11:32

These judgments indicate the reality of the spiritual condition of many people in this church. Hearing this letter read with a rehearsal of Paul's judgments, then told that they were weak, sick and asleep, when they thought that they were spiritually strong, healthy and alert ought to have made it clear to them that there was a very serious spiritual problem.

What is the Purpose of Chastening?

The purpose of our Lord's chastening is that 'we might not be condemned with the world.' Nothing in this passage suggests that people will avoid physical sickness if they 'rightly discern the Lord's body.' (11:31,32) Neither does Paul imply that one who has trusted Christ and repented of his sin could ever find himself 'unworthy'. However, by this examination exercise, the true believer knows that he will always find himself worthy, not because of his works, but because he has discerned the Lord's body and blood as payment for the penalty of his sin.

Consequences For Failing To Heed His Judgments

The consequences for failing to heed His judgments are twofold.

First, it is implied that spiritual weakness, sickness and sleep are consequences of failing to heed the Lord's judgment. (11:30,31) This is the evidence of guilt that exposes the trespasser to the penalty.

Secondly, some among them might by condemned with the world. (11:32, 34) Christ warned Nicodemus that he who does not believe is 'judged' or condemned already. (Jn. 3:18,19) Not having discerned the Lord's body, every unbeliever is already guilty. Paul exhorts everyone to judge himself in order to avoid condemnation. (11:31)

Paul's Practical Remedy To Minimize Distraction

Paul's had practical solutions to minimize distractions at the Lord's Table,

- Don't come when hungry. The Lord's Table was not to satisfy physical hunger.
- Don't be in a hurry. In Paul's day, circumstances were such that arriving at the same time was difficult. They didn't have clocks.

Bringing food for themselves, while others went hungry, shamed those who had little or none. (11:21,22) They were to continue to eat together and wait expectantly for each other.[141] Paul reduced the incentive for the 'unworthy' to come, since their appetites would not be satisfied at the Lord's Table. (11:33,34) Certainly, those who had eaten beforehand might also be unworthy participants at the Table. Outward etiquette does not achieve worthiness.

Literally, Paul said, 'that you might not come into condemnation.' (11:34; subjunctive mood) He did **not** say, 'that you will not come into condemnation. Rather than have an appetite for physical food, Paul wanted them to desire the spiritual food symbolized by the bread and the wine. Only then could they partake worthily.

---

[141] 'Wait' is to wait expectantly. In the other six places this word appears in the NT, the idea is to look forward to, to be eager: Jn. 5:3; Ac. 17:16; 1Cor. 16:11; Heb. 10:13; 11:10; Jas.5:7.

How Were They Guilty?

To be guilty of the body and blood of Christ is to share the same sentence and punishment as the Romans and Jews for their part in crucifying Christ. While the lambs were being slain for the Passover, Jesus was on the cross, but the Jews did not discern the Lord's body. For this, there is a penalty.

The selfish outward manner in which they participated at this Table was evidence that they had not discerned the Lord's body. Anyone who participates unworthily cannot discern the Lord's body for his spiritual life and nourishment. For that reason, he remains guilty of the body and blood of Christ and under condemnation. (11:27, 34)

Paul's Spiritual Remedy

The means by which one becomes worthy is spiritual. (11:29) The sinner who believes that Christ's death is essential and efficacious to pay the penalty for his sin, has discerned the Lord's body and blood. To rehearse the terms of salvation at every Lord's Table is the Christian's great delight!

SEPTUAGINT

Supposedly translated from older Hebrew manuscripts no longer in existence, the Septuagint is considered a valid Greek translation. The alleged circumstances and date of this translation are not within the scope of this project, however, because many believe that the LXX was used in the Greek churches and even synagogues, the following should be noted.

- It has not been shown how older must be better or more accurate. It's like saying that the JW's New World Translation is more accurate because it is older than the NIV.
- When Jesus referenced the Law and the Prophets, He would not have been adding credence to the flawed Greek LXX. (Matt. 7:12; 26:56; Jn. 6:45)
- Jesus' 'Scripture' had 'jots and tittles', which the Greek LXX would not have. (Matt. 5:17, 18)
- Jesus spoke words that pointed to the fulfillment of the written Law, Prophets and Psalms, not translations. (Lk. 24:44)
- Since not one jot or tittle of the Law would pass until all would be fulfilled, the manuscript Jesus and the Apostles had were no less deficient than earlier manuscripts, in Hebrew or Greek.

- Since Jesus and the Apostles would be well acquainted with Hebrew and Greek, they had no reason to borrow quotations from a defective LXX Greek translation.
- Quotations that bear no resemblance to the LXX indicate that NT writers used the "Scriptures", not a translation, giving evidence that they knew Hebrew and translated from it directly.
- Quotations that are **similar** to the LXX simply show that the LXX was not correct. The word of God is precise.
- The few quotations that appear to be **identical** show that translators independently translated the phrase the same.
- As a scribe and priest, why did Ezra not write translations of the Law when Israel returned 450 b.c.? The priests and scribes would not have authorized a translation like the LXX at this time in history. (Mal. 2:7; De. 31:24-26)
- Even at the time of Jesus and the Apostles the Aramaic translations were not written; it was orally targummed. It was not until the second century AD that they were written down – 'Onkelos' and 'Jonathan'. Given scribal and synagogue regulations, it is untenable that Jewry would authorize a 250-year-old Greek translation for public services, since that didn't happen with Aramaic till 150 AD.
- The noted Jewish preacher Apollos from Alexandria was mighty in the "Scriptures", not the LXX. (Ac. 18:24)
- It would be expected that if the Septuagint was highly valued that it would have been transcribed for the benefit of the entire Greek speaking world as the MT was for Jews.
- One last problem: language drift. One reason for new translations, is that the meaning of words change. English changes and so does Greek. It is particularly unusual that a more than 250-year-old Greek translation would not encounter some changes. A credible support for the alleged age of the LLX must demonstrate the changes, or why they did not exist.

CONCLUSIONS:

Apparent quotations from NT writers that appear similar or the same as the LXX is no proof that they used this supposed Greek translation. It only shows that two translators can independently translate short passages the same. Because the Apostles were inspired, it should be emphasized that where the quotations do not match, the LXX is wrong; where they are right, the LXX happened to translate correctly. Paul's quotations of the OT are inspired; the LXX translation quotations are not. Since Christ declared that Scripture had yet remained unchanged in His day, the only conclusions to draw are that differences between NT quotations of the OT and the LXX translation may indicate a common Hebrew manuscript or that the LXX plagiarized the NT. It should be noted that no LXX extant copies predate 320 AD.

NT writers are critiqued for their inexact quotations of the OT. However, there is no instance where they have contradicted the OT. Secondly, as inspired writers, they, by the Holy Spirit provided added commentary to OT authors.

The differences between the LXX and NT are due to mistranslation by uninspired LXX translators. This means that the NT inspired writers are the arbiters of reliability, not the LXX.

Paul and Peter are clear that all scripture is given by God. (2 Tim. 3:16; 2 Pe. 1:21,22) Translations are second-hand representations of truth in another language, therefore are not given by God.

The site below makes an honest attempt to scholarship regarding LLX. Please note: *Bad Arguments For A Correct Conclusion*, near the bottom of the page. They argue for the Masoretic Text as what God originally inspired.
https://creation.com/bad-arguments-mt-lxx

The link below also appears to be an objective regard for the methodology of translation. The King James wasn't the only Bible that came from the Textus Receptus.
http://www.textusreceptusbibles.com

VISIONS AND MIRACLES

Doubtless, the Bible records numerous visions and supernatural miracles. There was always a purpose for them. But are we still to expect visions and miracles today? Can personal experiences be misleading? Only the Scriptures can be trusted with the answer.

BIBLE VISIONS

God's purpose and guidance was occasionally delivered to Jew and Gentile by means of dreams and visions.

VISIONS SERVED TO UNITE JEW AND GENTILE

Commensurate visions of Peter and Cornelius were intended to unite Jew and Gentile in the faith of our Lord. Peter, a chosen Apostle of Christ, had not yet understood that devout believers, including Gentiles were to be received in the fellowship without prejudice. (Acts 10:28,29; 44- 48; 11:17)

PAUL WAS SILENT ABOUT HIS VISION

Though Paul personally saw visions of the Lord, he declared that there is nothing to be gained by declaring what he saw. (2 Cor. 12:1-6)

A VISION OF CHRIST IS OVERWHELMING

When John saw the exalted Christ, he fell as if one dead. (Rev. 1:9-17) Note that none of the dreams and visions in Lee Strobel's book elicit that kind of response! His examples invariably revealed a 'Christ' who made people feel shameless while still in their filthy sins. Even as a true believer, John 'fell before Christ as if dead'.

SUMMARY

Sometimes God provided guidance through visions and dreams. Because it is impossible to witness someone else's dream/vision, credibility is always in question. The listener never really knows what is true. But there is one exception. The Bible says that God revealed Himself to us through men He selected. (Acts 2:32) These men put this revelation in writing, which include 'authorized' visions and dreams that we can believe. Now, having a complete record of all that sinful humanity needs to know about God and what He has done for us, as there is no further need for more 'scriptures', there is no further need for dreams and visions.

Yet, testimonies of visions seen by Muslims are eagerly accepted as a means by which God draws them to Christ.

A worthwhile resource on this important subject is An Evaluation of *Muslim Dreams & Visions of Isa (Jesus)* by Dennis McBride.
http://www.biblicalintegrity.org/2012/03/01/muslim-visions-jesus/

The article above questions the means of subjective visions that allegedly have pointed many Muslims to Christ,

- Satan is attempting to direct worship from Christ to himself, which was his goal at the start. (Isa. 14:12-14; Matt. 4:9)
- Apparently, all accounts of dreams or visions equate 'Isa' of the Qur'an with 'Isa' (Arabic for Jesus) of the Bible.
- Visions of 'Isa' conform to his description in the Koran, not the Bible. Muslims think that someone else died in Christ's place.
- Dreams and vision of Christ dilute the "primacy, centrality and authority of God's Word by establishing faith based on subjective revelations and experiences." (John 20:24-29)
- Some outreach to Muslims encourage Christians to pray that Muslims will have visions, so more will be saved. Unbiblical!
- This 'phenomena' creates the expectation that Jesus will appear to them in times of difficulty and persecution.
- Having these visions, creates divisions in the body.

Writing to believers, Peter affirms their faith in, and love for Christ, despite the fact that they did not see Him. With the words, 'though now you see Him not', Peter implied that 'then you saw Him,' but now you do not. Anyone who saw Christ, as Peter had, was present when He died and rose from the dead. Peter also identifies another group with the words, 'whom having not seen'. Most, who would be reading his letter, however, had not been to Jerusalem before Christ died and rose from the dead. Since His resurrection, no one had seen Him. (1 Pe. 1:7, 8)

Neither Peter or the other Apostles hint that dreams and visions were a means of comfort and guidance during the intense trials they were enduring. If visions of Christ are a means of faith and spiritual growth today, then we would expect this experience to be a historic reality, especially during the apostolic era, when they were also experiencing hard trials. Therefore, with absolute certainty, we can say that no one has seen Christ, by dream, vision or in person since the time of the Apostles.

MIRACLES

Like visions, testimonies of God's supernatural intervention are myriad. But scripture is clear that the performance of supernatural miracles had purpose.

Below is the conclusion of an article written by Wayne Jackson entitled,

ARE 'MIRACLES' UNIQUE TO CHRISTIANITY?

https://www.christiancourier.com/articles/5-

Wayne Jackson concludes,

> "There is one final point of this presentation that needs to be pressed with great vigor. There is no alleged miracle being performed today by Pentecostals, or those of a similar "Christian" persuasion, that cannot be duplicated by various cults and non-Christian sects.
>
> Those who practice Christian Science, Mormonism, Catholicism, Transcendental Meditation, Yoga, Psychic Healing, Scientology, New Age Crystal Healing, etc., claim the same type of signs as the Pentecostals. In fact, more than 20 million Americans annually report mystic experiences (including healing) in their lives. (Psychology Today 1987, 64)
>
> Since the Scriptures clearly teach that the purpose of miracles, as evidenced in biblical days, was to confirm the message proclaimed, hence, to validate the Christian system, do the multiple alleged examples of miracle-workings indicate that the Lord has authenticated all of these woefully **contradictory** systems? Think of the implications of that – especially in the light of Paul's affirmation that God is not the author of confusion. (1 Corinthians 14:33)
>
> There is abundant evidence that genuine miracles were performed by divinely appointed persons in the first century, but there is not proof whatever that such wonders are being replicated in this modern age."

WHY DID CHRIST PERFORM MIRACLES?

Jesus graciously showed the works of His Father. (Jn.10:38) He didn't perform miracles to give everyone a happy life. It was certainly within His power to heal everyone, but He didn't.

Jesus of Nazareth was approved by signs and wonders. (Acts 2:22, 43) He was expected to be a miracle worker like Moses was – one who did signs and wonders. (De. 18:15)

When Jesus saw the faith of the four who opened the roof to let the paralytic down into the house were Jesus was, said to him 'Son, your sins are forgiven you.' Hostile Jews rightly understood that no one could forgive sins but God. They accused Christ of blasphemy. To prove he had the power to forgive sins, He commanded the paralytic to take up His bed and walk. (Mk.2:2-12)

When is the last time you heard someone claim to be healed of terminal cancer, boast of how God had forgiven him of his great and many sins?

What "Greater Miracles" Would The Disciples Do?

Another portion of Scripture is misunderstood to say that Christ promised that we would do 'greater miracles'. (Jn. 14:12) As shown the first chapter of this book, translations have ignored the genitive. Spoken to the disciples at the Passover meal, Jesus said to them that 'greater OF the works that I am doing you will do also.' The disciples were not doing the "greater" works that Christ was doing, such as washing feet.

Miracles Are Evidence Of Apostolic Authority

The message of the gospel salvation was confirmed to those who heard Him. God bore witness of the veracity of their message with signs, wonders, miracles and gifts. (Heb. 2:3,4) It should be noted that it is past tense. He is no longer 'bearing' witness.

Paul stated that signs, wonders and mighty deeds were the signs of an Apostle. (2 Cor. 12:12) There are only 12! The purpose of the supernatural signs was to authenticate the Apostles as God's messengers. The Apostles performed signs and wonders in the name of Christ among the people. (Acts 4:30; 5:12; 15:12) The signs and wonders were granted to the Apostles so that the people had no reason to question their message – the gospel. (Acts 14:3; Rom.15:18-20)

God's Revelation Is Exclusive To The Scriptures

The Bible does not command believers to perform miracles to convince the lost. Christ only commanded that the Gospel be preached. Miracles were never intended to be a 'name it and claim it' panacea for human suffering.

Miracle claims in books are always in the third person. They cannot be verified. Credibility becomes an issue because it is impossible to determine if the event has been rehearsed accurately, and without bias. Since, no one after the Apostles has been appointed to deliver God's revelation, there is no further need for miracles, visions and dreams.

But, we need witnesses.

The First Witnesses

Jesus declared to His disciples that they were witnesses. (Lk. 24:48) Jesus confirmed that the Galileans would be witnesses. (Acts 1:8) Peter declared that he was one of many witnesses. (Acts 3:15, 32) Peter declared himself to be one of a group of chosen witnesses. (Acts 10:39-41; 13:31) Jesus appeared to Paul to make him a minister and a witness. (Acts 26:16) Peter is a witness of the sufferings of Christ. (1 Pe. 5:1)

Timothy was not a "witness", but he was exhorted to take the things that he had learned from witnesses such as Paul and commit it to faithful men. (2 Tim.2:2)

It is important that witnesses have integrity. Only God would know who they were and for that reason chose 12 primary witnesses plus additional believing Galileans. This precludes any notion that we should consider contemporary claims visions of Jesus miracle experiences valid.

If we know that Christ has chosen men for the task of recording the truth pertaining to the experience of visions, dreams and miracles, then we have a propositional document upon which to depend. We can believe the testimonies of visions, dreams and miracles in its pages. However, our faith is in the Christ, who was central to the miracles, dreams and visions, who not only died but gave us His Word through His Apostles and Prophets.

We are to remember the words of the Prophets and the Apostles. (2 Pet.3:2; Jude 17)

Having presented the Bible as our standard, as God's revelation, it is now our task to examine a book that is deemed to be evangelical.

BOOK REVIEW

THE CASE FOR MIRACLES BY LEE STROBEL

Despite the many arguments of inspired Scripture marshalled against Pentecostalism, countless books tout personal experience over God's written Word. The Case For Miracles, by Lee Strobel, is a representative record of subjective accounts of miracles, dreams and visions, some 'Christian', some not. However, when analyzed logically and biblically, can these testimonies stand against God's propositionally revealed word?

STROBEL'S PREFERRED DEFINITION OF MIRACLE

Strobel's favors Purtill's definition of miracle,

> "A miracle is an event brought on by the power of God, that is a temporary exception to the ordinary course of nature for the purpose of showing that God has acted in history." (page 27)

ESSENCE OF BIBLICAL MIRACLES

Purtill's definition doesn't distinguish between natural and supernatural. (ie. Turning water into wine) Secondly, it excluded the permanent miracle of the new birth and sanctification.

The word translated 'miracle' in Acts 8:13 means power. Philip was doing miracles, some were temporary, however, some demons were permanently cast out. Salvation is the miracle or power of God. (1Cor. 1:18) Our bodies will be raised permanently in power or by a miracle. (1 Cor. 15:43) 'Miracle' is a process in the believer. (Eph. 3:20) Peter talks about the believer being kept by the power or 'miracle' of God (1 Pet.1:4,5)

'MIRACLE' IS DIFFERENT THAN PROVIDENTIAL CARE

Strobel cited Purtill's testimony of his personal severe illness, "God was, as usual, hiding divine action in plain sight amid the ordinary course of events." Purtell confused providential care with a truly biblical understanding of 'miracle'. Indeed, all apostolic miracles were providential, but not all of God's providential care is by means of miracles.

MIRACLE PRAYER

Strobel rightly differed with Pentecostals who cite Isa. 53:5 for physical healing. To him it was untenable that someone who prayed, 'Your will be done' lacked faith.

Scripture Use Out of Context

However, James 5:14 is not applicable for physical healing. P.25,27. James is referring to praying for the depressed and fearful, so that they might be strengthened in the faith. (Please see The Lord's Table, p.225)

Prayer For Miracles Is Available For The Cults

Strobel records that prayers of Protestants and Catholics for people to recover rapidly had better results than no prayer. (P.126-127) He doesn't make a distinction between truly saved and unsaved.

Answers to Healing Prayer Are Attributed to Angels.

One person testifies of tingles and temperature changes in the healing process. The healing was attributed to angels. (p. 136)

Veracity of Healing Prayers Was Not Based On Scripture

The child who received an answer to prayer as illustrated on page 17, experienced God's providential care, not a miracle. The child's answer to prayer was not supernatural. We are not informed how this child responded to other times when her prayers were not answered? Was this child ever taught to pray like the Apostle Paul did in Col. 1?

According to the Strobel, a physical miracle event is sometimes accomplished through prayer. Indeed, prayer is part of the life of every true believer. But when Paul prayed for the believers in Colossae, he did not mention anything about being physically healed or any other physical need! (Col. 1:9-12)

Integrity of Miracle Reports

He stated that miracle reports were established by individuals with 'unquestionable integrity.' It is soon apparent in Strobel's list of claimants that most of them are charismatic, charismatically inclined and Roman Catholic not to mention cults and Protestants with severely skewed doctrines. (P.122) Without sound theology, integrity is impossible.

Hume argued that witnesses cannot be trusted. (P.88, 89) This is partially true. The fact is that <u>not all</u> witnesses can be trusted. The problem is that we don't know which witnesses can be trusted. For that reason, 'official' witnesses were chosen for us by Christ.

Claiming 'unquestionable integrity' means different things.

Credibility Gap

Would you believe that as Creflo Dollar and Kenneth Copeland were speaking, a man was healed of his MS? Page. 255-257 *https://www.youtube.com/watch?v=Nx6pD61YKLY*

STROBEL CLAIMS MODERN MIRACLES PROVE BIBLE MIRACLES

Strobel argues that if temporal miracles are possible, they must be happening today. P.48. When Craig Keener was asked if he had accomplished what he had hoped for in his book, he said that his goal was to show that the New Testament should not be dismissed as legendary because as they report miracles, so also there are many firsthand claims of people today. This makes the credibility of the Bible dependent on contemporary miracles.

CULTS BELIEVE IN MIRACLES

Strobel makes his case for miracles with evidence from the cults. P.89 Having allowed 'born-again' Catholics to be part of the 'miracle' story, he has no basis upon which to deny the testimonies of other cults like the Mormons. So, because the 'queen' herself along with the physicians declared a healing performed by Jansenists, Strobel thinks the story becomes more credible.

WHICH PRAYERS DOES GOD ANSWER?

The author makes no distinction between the faith of Protestants and Catholics. (p.126-127) Strobel accepts Candy Brown's evaluation that prayers have better outcomes when born-again Christians pray, whether 'Protestant or Catholic'. Given the great doctrinal divide between Protestants and Catholics, it is impossible for a true Protestants to accept the observations of such a mixed group as valid. Catholics pray to Mary and to angels; they believe in salvation by works; they believe in penance and a host of other false doctrines, yet we are asked to accept false teachers as authorities on the subject of visions, dreams and miracles?

Mormons are just as 'born-again' as are Catholics, yet neither are biblically born again.

DIVIDING THE CHURCH

African and Asian students diminish western evangelicalism by claiming their 'Christianity' superior because they are surrounded by 'spiritual warfare'. Olson invited a Catholic priest from Nigeria to address his class. Rather than talk about doctrine, he taught that a common belief in miracles can draw 'Christians' together. (P. 228) It was the doctrine of Jesus, the same doctrine that these African and Asian students despise. A true doctrine of miracles must include the truth of Christ.

'Sense-ational' Conversion

Keener was led in a prayer of repentance and faith. He talked about a palpable sensation running through his body and overwhelming sense of God's majesty but said nothing of the forgiveness of sin and the fruit of the Spirit. Did his repentance have godly sorrow? (P,78-81)

Indeed, as Keener and Strobel indicated, coming to faith is a miracle, but here is where Strobel's miracle view is weak. When someone truly comes to faith in Christ, he is born again. As no one can claim to be his own midwife in his physical birth, neither can he claim to have been the cause of his own spiritual birth.

His 'sensations' and overwhelming 'sense' of God's majesty reminds me of Lk. 8:13 where the word was received with joy, yet only believed for a while, having no true sorrow for sin. (2 Cor. 7:9,10) The Bible does not say that evidence of a conversion is to feel something rush through your body. The conversion experience includes a godly sorrow for sin, after which there is the discovery that he now loves the things that God loves and hates the things that God hates and produces the fruit of the Spirit. (2Cor. 7:9,10; Rom.7: 22; Ga. 5:22-25)

His Book Teaches That Experience Determines Doctrine

He disagrees with the cessationist, not because he has studied the Scriptures on this subject, but because he has experienced miracles. (Page 225-226)

Conflict of Hybel's 'Nudging' Experience

Strobel cites Bill Hybels who wrote a book on the 'nudgings of the Holy Spirit'. (P.229-231) He said that not every miracle was a spectacular intervention of God's power. He also said that people are embarrassed by the supernatural. But what about the 'miracle' of being 'nudged by the Holy Spirit' not to commit adultery as he did? Rather, be concerned with the miracle of sanctification in the believer's life.

Feelings Are Deceptive

He cites Derren Brown, a self-confessed, atheist, illusionist, who speaks in 'tongues', touches them to make people fall backwards. He heals but does not believe it to be real. Yet, he makes his audience feel.

A physician says, 'I can't explain it'. (P.112-113) If lack of a rational explanation is reason to believe a miracle has occurred, then Derren Brown is a 'miracle worker'. All magicians, then are miracle-workers.

MEDICAL ANOMALIES

Strobel mentions various anecdotal accounts of individuals who have alleged to have recovered from serious physical illness or trauma that could only be explained by a 'miracle'. Is an event deemed to be miraculous, if we cannot understand it?

MEMORY RECOVERY

A medical doctor is cited, who claimed that he had a dream showing the information he needed to pass to become a medical doctor. Does God give dreams to help you pass an exam?

> "A 2010 Harvard study suggested that dreaming may reactivate and reorganize recently learned material, improving memory and boosting performance. The subjects were 99 healthy college students who agreed to avoid alcohol, caffeine, and drugs for at least 24 hours prior to the experiment. All the volunteers demonstrated normal sleep patterns before enrolling in the study."[142]

God has made us with the capacity to dream. Dreams may serve to enhance the memory to recover information already learned. For the believer this may occur as the result of prayer, but God has facilitated the answer by how he has created us. The dream was not a supernatural communication. It was providential memory recovery.

THE STORY JUST NOT BELIEVABLE

He tells of a young girl who had apparently been bitten by a poisonous snake, then carried by her mother for three hours on her back and then raised from the dead, when her pastor prayed for the girl. (P. 98)

DIAGNOSTIC ERRORS

Similarly, the mother of a girl, who didn't want to wear a hearing aid the rest of her life, felt a compulsion to pray for her daughter. Examined later, the doctor said that the medical report could not explain what happened. (P.100) There are a lot of things in medicine that cannot be explained. Many mistakes are made in diagnosis.

THE STORY CONFLICTS WITH ITSELF

In Missouri x-rays confirmed that Carl's ankle was broken. The orthopedist wanted him to stay overnight. During the night, he

---

[142] https://www.health.harvard.edu/staying-healthy/learning-while-you-sleep-dream-or-reality

'experienced a voice from the Lord.' Contrary to the radiologist report, the voice said, "The ankle was not broken." After returning to Michigan, (not told how many days later) his ankle was x-rayed again, this time showing no breaks. (P. 106) The story itself makes the 'voice' a liar. He had felt excruciating pain, the Missouri x-ray showed that it was broken and the 'voice' says it "was" not broken when it was. Yet, we are asked to accept both x-rays?

Rare Occurrences

On page 108, the surgeon said that he hadn't seen spontaneous closure in an 8 year old 'very often'. It is amazing that he even uses this as part of his case for miracles. Is it a 'miracle' too that after an appendectomy the body heals and the body returns to normal?

Incorrect Equipment Settings

A cardiologist 'feels' God telling him to turn around and pray for a patient who the medical team had failed to resuscitate. He prayed that in Jesus' name that He "would raise him from the dead". After his brief prayer, he urged the other doctor to shock him one more time. The patient's heartbeat jumped from a flatline to about 75 per minute.

It had been suggested by some reading the newspaper reports that his heart had not completely stopped. The cardiologist's reply was that normally the electric shock applied in such circumstances would not accomplish anything. The unanimous verdict of the attending medical team was that this patient was dead. (P.109-110)

Patients cannot be restored to a normal heartbeat with a defibrillator after the heart has flatlined.[143] Note an incident where an incorrectly adjusted heart monitor rendered a false flatline reading,

> "Meanwhile, patient developed ventricular fibrillation (VF) Even after 20 min of resuscitation following advanced cardiac life support (ACLS) protocol, no evidence of cardiac activity was noticed. (Flat line seen in the ECG monitor) We were about to declare death when a timely intervention prevented a major error. We increased the gain of ECG on the monitor from 0.5 to 7, and there was perfect normal sinus rhythm. On checking carotid pulse was present. Surgery was completed, and the patient was shifted to the post-anaesthesia care unit. Patient's

[143] TV Myth: Shocking a Flatline Heart Rhythm Will Revive Patient
http://www.aed.com/blog/tv-myth-shocking-a-flatline-heart-rhythm-will-revive-patient/

> post-operative ECG and cardiac enzymes were normal, confirming that high-quality CPR was administered (and successful)." [144] (emphasis added)

Dr. Chauncey Crandall is a 'slain-in-the-spirit' charismatic and has appeared with Pat Buchannan on the 700 Club. He believed that he prayed this man to life. I don't.

Psychosomatic Recoveries

Strobel and Brown admitted that improvements to patients' health could be psychosomatic, with 'direct-contact' prayers. When Jesus healed with the direct-contact, the recovery was not psychosomatic. (P.132-133)

'Healings' can be attributed to a placebo effect.

Healings That Were Not Instant

Working with charismatic missionaries in Mozambique, Brown observed that improvements were "significant". (134-135) Healings were not instantaneous, yet everyone improved to one degree or another. (p. 136) The believer can be thankful for improvements in health, but they are not miracles. When Jesus healed, the recovery was 'instant'!

Allergy Recovery

A girl 'sensed' after a prayer that she had been immediately healed of an allergy. She was so convinced that she immediately put on a latex wristband that she was allergic to. Why, if she was allergic would she have a latex wristband with her? And from where did the apple to which she was allergic suddenly appear? This sounds staged! (P. 255-257)

Children outgrow allergies.

https://www.todaysdietitian.com/newarchives/050113p12.shtml

Cult Healings

Pascal's niece was healed of an eye problem in a pagan institution known as the Jansenists. P. 89

Summary

Professing believers ignore Scripture, when identifying miracles.

Physician's Error

Despite a physician's best efforts, they are human and make diagnostic errors. To use a physician's diagnosis as evidence, does not prove a

---

[144] *Indian Journal of Anaesthesia*
https://www.ncbi.nlm.nih.gov/pmc/articles/PMC4551041/

miracle. Doctors mis-diagnose.[145] The other examples of supposed 'healing' bear no resemblance the record of miracles in the Bible.

Confirmation Bias

People claim to have seen a miracle because it accords with a bias that miracles are not only possible, but are happening. This is 'confirmation bias'. Both sides of an issue may interpret the evidence to fit their bias. But the veracity of a bias can only be determined by an independent authority. It must be emphasized that all third-party observations of supernatural miracles in the Bible were certified as appointed holy men of God, who spoke as they were moved by the Holy Spirit. (2 Pe.1:19-21)

The Pagan Also Believes In Miracles

It is not necessary to believe the Bible to believe in miracles. The magicians of Egypt believed in miracles. Unbelievers also believe in miracles, even supernatural miracles.

The Spiritual Miracle

Psalm 103 is often used out of context to refer to physical diseases. All the people, who read that Psalm throughout the ages, died! Man needed a spiritual deliverance. Unfortunately, Strobel diminished the salvation supernatural miracle that God wrought in His children (P.78-81)

PURPOSE OF THE MIRACLES

What does Lee Strobel think the purpose for the miracle events in the Bible are? Does he have support for his view?

THE STARTING OF A KINGDOM

The author said that miracles were a sign for the 'inbreaking' of the kingdom. (P.86) Luke wrote that the reason why Christ did the miracles was to show Himself as approved by God. (Acts 2:22

HE CITED 'STATS' THAT MIRACLES STIMULATE EVANGELIZATION

Strobel cites statistics to show that where there is 'revival', there are signs wonders and healings. A miracle is performed for someone who defied Christ, after which he and tens of thousands came to faith in Christ in Suriname as a result. (P.114 - 115) Why didn't John the Baptist think of performing a miracle for King Herod?

---

[145] *The Incidence of Diagnostic Error in Medicine* https://qualitysafety.bmj.com/content/22/Suppl_2/ii21

But feeding 500 by the supernatural multiplication of the boy's lunch did not result in their evangelization. (Jn. 6:26-27) Neither would Lazarus rising from the dead cause the rich man's brothers to repent. And we are asked to believe that tens of thousands were saved as a result of a 'miraculous' healing?

Nothing is said about a revival of repentance. His examples of 'believers' appear to be biblical illiterates, if not fake believers.

VISIONS AND DREAMS

Ravi Zacharias stated that there is no other religion that had a more intricate doctrine of angels and visions. (P. 142) Because of their sensitivity to angels, Ravi is convinced, without biblical support, that God reveals Himself in them.

NABEEL WAS MISLED

Nabeel was a Pentecostal who believed that, like the disciples of Jesus, we also have been given the authority to cast out demons and heal all manner of sickness.[146] He based his healing sermon on Matthew 9:35-10:1. His sermon teaches that healing is a means by which someone is led to the Lord. As an ordained Southern Baptist preacher, he confessed that the message that he was preaching at this Pentecostal Church, he would not preach to other churches. Why? If it is the truth, why?[147] Many of Nabeel's charismatic friends came forward to prophesy that he would be healed from his own terminal cancer. His healing didn't happen.[148]

This is not intended to question Nabeel's Christian conversion. [149] Unfortunately however, Nabeel had not been mentored well regarding the profound differences between Roman Catholicism, 'Charismaticism' and Protestantism. He associated with Ravi Zacharias, who appeared in shows

---

[146] The command to His disciples is that they would pray that the Lord of the harvest would send laborers into the harvest. We do not see them praying that others would join with them in working miracles. The second error he makes with Mat.10:1 is that he applies it to every believer. Jesus just gave this authority to the Twelve! If it was intended that prayer could be made that anyone receive this authority, why then did He only give it to His disciples?
https://www.youtube.com/watch?v=CCKrB1oHnxE

[147] Michael Brown, *Nabeel Qureshi and the Futility of Charismatic "Healing"*
https://pulpitandpen.org/2017/09/20/michael-brown-nabeel-qureshi-and-the-futility-of-charismatic-healing/

[148] 'So Many People Prophesying That I Would Be Healed'
https://hellochristian.com/4532-nabeel-qureshi-so-many-people-are-prophesying-that-i-will-get-healed

[149] Nabeel Qureshi Redux
https://pulpitandpen.org/2016/07/31/nabeel-qureshi-redux/

with Charismatics like Joyce Meyer and ecumenical events such as Reset 2016. Given Nabeel's lack of understanding of vital and important fundamental differences within what is called Christianity, it is expected that his teaching and testimony be tested with the greatest of care.

Nabeel's Testimony

Nabeel says that he had a dream with a door slightly ajar. He claimed he dreamt the parable in Luke 13:24-28, which he had not read before. Therefore, this must have been divine communication. (P. 140-141)

But dreams are stimulated by what we already know. Nabeel knew Islamic tradition,

> "Islamic tradition describes Jannah, or heaven as having eight doors or gates. Each door has a name that describes the types or characteristics of the people who will be admitted through it. Some scholars surmise that these doors are found inside Jannah after one enters the main gate. The exact nature of these doors is unknown but they were mentioned in the Quran and their names were given by the Prophet Mohammed."[150]

One can understand why a Muslim might be dreaming about doors, wondering, if he will qualify to go through it. Given the exposure of this imagery in the Koran, there is no reason to accept the notion that this was a 'divine' revelatory communication. Why did Strobel not mention this?

Nabeel alleges, as do others, that thousands of Muslims are being saved through dreams and visions. But Strobel does not tell us about those who have reverted to Islam.[151]

ANGEL VISIONS

Incidents are cited where two people have the same dream, or 'Jesus' tells them something they could not otherwise have known. Again, dreams like this are personal testimonies that cannot be verified. The Bible tells us to test the spirits. We are not asked to believe another person's testimony.

---

[150] *Doors of Jannah*
https://www.learnreligions.com/doors-of-jannah-2004342

[151] Reversion: Why Do 'Christian Converts' From Islam Return To Their Old Religion?
https://network.crcna.org/global-mission/reversion-why-do-'christian-converts'-islam-return-their-old-religion

The Possibility Of The Demonic

Another important aspect of this 'vision' phenomena is that it can be demonic. Muslims believe in Isa. It is conceivable that Satan would come to some as an angel of light and love. But this 'angel' certainly would not 'talk' to them about personal sin.

Feeling No Shame

An example is given of a woman who claimed she had a vision of Jesus. The man in the dream said he died for her and loved her. When Jesus appeared to persecutor Saul on the way to Damascus, he fell on his face! Saul did not assume – he asked, 'Who are you Lord?' These Muslims didn't even ask who it was that appeared to them. Persecutors of Christians like Paul, yet, we are to believe that 'Jesus' made them feel great. Did Saul "feel" loved when Jesus met him?

Even when the angel of God appeared to Cornelius in a vision, he was fearful, until he was informed that his prayers had come up as a memorial before God. (Acts 10:1-5) Unlike Muslims, Cornelius was already a true worshipper of God.

Noor said that for the first time she felt no shame. She did not testify that Jesus had exposed her as a sinner, that she repented of her sin and was cleansed by His blood. Again her dream could not be verified, therefore not believable. (P. 145-148.) Satan deceives people with a no-shame salvation.

John tells us that when Christ appears that those who are not His will be ashamed at His coming. (1 John 2:28)

A 'Jesus' Who Was Concerned About Career Choice

The 'Jesus' who 'appeared' to one Muslim in dreams was not concerned about repentance for his terrorism, just about a destructive career choice. (P. 148-149) Again, where was the godly sorrow?

Shame/Honor Culture

It is implied that the sighting of Jesus in their dreams and vision conform to the shame/honor culture of Muslims. But rather than shame, "they feel love, grace, safety, protection, affirmation, joy and peace." (page 151, 158) Their 'Jesus' is not the Bible Jesus.

Strobel cites Zacchaeus, the Samaritan woman, the blind and crippled as examples of this. But the Bible does not record incidents where Jesus wanted to confer honor. We know that Jesus did not meet with Nicodemus to make him feel good. He said to him, 'Are you a teacher in

Israel and do not know these things?' To the woman who was caught in adultery, he said, 'Neither do I condemn you, go and sin no more.' To the Samaritan woman, He said, 'You have had five husbands...'. He did not meet with people to given them self-esteem. Why didn't He make the Pharisees and scribes feel wonderful about themselves? They were also religious enemies of the Savior, as are the Muslims. Nicodemus, the woman caught in adultery and the Samaritan woman personally met Christ. He administered His grace to each of them, but He was not complimentary.

Jealousy of Those Who Have Dreams

Strobel confessed a jealousy of people who have 'Jesus dreams'. Apparently, God's revelation in His word is insufficient to satisfy his spiritual longings. (P.155) It is one thing to desire to see our Savior face to face, but it is quite another matter to desire to have a 'vision' of Jesus, like others have had. Why not desire to know more of His will already revealed to us in Scripture?

Dreams Are Based On Experience

Strobel said that he had had a dream of an angel who told him that going to church and behaving well doesn't qualify one for heaven. (P.156-157) But it should be noted that his parents made him learn the Lutheran catechism, so he would have dreamt about truth he had already heard. His 'angel' and the message of the 'angel' was a product of his own mind.

CLOSING SUMMARY

The miracles that Christ and the Apostles performed were supernatural. When Jesus commanded both the wind and the sea to 'be still', natural law was suspended. When people recover even from a grave illness today, it cannot be attributed to a supernatural event. With the assistance of the medical profession, the body still recovers naturally.

The 'miracle' stories in this book are not believable for the following reasons,

- It is impossible to verify all healing stories.
- 'Miracles' happen to heretics like Mormons, Mystics Charismatics and Roman Catholics to name a few.
- No distinction is made between prayers of unbelievers and prayers of believers. Catholics pray to Mary and other 'saints'.
- Strobel equates the miracles of Jesus with charismatic healings of today.

- Scripture is rarely applied and when it is referenced, it is out of context and misinterpreted.
- The 'miracle' stories are contradictory and incomplete.

Some of the physical recoveries, touted as 'miracles' were medical anomalies, misdiagnosis or misrepresented. Human inability to explain a physical recovery does not qualify as a supernatural event.

There is only one source for credible supernatural events. They are recorded in Scripture by chosen men of God. Since then, no one has been chosen to reveal new information. The miracle/vision case is closed.

Do Witnesses Determine Reality?

Strobel admitted that spontaneous remissions occur, charlatans deceive, that doctors have erred, x-rays are misread. He agrees that people have a motivation to lie. He agrees that honest people will misperceive, that memories will fail and the apparently dead will survive. Yet, he insisted, on the basis of the sheer number of witnesses, that some of them must be correct. (P. 260-261) How does 'sheer numbers' of witnesses help, if there are liars in the bunch?

Whether few witnesses or many witnesses, the majority are inclined to interpret an event according to one's personal bias. Witnesses will misinterpret the 'miracle'. The more witnesses there are, the more cross-examination is needed. Unless witnesses are trained by an objective standard, it is impossible to acquire credible testimony. Modern day 'witnesses' do not determine whether a miracle has occurred. The written word of God does. The Bible is to be trusted, not uninspired modern 'witnesses', who when "tested", are found to contradict the Scriptures.

Another major error of 'miracle' hunters is made when it is presumed that when an event cannot be explained, it must be a miracle. This is graphically illustrated with the author's own inclusion of the atheist illusionist Derren Brown.

Contrary to his claim that at the bottom of 153, he has not checked "everything against scripture."

Visions and Dreams

In God's providence, He is certainly able to stimulate interest in the Gospel with a natural dream. He may dream <u>about</u> heaven, <u>about</u> hell, <u>about</u> good angels, even <u>about</u> Jesus, but never are these images real. They are not revelatory. Anyone who claims to have seen a vision of the Lord, or an angel from the Lord, is not to be believed. Note the following Scripture,

- Peter tells about the revelation of Jesus Christ, 'whom having not seen you love.' (1 Pet. 1:7,8)
- Speaking as one of the Apostles, John states that "we have seen and testify..." (1 Jn. 4:14)
- Paul tells us that we walk by faith not by sight. (2 Cor.5:7)
- John asks the question, 'How can one not love his brother whom he has not seen, yet claim to love God whom he has not seen.?' (1 Jn. 4:20)

A vision of the Lord would be a revelation. The Bible precludes further revelation from the Lord. We have all we need in the Bible. As other commentators have warned, those who claim to have seen Jesus in a vision, love the 'person' in that vision.

Having analyzed Strobel's case for miracles, I found no Scriptural support for any of his reports for visions and miracles. If it were possible to access all the missing data for each 'miracle' and 'vision' in this book, we would know the illusion they are, as we would Derren Brown's magic. An event that cannot be explained is no more supernatural than not being able to explain a magician's trick. (Derren Brown)

Thankfully, despite the absence of details for these supposed supernatural events, we have the Scriptures that give us the answer.

The Believer's Common Miracle Experience

Rather, confess the miracle of new birth, the fact that you've been made a new creature in Christ, that you were absolutely and totally dead in your terrible trespasses and sins, that God inaudibly spoke to your heart and caused you as one of his elect children to come to spiritual life, to be born again! That is the common 'miracle' experience which every believer can and should testify about. (Rom. 10:9-11)

ABOUT THE AUTHOR

Raised by Christian parents in conservative churches, Bible teaching has greatly benefited Howard Boldt from childhood. Since Bible College, he served in church administration, music, and teaching Sunday and mid-week Bible classes. With his growing interest in the Scriptures, Howard became particularly concerned about the negative impact doctrinal errors were having upon Christians. From teaching to essays to books, he has attempted to articulate biblical reasoning for his views. Happily married to his wife of 51 years, he has also experienced the joys of family life. He lives in Alberta, Canada.

www.ingramcontent.com/pod-product-compliance
Lightning Source LLC
Chambersburg PA
CBHW071411090426
42737CB00011B/1424

* 9 7 8 1 7 7 3 5 4 3 6 3 5 *